Masks, Modes, and Morals:
The Art of Evelyn Waugh

Also by William J. Cook, Jr.

CONFIDENCE IN FACT

Masks, Modes, and Morals:
The Art of Evelyn Waugh

William J. Cook, Jr.

Rutherford • *Madison* • *Teaneck*
Fairleigh Dickinson University Press

Associated University Presses, Inc.
Cranbury, New Jersey 08512

ISBN: 0-8386-7707-X
Printed in the United States of America

Quotations from the following books by Evelyn Waugh by permission of Little, Brown and Co.

Decline and Fall, Copyright 1928
Vile Bodies, Copyright 1930
Black Mischief, Copyright 1932
A Handful of Dust, Copyright 1934
Scoop, Copyright 1937, 1938
Put Out More Flags, Copyright 1942
Brideshead Revisited, Copyright 1944, 1945
Men at Arms, Copyright 1952
Officers and Gentlemen, Copyright 1955
Unconditional Surrender (American title: *The End of Battle*),
    Copyright © 1961

Quotations from *Evelyn Waugh: Portrait of an Artist* by Frederick J. Stopp by permission of Little, Brown and Co. and Chapman and Hall Ltd.

Selections from Northrop Frye, *Anatomy of Criticism* (copyright © 1957 by Princeton University Press). Reprinted by permission of Princeton University Press.

To
Judy, Vonda, Jennifer, and Jill

and
To
Carl Benson

Contents

Preface   9
Acknowledgments   11
1 WAUGH AND HIS ART   17
   The Enigmatic Mode   21
      Identification of Mode   23
      Disparities in Mode   30
      Toward Reconciliation   36
   The Complexity of Mode   42
      Thematic Possibilities of Mode   46
      Technical Exigencies of Mode   49
      Waugh's Personae Technique   53
2 THE ESTABLISHMENT OF MODE   60
   Decline and Fall   61
   Vile Bodies   82
3 VARIATION IN MODE   100
   Black Mischief   101
   A Handful of Dust   122
4 EXTENSION OF MODE   145
   Scoop   148
   Put Out More Flags   165
5 MODE SUSPENDED—*Brideshead Revisited*   193
6 ADAPTATION OF MODE   236
   Men at Arms   238
   Officers and Gentlemen   271
7 THE FINALITY OF MODE   297
   Unconditional Surrender   297
   Conclusion   337
Bibliography   345
Index   350

Preface

Although recent criticism has been increasingly friendly
to Evelyn Waugh, his status as a novelist is still tentative:
on the one hand he is commercialized as a "major novelist" of the twentieth century; on the other, as a "brainless
genius" who can lay no claim whatsoever to that ambiguous
but distinctive designation, "major novelist." Perhaps this
divergence of opinion exists because critics and the general
reading public do not always know exactly how to approach his fiction; they are puzzled by the great variety of
novels and find it difficult to detect significant relationships between even the most similar works. While finding
reasons to praise or condemn individual works, critics have
been generally hard pressed to arrive at a theory of fiction
that will both account for the variety of his fiction and
provide a valid basis for the evaluation of all his novels.
In many cases, Waugh is approached with preconceived
notions regarding the craft of fiction, the aspects of the
novel, or the proper relationship of dogma and art. The
result is that the critical consensus now holds that Waugh
intentionally violates the traditional art theories regarding the novel, that he abandons at mid-career all concern
for artistic achievement in favor of moral pronouncement,
and that his career is characterized by early success and
promise but later decline and failure. Waugh thus becomes
something less than a conscious craftsman, something other
than a serious novelist—assuredly not a "major novelist."
   This study proposes to overcome some of the misconcep-

tions regarding Waugh's fiction and to offer a new, perhaps more valid, approach to an evaluation of Waugh as novelist. First, it will advance the thesis that Waugh's fiction is unified by constantly maturing artistry and theme; second, it will examine the way in which artistry and theme steadily and simultaneously develop from the early satires to the later more conventional novels. Attention will be focused through close textual analysis on Waugh's single fundamental technique, a technique central to every aspect of every Waugh novel. This technique, which is formulated within the ironic mode, arises initially out of the artistic demands of satire and the temperament of the author, but, modified, serves as the primary technique of every subsequent work, even the later realistic novels.

Waugh's uniquely contrived personae technique, in essence the relationship of a narrator-persona with a character-persona, is central to the varied and maturing narrative formulation; it sustains, discovers, and embodies the increasing seriousness of the central theme; it controls and informs the gradually deepening tone of the novels. In this way, Waugh's fiction moves inevitably from satiric denunciation, to comic criticism, to romantic optimism, and, finally, to ironic realism. As testimony to his novelistic skill, Waugh brings to a high degree of refinement the individual novels at each stage of his career; as evidence of his concern with human values, the dominant continuing theme of all the novels moves from fantasy to reality and the tone from scathing satire to a mellow, yet hopeful, resignation. At the end of his career, in the war trilogy, he demonstrates the mature artistry and the moral seriousness characteristic of a major novelist.

Acknowledgments

I wish to thank the following publishers for giving me permission to quote from published works:

Bookman Associates, for permission to quote from A. A. DeVitis, *Roman Holiday: The Catholic Novels of Evelyn Waugh*, 1956.

Chapman and Hall, Ltd., for permission to quote from Frederick J. Stopp, *Evelyn Waugh: Portrait of an Artist*, 1958.

College English, for permission to quote from James W. Nichols, "Romantic and Realistic: The Tone of Evelyn Waugh's Early Novels," 24 (October, 1962): 46–52.

Collins Sons & Co., Ltd., and Harper & Row, Publishers, Inc. to quote from Søren Kierkegaard, *The Concept of Irony*, London: Collins Sons & Co., Ltd., 1966.

Farrar, Straus & Giroux, Inc., for permission to quote from Frederick R. Karl, "The World of Evelyn Waugh: The Normally Insane," *The Contemporary English Novel*, 1962.

Harvard University Press, for permission to quote from David Worcester, *The Art of Satire* (Cambridge, Mass.: Harvard University Press, copyright 1940 by the President and Fellows of Harvard College; 1968 by Eloise Worcester Spencer Wade). Reprinted, New York: Russell & Russell, 1960.

Iowa State University Press, for permission to quote from

Leonard Feinberg, *The Satirist: His Temperament, Motivation and Influence,* 1963.

Little, Brown and Company, for permission to quote from the works of Evelyn Waugh. Also for permission to quote from Frederick J. Stopp, *Evelyn Waugh: Portrait of An Artist,* 1958.

Longman Group, Ltd., for the British Council, for permission to quote from Christopher Hollis, *Evelyn Waugh,* 1966. (*Writers and Their Work series.*)

St. Martin's Press, Inc., MacMillan & Co., Ltd., for permission to quote from A. E. Dyson, *Evelyn Waugh: And the Mysteriously Disappearing Hero, The Crazy Fabric: Essays in Irony,* 1965.

A. D. Peters & Company, for permission to quote from *Decline and Fall,* copyright 1928, by Evelyn Waugh; *Vile Bodies,* copyright 1930, by Evelyn Waugh; *Black Mischief,* copyright 1932, by Evelyn Waugh; *A Handful of Dust,* copyright 1934, by Evelyn Waugh; *Scoop,* copyright 1937, 1938, by Evelyn Waugh; *Put Out More Flags,* copyright 1942, by Evelyn Waugh; *Brideshead Revisited,* copyright 1944, 1945, by Evelyn Waugh: *Men at Arms,* copyright 1952, by Evelyn Waugh; *Officers and Gentlemen,* copyright 1955, by Evelyn Waugh; *Unconditional Surrender* (American title: *The End of Battle*), copyright © 1961, by Evelyn Waugh. Reprinted by permission of A. D. Peters & Company.

Princeton University Press, for permission to quote from Northrop Frye, *Anatomy of Criticism.* Also, for permission to quote from Gilbert Highet, *The Anatomy of Satire* (copyright © 1962 by Gilbert Highet). Reprinted by permission of Princeton University Press.

Texas Studies in Literature and Language, for permission to quote Robert Murray Davis, "Evelyn Waugh's Early Work: The Formation of a Method" (Spring,

1965) 7: 97–108, copyright 1965 by the University of Texas Press.

University of Toronto Press, for permission to quote from G. C. Sedgewick, *Of Irony, Especially in Drama,* 1948.

University of Washington Press, for permission to quote from James F. Carens, *The Satiric Art of Evelyn Waugh,* copyright 1966 by University of Washington Press.

A. P. Watt & Son and Curtis Brown Publishers, Ltd., for permission to quote from Sean O'Faolain, *The Vanishing Hero: Studies in the Novelists of the Twenties,* 1956.

The Yale Review, for permission to quote from Alvin B. Kernan, "The Wall and the Jungle: The Early Novels of Evelyn Waugh" (Winter, 1963) 53: 199–220.

Yale University Press, for permission to quote from Stephen Jay Greenblatt, *Three Modern Satirists: Waugh, Orwell, and Huxley,* 1965. Also, for permission to quote from Alvin B. Kernan, *The Plot of Satire,* 1965. Also for permission to quote from Alvin B. Kernan, "A Theory of Satire," *The Cankered Muse.* (Reprinted in *Modern Satire,* Harcourt, Brace & World, Inc., 1962.)

I am greatly indebted to the library staff at Auburn University, particularly Mr. Grady Geiger, for their splendid cooperation in obtaining sometimes obscure secondary materials; to Mrs. Rebecca Roden for consistent excellence in preparation of the manuscript; and to professors Leo Gosser, Eugene Current-Carcia, Walton R. Patrick, Franklin T. McCann (deceased), James R. Woodall, and especially Carl Benson for their guidance and encouragement. And to my wife, who is indeed a wife.

Masks, Modes, and Morals:
The Art of Evelyn Waugh

The blossoms of the apricot
        blow from the east to the west,
And I have tried to keep them from falling.
                                                    Canto XIII
                                                    Ezra Pound

1
Waugh and His Art

In a study which proposes an appraisal of the artistic achievement of Evelyn Waugh by examining the tenuous and intricate relationships between his basic technique and the dominant thematic emphasis of his novels, several problems arise which threaten to extend the discussion beyond all reasonable proportions. The necessary method of investigation involves complexities hardly reconcilable even by studies directed expressly toward that end; Waugh's fiction itself seems diverse beyond the point of incongruity, verging on paradox and contradiction, often within a single novel. The first of these difficulties may be dealt with somewhat out of hand by limiting the scope of the probings into technique and theme; that is, the critic may be selective in his approach. His choice must be based on literary discernment and motivated by serious purpose, not happenstance or presuppositions. But the second must be grappled with directly, if awkwardly, for no amount of selectivity or limitation can significantly diminish the enigmas encountered in Waugh's fiction.

Any attempt to evaluate the accomplishment of an artist must begin with a consideration of the nature of his primary medium of expression; in the case of Waugh, determining this medium can become a rather frustrating task. But the consensus of the criticism regarding Waugh is that it was in the medium of the satiric novel that he was most comfortable and achieved his greatest literary success. Because of this, and for other reasons that will become apparent later in the discussion, it is necessary to consider Waugh first as a satirist in view of both contemporary criticism and the general though unsettled rules of that ancient art.

Most of the critical attention which Waugh has received seems to be concerned primarily with clarifying his philosophy—personal, political, social, or religious—through analyses of the more superficial and obvious features of his fiction and especially through identification of the objects of his scorn. From such studies emerges, it is supposed, a mosaic reconstruction of the personality of the author himself, Evelyn Arthur St. John Waugh. Though these studies may be profitable, they do not consider Waugh the artist; they fall short of establishing with any degree of permanency a critical estimation of the author's artistry. Only recently has serious attention been given to analysis of the form and the interworking of method in his fiction, an area that in other than satirical novels has grown attractively complex in the twentieth century, at least to critics.

There is only one full-length study of Waugh's artistic techniques and achievement, and a few shorter discussions which deal directly with some specific feature of his technical ability.[1] Waugh the artist has suffered possibly because the art of satire strangely enough has been neglected in favor of its more superficial elements. This study will investigate the more intrinsic, aesthetic qualities and, therefore, is based in large part on the principle implied

---

1. The book-length study is by James F. Carens, *The Satiric Art of Evelyn Waugh* (Seattle: University of Washington Press, 1966); two of the best restricted studies of Waugh's early technique are by Robert Murray Davis, "Evelyn Waugh's Early Work: The Formation of a Method," *Texas Studies in Literature and Language* 7 (Spring, 1965): 97–108, and James W. Nichols, "Romantic and Realistic: The Tone of Evelyn Waugh's Early Novels," *College English* 24 (October, 1962): 46–56. These studies will be used extensively in this discussion.

by Kernan who, assessing the contemporary critical view of satire, has observed that in most criticism of satirical works:

> Our attention is . . . directed away from the satiric work itself and toward some second object, the personality of the author or the contemporary social scene. In this way satire is denied the independence of artistic status and made a biographical and historical document, while the criticism of satire degenerates into discussion of the author's moral character and the economic and social conditions of his time.[2]

Maintaining that the art of satire includes more than the fancy manipulation of language, burlesque, irony, caricature, and invective, he suggests that the study of satire be conducted in much the same manner as other literature:

> We need to approach satire in the way we do other poetry—as an art; that is, not a direct report of the poet's feelings and the literal incidents which aroused these feelings, but a construct of symbols—situations, scenes, characters, language—put together to express some particular vision of the world.[3]

If this approach is valid with verse satire, then there must also be some value in approaching the modern satirical novel in somewhat the same way. It is true that the satirical novel, hybrid as it is, cannot be examined fully nor can it be completely understood solely within the framework derived from classical formal verse satire, although there are many features common to all satirical works which may provide a basis for comparison and evaluation. On the other hand, satirical novels may not be judged altogether by the standards of the novelist's craft. In fact, some critics have suggested that Waugh's early works are not novels at all:

2. Alvin B. Kernan, "A Theory of Satire," *Modern Satire*, Alvin B. Kernan, ed. (New York: Harcourt, Brace & World, Inc., 1962), p. 165.
3. *Ibid.*, p. 166.

The word "novel" is, of course, a catchall term, but it is inescapable: we use it even knowing that we should make more precise distinctions. Properly speaking, Evelyn Waugh's early novels are satiric romances with some of the qualities of the novel.[4]

But another critic has attempted to define the satiric novel in such a way as to incorporate Waugh's early fiction into the category:

A "satire," as far as the novel is concerned, is a novel so constructed and so written as to embody a point of view which adversely criticizes the manners and morals of its characters—and often the society to which they belong, as well. Even a casual reading will make plain that most of Waugh's early novels are intended to be satiric, as well as comic.[5]

Although apparently disagreeing, both these statements deny Waugh the status of novelist and hence the prerogative to be judged by the discipline of that craft—the first directly by the substitution of an alternate genre; the second indirectly by extending the borders of the novel form to encompass even the most satirical work of Waugh. Yet, because satirical "novels" do most nearly approximate the novel in form, although they may not be judged as novels, in many ways they may be approached critically as novels. This is particularly true of Waugh's fiction because, in the course of his career, he seems to become less a strict satirist and more a novelist.

Proceeding on the assumption that the modern satirical novel, which is the current major form of satire, may be profitably approached as an art, this initial discussion will attempt to accomplish three necessary prerequisites for a detailed study of Waugh's artistry. First, it will seek to establish with reasonable accuracy Waugh's primary mode; specifically, it will attempt to determine whether and to what degree he is a satirist, and to survey critical opinion

---

4. Carens, p. xii.
5. Nichols, p. 46.

regarding his achievement in this mode. Second, it will examine as precisely as possible and in the detail necessary the constituent thematic and technical factors of this mode and their relationships, particularly as applicable to Waugh's fiction. Third, it will attempt to identify the fundamental technique which arises within this mode, a technique which is not only central to Waugh's satires but also essential to his artistic development and thematic expansion beyond the limits of satire.

THE ENIGMATIC MODE

Although Waugh's fiction, because of its diversity, defies generalization or relegation into any specific category, he is considered by most critics a major satirist of the twentieth century; however, he is not deemed a major novelist. At present, as for more than twenty-five years, few if any hear the slightest discord in the now traditional designation of Waugh as "satirist." In statements such as, "Waugh's career as a satirical novelist began in 1928";[6] or in almost casual references to him as a "modern satirist";[7] or in his being dutifully included in a critical study of "three modern satirists"[8] more may be revealed about the depth of criticism than about Waugh's fiction. Critics and the popular reading audience alike appear content to accept him as a satirist, with few if any questions or stipulations. In fact, only recently has been quelled the once prevalent rumor that he is a "satirist of the upper classes."[9]

It is regrettable in a sense that the first two novels, *Decline and Fall* (1928) and *Vile Bodies* (1930), were

6. Carens, p. v.
7. Nichols, p. 46.
8. Stephen Jay Greenblatt, *Three Modern Satirists: Waugh, Orwell, and Huxley* (New Haven: Yale University Press, 1965).
9. Alvin B. Kernan, "The Wall and the Jungle: The Early Novels of Evelyn Waugh," *The Yale Review* 53 (Autumn, 1963): 202.

such brilliant successes and therefore received immediate critical acclaim which established the twenty-five-year-old author as an accomplished satirical virtuoso.[10] This initial response has seriously restricted unbiased criticism of the later works and has consequently lessened the critical esteem with which these works might have otherwise been favored. Thus, the status of Waugh's fiction has been adversely affected in at least two ways. First, the early novels and the ensuing reputation so firmly established Waugh as a satirist that the majority of critics since that time have been predisposed to think of him almost exclusively as a satirist who writes the unique sort of lambast typified by *Decline and Fall.* Second, there has therefore been engendered a critical mood which encourages the judging of the later works, from *Brideshead Revisited* to *Unconditional Surrender,* by the standards implied in the early satires. Thus, although it has been suggested that because of their reflection of a social milieu long past, the "comic performances are in eclipse,"[11] and although *Brideshead Revisited* has received a great deal of attention, even the most recent criticism has dealt with the satires of the early period and has generally exalted the works from *Decline and Fall* through *Handful of Dust.*[12]

If such a reading of Waugh is correct, then there is

---

10. Both these novels have been considered "experimental" novels by some critics: Nichols refers to *Decline and Fall* as an "apprenticeship novel" (p. 46); Greenblatt describes *Vile Bodies* as "experimental" (p. 13). However, Davis has shown that they were not amateur novels because of even earlier experimentation which had "perfected" techniques (p. 97), and George Greene in "Scapegoat with Style," *Queens Quarterly* 71 (Winter, 1964–1965), has noted that "In *Decline and Fall, Vile Bodies, Black Mischief,* and *Handful of Dust* one is awake to the presence of a true artist, a maker" (p. 491).
11. Don W. Kleine, "The Cosmic Comedies of Evelyn Waugh," *South Atlantic Quarterly* 61 (April, 1962) : 533.
12. Although various divisions of Waugh's fiction are made by different critics, the most common is the concept which sees the novels in two groups: the early novels, *Decline and Fall, Vile Bodies, Scoop, Black Mischief, Handful of Dust;* and the later novels, *Brideshead Revisited* and all that follow. This division may prove a bit inaccurate as the study progresses, but, for purpose of discussion, this initial chapter, particularly, will consider them in this way.

little unity in his fiction, and rather than continuity in thematic expression and artistry there is a sudden and lasting decline beginning with *Brideshead Revisited.* That there are grounds for this view cannot be disputed; but to suggest that it is the final assessment of Waugh's fiction bespeaks naïveté void of both perceptive analysis and awareness of subtleties in art. If Waugh is to be understood and his artistry appreciated, the totality of his fiction must be seen as deriving from the same mode, even though there is a variety of applications of modal qualities.

Identification of Mode. In addressing the first of the problems mentioned above, that is, Waugh's universal acclaim as a satirist and the obvious discrepancy in this reputation, it must be pointed out that although the early novels cannot be taken exclusively as his whole contribution to the world of letters, nor as the extent of his message and method, an understanding of the mode of these works and the relationship of these early novels to the later ones is crucial to an appreciation of Waugh. An understanding of these novels allows insight into their nature and into the critical problems surrounding them and will provide a basis for a more detailed, comprehensive study of his artistry as it grows and develops in later works.

Although held in high regard, the early novels nevertheless provoke considerable friction ranging from disagreement over basic points to shadings of meaning and emphasis. No doubt it is the variety in the early works that has caused bickering over whether the early stories are actually satires. Critics on both sides of the argument seem oblivious to a fact particularly applicable to modern satirical works; Carens, noting that "Satire, both as a term and as a means of expression, constantly provokes controversy," suggests:

Many discussions are unsatisfactory because they are based on *a priori* views of what satire can do and must be. But it is impossible to prescribe the exact nature of a spirit that has endured in various prose forms since the time of the Greeks.[13]

Waugh himself, moreover, has encouraged controversy over this point. In a well-known essay, written in 1945 just after the publication of *Brideshead Revisited,* he denies that his novels, at least to this period, were meant to be satirical. To the question, "Are your books meant to be satirical?" he replied:

> No. Satire is a matter of period. It flourishes in a stable society and presupposes homogeneous moral standards—the early Roman Empire and the eighteenth Century Europe. It is aimed at inconsistency and hypocrisy. It exposes polite cruelty and folly by exaggerating them. It seeks to produce shame. All this has no place in the Century of the Common Man where vice no longer pays lip service to virtue.[14]

This interesting comment has spawned disagreement not only over whether Waugh was serious in this description of his own fiction, but also whether his critical view of literary history is accurate. Toward what end this latter point is argued one cannot be sure; of the profit in discussion of the former, one is doubtful. Nichols has disregarded the statement because "the tone of the article suggests that he was not entirely serious";[15] he has therefore concluded that Waugh, like the traditional demuring satirist, was being either ironic for the sake of preserving his artistic stance or merely facetious. While it may be true that the entire article from which this comment is taken is characterized by an air of friendly good humor, this is not sufficient reason to refuse to consider the comment seriously; in fact, there is a noticeable change in tone at the beginning of the paragraph which contains this disclaimer.

---

13. Carens, p. xii.
14. "Fan-Fare," *Life* 20 (April 8, 1946) : 60.
15. Nichols, p. 46.

But not all critics disparage the value of the self-criticism. Stopp takes Waugh rather at his word, suggesting that "the besetting weakness of many critics of Mr. Waugh is to infer satire when it is not uniformly present, but only the mixed ingredients of farce, satire, and the comedy of manners."[16] Specifically regarding Waugh's comment, he says:

> It is tempting to whittle away at this assertion; to say that here is the later Waugh who has lost touch with his earlier intentions; that satire has flourished in disintegrating societies—such as the Middle Ages—as well as in stable ones; that the satirist always pretends his own society to be disintegrating. All this is to the point; but there is some truth in the writer's disclaimer.[17]

Assuming as others have that "the element of moral indignation" is necessary for satire and noting that this quality is absent in Waugh's early attempts, he charges:

> It is preposterous to assume that Mr. Waugh's entertainments, especially the earlier ones, are quite simply, satirical, since we would have to infer that he was inspired by moral indignation against a variety of social phenomena too varied to be adequately listed. . . . Many critics, however, tend to take farce for satire, fooling for serious comment, and make up for some deficiency in fantasy by a touch of didacticism.[18]

Stopp concludes his remarks with the observation that "Mr. Waugh's earlier comic extravangazas are to traditional, objective satire as existentialism is to academic philosophy."[19]

Carens, however, believing that Waugh is a satirist, takes issue with Stopp's interpretation and questions the straightforwardness of Waugh's statement. He notes that the claim that satire can be written only in a stable society is an unsupportable assumption:

---

16. Frederick J. Stopp, *Evelyn Waugh: Portrait of an Artist* (Boston: Little, Brown and Company, 1958), p. 190.
17. *Ibid.*, p. 195.
18. *Ibid.*, pp. 190–91.
19. *Ibid.*, p. 195.

Nevertheless, it is just as possible that satire may be written during periods of instability, when the artist feels that traditional or peculiarly personal values are challenged. Aristophanes and Juvenal certainly did not regard their own times as stable ones, and probably one of the impulses behind their satires is the resentment at the absence of homogeneous values. . . . It is clear that the satirical novelists of our times belong to [this] class . . . writing from values which are not commonly held by their fellows.[20]

He goes on to point out that even the twentieth century "common man," as Waugh called him, is "not so barbarized that [he] is unable to respond to traditional appeals to reason and order." Yet, Carens's most valuable observations are in regard to the nature of satire itself; his more common-sense concept of satire, particularly in modern literature, makes the "traditional" rigid views of satire appear rather narrow, even impossible.

Sometimes satire aims to correct or reform; but probably even more often satire is written, as Wyndham Lewis argued it could be, for its own sake. Sometimes humor is a recognizable element of satire. But the range of satire, and its techniques of expression, are so extensive that within the satiric speculum are various shadings of the comic, the grotesque, the shocking, and the disgusting. Sometimes satire is a purely destructive force; but just as often it is creative too.[21]

Again, he very succinctly notes that:

Modern satire is not a genre but an attitude toward man and society that may be given expression, by means of certain traditional techniques, in any literary form . . . In the novel, as in other forms, satire may be given different degrees of emphasis: the spirit of satire may lightly brush the surface of a novel: it may lend a pronounced color to other significant elements; it may deeply suffuse the whole.[22]

Whatever value these remarks have in determining

20. Carens, pp. 57, 58.
21. *Ibid.*, p. xii, xiii.
22. *Ibid.*, p. xi.

Waugh's basic mode, the novels themselves demonstrate clearly that from the very beginning his work is characterized by the essential trademarks of satire. Frye has suggested two basic requirements of satire:

> Two things, then, are essential to satire; one is wit and humor founded on fantasy or a sense of the grotesque or absurd, the other is an object of attack.[23]

Highet, similarly, observes that "The final test for satire is the typical emotion which the author feels, and wishes to evoke in his readers. It is a blend of amusement and contempt."[24]

Regarding the first of the requirements, Kernan has specifically called attention to the objects of attack most common in the works of modern satirists:

> [Contemporary satires] attack some variety of the modern belief that man and his institutions are better than they were in the past and that our morals, our social institutions, our technology, and our wisdom are all approaching perfection. In each work the satirist has contrived some clever technique for confronting these beliefs with the inescapable facts of existence which make simple views of progress ridiculous and untenable.[25]

Studies of Waugh's early works have concluded that his one obsession was the decadent state of modern civilization compared to the authoritarian, romantic, chivalric traditions of the past, particularly of the Middle Ages. So strong is this disavowal of all that is modern that at least two critics have been so bold as to classify Waugh as a writer of "decadent novels."[26] Less harsh, however, and probably more accurate is Rolo's estimation:

---

23. Northrop Frye, *Anatomy of Criticism* (Princeton: Princeton University Press, 1957), p. 224.
24. Gilbert Highet, *The Anatomy of Satire* (Princeton: Princeton University Press, 1962), p. 21.
25. Kernan, "Introduction," *Modern Satire*, p. v.
26. Richard A. Long and Iva G. Jones, "Toward a Definition of the 'Decadent Novel,'" *College English* 22 (January, 1961): 245–49.

In Waugh's view, the Modern Age has crazily destroyed and can-nibalized what he finds supremely valuable—veneration for the past and for the heirarchical principle; the aristocratic way of life; the former greatness of England and the supremacy of the Catholic Church throughout Western society.[27]

Noting the symbolic significance of the "wall" in *Helena*, especially as it relates to the early works, Kernan has summarized the dominant thrust of the novels:

> While actual stone walls of culture are not always present in Waugh's scenes, the immaterial walls of culture are. The tradi-tions, the social institutions, the ritual language, the buildings, the manners, the morals, the codes of service, the esthetic values, "all that seeming-solid, patiently built, gorgeously ornamented structure of Western Life," are for the classicist like Waugh the walls protecting sense, order, and meaningful life from riot and savagery.[28]

Of course, as a result of this position, Waugh has been accused of snobbery and, possibly more frequently, of contumacious ultraconservatism. In fact, it is popular to think of him as Stopp has suggested—"writing out of a personal myth which is something between that of a Knight of the Round Table and an English eighteenth-century squire."[29] Yet, these and other similar opinions seem to overlook an important sentiment, seldom quoted, near the end of the paragraph in which Waugh makes his controversial disclaimer. Still denying the role of the satirist, he says:

> The artist's only service to the disintegrated society of today is to create little independent systems of order of his own. I foresee in the dark age opening that the scribes may play the part of the monks after the first barbarian victories. They were not satirists.[30]

---

27. Charles J. Rolo, *The World of Evelyn Waugh* (Boston: Little, Brown and Company, 1958), p. vi.
28. Kernan, "The Wall and the Jungle," p. 201.
29. Stopp, p. 57.
30. "Fan-Fare," p. 60.

This image is interesting not only because of the question of its appropriateness but also because it may reveal much about Waugh's true feeling toward his work. Here is described a lonely, dejected observer of ruin and chaos, isolated and guarded by a citadel of learning and religion, and therefore order and authority. The image suggests his well-known "exiles" statement, "To have been born into a world of beauty, to die amid ugliness, is the common fate of all us exiles." There is a note of seriousness here and a sense of genuine concern similar to that implied by Carens's final comment on the nature of the satirist:

> Whatever else the satirist may be, he is a man who cannot help but expose foolishness and vice and absurdity; and he does have standards (whether they be personal, social, political, theological, moral, aesthetic, or metaphysical) by which he judges, even if those standards remain implicit rather than explicit in his writing. He must know "good" if he is to expose and ridicule man's imperfections.[31]

Regarding the second necessary trait of satire, that is, comedy, Bredvold has suggested that "although much great satire can probably be read only with a grave countenance and a pain in the heart, nevertheless all satire is related to laughter through the common element of the comic."[32] He continues, "any sound theory of [satire] must be adjusted to our theories of the comic and of laughter."[33] Strongly reflecting a sentiment similar to Frye's, he maintains that "It is [this] combination of the moral judgement with the comic experience which gives satire its distinctive character."[34] Although Waugh has been accused of lacking any serious moral purpose in his "satires," and of neglecting to imply moral norms in his

---

31. Carens, p. viii.
32. Louis I. Bredvold, "A Note in Defence of Satire," *A Journal of English Literary History* 7 (December, 1940): 255.
33. *Ibid.*
34. *Ibid.*, p. 260.

early fiction particularly, it is readily apparent even from a casual reading of the novels that comedy is a paramount feature in the early novels and a pervasive leavening influence in the later ones. Because the discussion immediately to follow will explore in some detail the several problems connected with this aspect of Waugh's fiction, it will not be necessary here to engage in an analysis of the comedy in Waugh's novels. Suffice it to say merely that his fiction by universal assent possesses the second requirement of satire, comedy.

In light of these remarks, it may be suggested that although Waugh's fiction does not adhere to any rigid set of rules, classical or modern, his fiction is characterized nonetheless by the traditional elements of the satiric mode however freely manipulated and diversely applied, and therefore must be considered as belonging essentially to that mode. But Waugh can be accepted as a satirist only with certain stipulations, for his art is much too complex to be confined to the relatively narrow range of satire. This is not to say that all the novels are not to some degree satirical; they are, even the Crouchback novels, but not purely that. Nevertheless, there are from the earliest of his fiction elements of the satirical mode which with varying emphases are present in all his fiction—even in the so-called romances of the later period—the understanding of which gives insight into the unified complexity of his craftsmanship and appreciation of continuous augmentation of theme.

Disparities in Mode. The second of the problems encountered in trying to evaluate fairly the artistic accomplishment of Waugh, while not as nebulous as the first, is nonetheless intricate and therefore a matter subject to confusion on the one hand and oversimplification on the other. It has been indicated earlier that critical consensus holds that with the publication of *Brideshead Re-*

visited there was a marked change in Waugh's fiction. And it must be admitted that there are apparent differences between the first six novels and the later ones, but not to the extent urged by critics who would group the novels in two or more camps, parade them under flags of opposing genres, and send them to do battle in a war that does not exist. Therefore, there is a danger of prematurely assuming a dichotomy in Waugh's fiction which is not actual and which seriously hampers fair evaluation of the later works. This initial discussion, while also providing a basis for later study, will suggest that the change that takes place during the course of the novels is more a change in technique than in thematic concern and less a change in both than is generally suspected. It will attempt to overcome, at least to some degree, the dual-Waugh concept by recognizing the distinction that must be made between aberration and logical progression.

The general theme of Waugh's fiction was noted in the previous section dealing with mode, but it was not theme which brought the early satires their success nor which was responsible for the lesser success of the later works. The early novels were and are primarily noted for the amazing control of objectivity and the masterful handling of the ironic authorial stance which is vital to any successful satiric work. Because it is difficult within the context of these novels to pinpoint with accuracy the author's real opinion, so ambiguous and indifferent is he, these novels are thought to be more artistic than the novels of the later period. Rolo reflects the view of several other critics in his observation:

> At his best—that is, when he remains detached—Waugh is certainly the finest comic artist to emerge since the 1920's. Edmund Wilson calls him the "only first-rate comic genius that has appeared since Bernard Shaw."[35]

---

35. Rolo, p. x.

Again, Rolo represents a popular critical view in his brief summary of Waugh's early works:

> Total repudiation, coupled with almost total detachment which Waugh initially maintained in his comic fiction, makes for a peculiar purity of comic vision . . . . In this lies Waugh's special genius: he isolates and magnifies aspects of reality—the cockeyed, the fantastic, the eccentric—which the ordinary eye glimpses only fuzzily through the haze of custom and cant.[36]

Perhaps the detachment is too perfect, for, while praised as excellence in artistry on one hand, on the other it brings unjust criticism of Waugh's personal feelings toward humanity from those critics who would seek the man behind the fiction. Unfortunately, as indicated by the identification of "total repudiation" with total detachment" as in the statement above, it is easy to confuse artistic detachment with personal repudiation. Lack of precision in judgment leads to the belief that "complete rejection of the modern world is the source of both what is best in Waugh's work and what is most vulnerable to criticism."[37] But as Bredvold notes there is a great deal of difference between "derision" and "indignation."[38] With Waugh, as in every similar case, "detachment, or the pose of detachment, exposes the satirist to the charge of callous indifference."[39] Feinberg, in discussing the danger of absolute detachment, notes as an example the extreme to which Waugh pushes the detached stance, if it is indeed only a stance:

> Detachment can be carried to extremes, and Evelyn Waugh is quite willing to oblige. In her analysis of Waugh's *The Loved One,* Joan Griffiths says, "His vision is no longer that of the suffering participant . . . . He has gained his apotheosis; he is

---

36. *Ibid.,* p. ix.
37. *Ibid.*
38. Bredvold, p. 258.
39. Leonard Feinburg, *The Satirist: His Temperament, Motivation, and Influence* (Ames, Iowa: Iowa State University Press, 1963), p. 171.

dehumanized. And to us this seems the crux of all Waugh's work."[40]

It is not uncommon then to find critics who while praising the works generally as satires at the same time note with displeasure the harsh nature of Waugh's detachment and malign the author because of his "hardness of mind."[41] For some critics the novels are "comic *tours de force*";[42] for others, "inverted horror stories, burlesques of a metaphysical nightmare";[43] or, strangely enough, "nihilistic fun."[44] Accusations of "urbane savagery" and insinuations of the "carelessness of the Waugh Universe" culminate in the charge that Waugh lacks the moral seriousness of a good satirist, to say nothing of a good novelist.

> It would be nearer the mark, possibly, to say that though he lacks the moral seriousness which major writers in one way or another share, he does, to a high degree, have the gift of creating his own world . . . . Swift and O'Neill are great writers in a way Waugh is not. The experience they offer . . . includes important partial truths shot through with deep human concern. This concern is exactly, I have argued, what Waugh lacks. His novels do not extend our awareness of *why* people are as they are, and they inhibit rather than create compassion.[45]

But such detachment is surely a masterfully controlled stance, not the result of misanthropy. In fact, it has been observed that in the progression of the novels (viewing them especially in retrospect) Waugh may not be so de-

---

40. *Ibid.*, p. 173.

41. Sean O'Faolain, *The Vanishing Hero: Studies in Novelists of the Twenties* (London: Eyre & Spottiswoode, 1956) , p. 50.

42. Greenblatt, p. 9.

43. Kleine, p. 536.

44. Bernard Bergonzi, "Evelyn Waugh's Gentlemen," *Critical Quarterly* 5 (Spring, 1963) : 23.

45. A. E. Dyson, "Evelyn Waugh: And the Mysteriously Disappearing Hero," in *The Crazy Fabric: Essays in Irony* (New York: St. Martins Press, 1965) , pp. 195, 196. (Also published in *Critical Quarterly* 2 (Spring, 1960) : 72–79.)

tached, so cold-blooded a portrayer of human foibles and evils as he is reputed to be. There seems to be an increasing identification with the plight of the creatures in his fictional world and for that matter with those in the real world. Fielding says:

> The pain that is behind all satire was more subtly concealed in his than any precursor; but like a sensory mesh it still lay just beneath the surface of his perception.[46]

Rolo observes that "always within his comic vision" there is "a core of tragic awareness which gives his comedies dimension of serious art";[47] and Ruff maintains that there is always a "definite ethical/didactic purpose in Waugh's highly stylized, craftsmanlike prose."[48] Carens, who takes the titles of Waugh's early satires as "important keys to the seriousness of the attitude which informs them,"[49] quotes G. S. Fraser in suggesting that:

> Waugh's novels of the thirties are among those works "written superficially in terms of comedy or even farce, but with an underlying very disturbed note of bitterness, the nerviness, the unhappiness, the lack of purpose and the lack of love, in much contemporary British life."[50]

O'Faolain well describes the effect of the early novels:

> The effect of this genuine but ambiguous detachment of Waugh's is that the laughter of his first six novels is our happy tribute to the delicate balance he strikes between his detachment from characters which allows him to satirise them and his affection for them which allows him to pity them.[51]

---

46. Gabriel Fielding, "Evelyn Waugh: The Price of Satire," *The Listener* 72 (October 8, 1964): 541.
47. Rolo, p. x. Also, in this regard, Greene has noted what he terms "vision beneath the moral and social disarray" (p. 492).
48. Lawrence A. Ruff, "Comments on the 'Decadent Novel,'" *College English* 23 (October, 1961): 64.
49. Carens, p. 13.
50. *Ibid.*, p. 4.
51. O'Faolain, p. 53.

What Waugh has actually accomplished in these novels becomes more clearly perceived when one recognizes the difference between "detachment of method" and "personal disinterestedness."[52] As Feinberg has explained:

> The satirist uses objectivity as a technique, a method of contrasting unpleasant or shocking material with calm, restrained, dispassionate expression. It does not prove that he does care about the events he is describing; it simply means that he has chosen a particular artistic form to describe those events.[53]

It should not be too surprising, then, to read that "It becomes unmistakably clear that his early comedies and his later novels—however different they may be in manner and tone—are expressions of the same viewpoint."[54] This statement not only asserts a continuing note of seriousness in Waugh's fiction, but also specifies the basic distinction to be made between the early and the late works. The "manner and tone" of detachment do not continue through all his fiction. Allegedly, there is an abrupt shedding of the objective stance in favor of obvious, even maudlin, subjectivity.

It is critical consensus that *Brideshead Revisited* marks a change in the artistic stance and temper—a loss of detachment: "Hereafter Waugh's opinions, previously kept below the surface by the restraints of the ironic approach, are often projected into his fiction."[55] It is generally held that with this novel Waugh suddenly lost control over his material—or, rather, relinquished it; that he became too concerned with preaching moral norms rather than indirectly implying them as he had done previously. As a result, he is supposed to have degenerated into an incurable romantic, oblivious to or careless of artistic requirements of fiction. Stopp is in agreement with

52. Feinberg, p. 179.
53. *Ibid.*, p. 171.
54. Rolo, p. vii.
55. *Ibid.*

O'Faolain that Waugh, beginning with *Brideshead Revisited,* sacrificed art for moral pronouncement.

> The charge is that Mr. Waugh has abandoned his old detachment, and has declared his loyalties—excellent things, loyalties, comments Mr. O'Faolain, but fatal for an artist. "A religious theme given institutional treatment is always liable to get lost in the embroidered folds of ecclesiasticism," is his comment on *Brideshead Revisited.* In stylistic terms the charge is that he has abandoned the stringency of satire for the sweetness of romanticism.[56]

O'Faolain himself probably best summarizes the general disappointment felt by critics with the appearance of *Brideshead Revisited:*

> In his early and, I think, best books Waugh . . . was much too finely equilibrated a humorist to utter explicit statements, and so long as he could imply his norm he apparently felt no need to project a positive hero to represent it . . . . It is the mark of the moral satirist who, like all universal moralists, has detached himself from the accidentals of life by withdrawing to the remote ground of [general] principles . . . .
> This admirable detachment disappeared with the publication of *Brideshead Revisited* in which Mr. Waugh changed ground. Ceasing to be a moral satirist he became a writer of romances.[57]

Clearly suggested in this observation are several important factors regarding Waugh's fiction which are, to a greater or lesser degree, reflected in the writings of critics of Waugh. This comment implies that Waugh from the beginning was moved to write by serious moral purpose; that his detachment in the early novels was more than mere British reticence; that as his fiction progressed there was a loss of objectivity to the extent that the later works are directly moralistic, didactic; and that, as a result, it seems that Waugh lost all aspiration to artistic creativity.

Toward Reconciliation. If it is true that Waugh did

---

56. Stopp, p. 48.
57. O'Faolain, pp. 60–61.

abandon the detached method in *Brideshead Revisited,* then it must be that from this point onward he is something more or less than a satirist because he has violated a very important traditional and necessary requirement of the mode. Only once after this novel did he return to the purely satirical vein in *The Loved One,* a work which Stopp considers the only genuine satire he ever wrote.[58] Since the Crouchback trilogy, an increasing amount of scholarly attention has been given to the frustrating problem of reconciling not only the technical differences but also the thematic differences between the early novels and the later ones. The question arises as to why, if at all, the "change in matter and tone" occurred, and how, if at all, the later novels are related to the first.

In trying to answer these questions, most commentators have turned to biographical material to account for any differences in the novels, and indeed it may be possible to correlate certain aspects of Waugh's fiction with his personal life. Inevitably, there is little satisfaction gained in this venture; usually, there is only one explanation offered, that is, his conversion to Catholicism, the religion which he embraced early in his career but which supposedly does not show up in his fiction until *Brideshead Revisited.* Catholicism, in one way or another, does seem to dominate the theme of this novel, possibly affects the artist's technique, and obviously pervades the later fictions. But the fact that he was converted to this religion in 1930, more than a decade before work was begun on *Brideshead Revisited,* is generally overlooked by critics. However, Wasson traces the influence of Catholicism on his fiction as far back as *A Handful of Dust* (1934) ;[59] and Bergonzi, going yet a step further, suggests that a

---

58. Stopp, p. 192.
59. Richard Wasson, "*A Handful of Dust:* Critique of Victorianism," *Modern Fiction Studies* 7 (Winter, 1961–1962) : 327.

kind of Catholic temper is evident from the very first novel, *Decline and Fall*.[60]

It is not within the scope of this study to attempt to ascertain the reasons for the change or progression in Waugh's fiction; perhaps those studies which have approached this problem from a biographical point of view are sufficient to answer this question. But this study does propose to explore the manner in which the progression occurs and to discover thereby not only the thematic unity but also the firmly established and positively directed artistic consistency in his works, both early and late. It seems that within the novels themselves there is an unmistakable and steady development of both technique and theme that is not interrupted by *Brideshead Revisited,* nor, for that matter, in any of the later works. Though it cannot be argued that Waugh's own personal bias and religious faith are obvious in this novel and to a large degree in the ones that follow, technically and thematically the later major novels are in complete harmony with the developing artistry and maturing world vision of the novelist, and may therefore represent not simply aberration and decline, but a necessary and logical stage in continuity and achievement. A close examination of Waugh's technique as it discovers and develops theme in novel after novel will show that the later works are in direct line of succession from the early "entertainments" and may in retrospect shed a new light of seriousness on the early works.

As Schorer has observed, "technique is the means by which the writer's experience, which is his subject matter, compels him to attend to it; technique is the only means he has of discovering, exploring, developing his subject, of conveying its meaning, and, finally, of evaluating it."[61]

60. Bergonzi, p. 23.
61. Mark Schorer, "Technique as Discovery," from *Approaches to the Novel,* Robert Scholes, ed. (San Francisco: Chandler Publishing Company, 1961), p. 249. (Originally published in *Hudson Review,* Spring, 1948.)

In the same well-known essay, Schorer suggests the two basic elements of technique:

> Technique in fiction is, of course, all those obvious forms of it which are usually taken to be the whole of it, and many others; but for the present purposes, let it be thought of in two respects particularly: the uses to which language as language is put to express the quality of the experience in question; and the uses of point of view not only as a mode of dramatic delimitation, but more particularly, of thematic definition.[62]

Both these aspects of technique, as indeed all technique must be, are refinements of specification describing the author's artistic and moral identification with his fictional material.

Carens, in his recent book dealing with the satiric art of Evelyn Waugh, has noted the necessity of "an explanation of Waugh's techniques" to a real understanding of his fiction, and upon his own recommendation he has produced what is probably the most comprehensive study of this rather involved subject. Unfortunately even he does not fulfill the expectations aroused by this intriguing suggestion, but he does offer some worthwhile comment regarding Waugh's technique. First, he agrees with many others who have said that "Waugh's awareness of the comic possibilities of incongruity in language is not confined to the adjective."[63] He explains, "Waugh's way of seeing people, then of selecting from that vision, is just as ineluctably satirical as his manner of using language or responding to situation."[64] Again, he notes another large narrative device common to Waugh's fiction, that of "counterpointing":

> In the works before *Brideshead Revisited,* plot is usually farcical, a distortion of reality. Scene, or episode, on the other hand, is treated ironically through "counterpoint" or montage; the tech-

---

62. *Ibid.,* p. 251.
63. Carens, p. 59.
64. *Ibid.,* p. 60.

nique is most obvious in the earliest novels, and it has persisted, though significantly modified in *Brideshead* and the novels following it, right down to the Crouchback trilogy, where it is again a prominent element.[65]

Carens summarizes his discussion of Waugh's techniques by saying:

> These different but related satirical modes (irony of manner in the treatment of the *ingénus,* understatement in the characterization of some subordinate figures, varieties of burlesque in the delineation of grotesque characters) and the different but complementary structural devices (extravagance of action, irony of episode) are thus at the basis of Waugh's satirical expression.[66]

Carens's analysis, while implying two major aspects of Waugh's technique, characterization and plot manipulation, provides only a hasty, superficial explanation of these devices and quite overlooks Waugh's essential technique. Probably the most incisive short discussion of Waugh's technique is that of Nichols, who begins with the premise that the satirist "has to establish *within* the satire a moral norm which his audience will accept."[67] Referring specifically to Waugh, he then says:

> One way of doing this is to let the reader know that a character is intended to represent the author's point of view. His actions or comments, then, can embody or focus the satiric attack. Waugh seldom did this in the early novels. Instead, he chose to let the tone—his implied attitude toward characters, events, social scene— bear the burden of . . . establishing a standard . . . and . . . of embodying . . . adverse judgment."[68]

Establishing of the tone of a novel requires either authorial intrusion or technical skill; and Nichols considers Waugh a conscious craftsman, at least in the early

---

65. *Ibid.,* p. 64.
66. *Ibid.,* p. 66.
67. Nichols, p. 46.
68. *Ibid.*

works. Waugh's technique, according to Nichols, consists of three basic methods of tone control: first, "he stakes out points of reference to guide the reader" which, although "they have no bearing upon the gyrations of the Bright Young Things," "serve to indicate a more conservative system of values."[69] Second, Waugh establishes the point of view by ordering "the structure of the novel itself to imply it."[70] The device of contrasting scenes (noted by Carens) is essential to this method. But, third, he says, "The most important of these devices . . . is the explicit commentary of the characters themselves."[71] Nichols's study is too short to explore in any depth the methods he finds in Waugh's fiction; nevertheless, he focuses attention on the crux of Waugh's technical skill—authorial narrative, thematic, and tonal control without obvious intrusion.

Another critic, Davis, has been concerned with even more precise technical matters in Waugh's fiction. Although many of his observations will be referred to later, suffice it here to say that he centers his study on the problem of "authorial distance from the characters" and from the material. He first points out that Waugh had in the very earliest fiction—that even before *Decline and Fall*—learned to detach himself emotionally from his material. Once he had learned to do this, Davis says, novels like *Decline and Fall* became possible.[72] This "emotional detachment . . . enabled him to select and alter events and, even more important, to adopt as a narrator a stance suited to the narrative devices he had developed in 'The Balance.' "[73] Davis then notes that Waugh uses this technique to gain emotional emphasis, to understate emotion, or to refuse to comment at all.[74] In his study, Davis comes

69. *Ibid.*, p. 53.
70. *Ibid.*, p. 70.
71. *Ibid.*, p. 53.
72. Davis, p. 97.
73. *Ibid.*, p. 102.
74. *Ibid.*, p. 104.

extremely close to identifying the basic technique of Waugh—often hinted at, but never fully realized—which is central to his thematic continuity and constantly developing artistry. Although comment has been made about various elements of the satiric mode and Waugh's unique application of these, especially in the early works, no study has been made of the primary technique by which he discovers and defines the thematic possibilities of the action—a technique which, if understood in its full implication, encompasses all the various *sub-specie* techniques which may be more obvious in the context of a novel, and will explain any supposed artistic or thematic discrepancy between the early novels and the later ones.

Waugh's consistent use of a single specially contrived character in every narrative—the central figure—and the relationship of the narrator to this character is the essence of his technique and the key to a proper understanding of theme. The genius of Waugh is demonstrated in his technique of developing theme through this persona-like character through whom the world is viewed, explored, and evaluated, and by whose experiences a significant new dimension is given to the traditional thematic range of satire, that is, the plight of the sensitive, innocent individual in a barbarous, chaotic age. But before this suggestion can be pursued certain modal characteristics and possibilities must be recognized.

THE COMPLEXITY OF MODE

It is at this point that the special affinity of satire and irony and the nature of the ironic-satiric mode become crucial to an understanding of the intricacies of Waugh's art, technically and thematically. Everyone who has written on the subject of satire has noted at least some interrelationship of satire and irony, but because neither can be satisfactorily defined, there is no agreement among such studies. It is neither possible or necessary to review here all the theories that have been advanced, either historical or abstract,[75] but it seems that there are three basic critical concepts of the relation of satire and irony.

First, satire and irony have been considered as similar but separate modes, differing only in method and purpose. Kierkegaard observes that "it might seem that irony were identical with ridicule, satire, persiflage, etc. Naturally it has an affinity with this insofar as it, too, perceives what is vain, but it differs in setting forth its observations."[76] However, this concept, owing to recent critical insights, is at present not very popular.

Second, irony most commonly has been thought of as an element or device of satire. Worcester suggests that this concept of irony places it "within the larger orbit of satire," and that "the general elements of satire [are] invective, burlesque, and irony."[77] Similarly, Johnson considers irony a "method" or a "device" of satire:

> No satirist uses a single method only, but each has his favorites. Swift's was irony.[78]

> Irony is one of the most powerful devices of indirect satire.[79]

Based on this concept of irony, certain critical terms which designate specific ironic methods employed by authors have arisen and threaten to solidify the idea that irony is subservient to satire: "irony of language (or statement)," which obviously involves the author's use of lan-

---

75. For an excellent historical account of irony, see Norman Knox, *The Word Irony and its Context, 1500–1755* (Durham: Duke University Press, 1961), pp. 3–23; for a brilliant examination of irony in theory and in practice, see David Worcester, *The Art of Satire* (New York: Russell & Russell, 1960), pp. 73–144.

76. Søren Kierkegaard, *The Concept of Irony*, Lee M. Capel, trans. (London: William Collins Sons & Co., Ltd., 1966), p. 273.

77. Worcester, p. 75.

78. Edgar Johnson, *A Treasury of Satire* (New York: Simon and Schuster, 1945), p. 13.

79. *Ibid.*, p. 24.

guage; "irony of manners," involving his relationship to
the characters; "irony of fact," indicating the incongruous
juxtaposing of scenes as the author chooses; "dramatic
irony," implying concealed knowledge by the author and
the audience or reader.

Third, and more in accord with twentieth-century notions, is the concept of irony as a mode which is fundamental yet which looms large enough to encompass not
only satire but other variations of mode as well. Worcester has noted that irony "has evolved from a fixed, specific
form to abstract, freely combinable elements," and further that "irony in its own right has expanded from a
minute verbal phenomenon to a philosophy of facing
the cosmos."[80] As he says, "We begin with verbal irony;
we end with cosmic irony."[81] Johnson also has noted that
irony is more than a "device" of satire:

> Irony, then, has large bounds than are contained within a biting
> epigram or the stab of a sarcasm. The larger ironies are cosmic;
> they are entwined in human fate. . . . They may inspire the in-
> sights that shape a satirist's entire design . . . . Irony has been the
> animating spirit of the skeptical philosophers among satirists.[82]

Again, Worcester describes "romantic irony" as "the internal attitude of the mind of its author,"[83] but one of his
most meaningful comments is that "Cosmic *irony* is the
satire of frustration."[84] Perhaps this last statement begins
to shed light upon the relationship of irony and satire,
particularly in modern literature. Even more illuminat-
ing is Sedgewick's description of "Socratic" irony, which
becomes for the ironic observer a whole way of life:

> One of the commonest [the newer ironies which have so afflicted
> the literature of the last century] is the irony of Detachment or

---

80. Worcester, p. 75.
81. *Ibid.,* p. 76.
82. Johnson, pp. 27, 28.
83. Worcester, p. 124.
84. *Ibid.,* p. 129.

Spiritual Freedom. By this we mean the attitude of mind held by a philosophic observer when he abstracts himself from the contradictions of life and views them all impartially, himself perhaps included in the ironic vision.[85]

It is Frye who has elucidated this matter to the point of practicality. In his brilliant study of fictional modes, he identifies as the fifth and final basic mode that of the ironic mode. Irony is at last recognized as something more than a kind of device employed in satire and as something other than a mode separate from but equal to satire. It becomes rather a fundamental mode which contains intrinsically the essential ingredient of comedy, tragedy, and satire. This concept makes the relationship of irony and satire reasonably clear and very practical. Specifically, Frye says that "the chief distinction between irony and satire is that satire is militant irony."[86] It is clear that in this statement he is not equating satire with irony, but is in fact including satire in the mode of irony; satire is conceptually based on the reality of irony and its expression is then formulated by "devices" of irony. Frye's entire discussion of modes bears out this interpretation, but certain of his concepts are nowhere better reflected than in pronouncements such as "satire is irony which is structurally close to the comic";[87] or "Irony with little satire is the non-heroic residue of tragedy."[88] From the same point of view, he can, in describing *Jonathan Wild,* use the phrase "satiric irony,"[89] but he seems to recognize that it would be redundant logically to conceive of "ironic satire." Satire is characterized by irony, but irony is not always satire, even though it implies that potentiality. Irony *is*; in itself it is purposeless.[90] Satire

85. Garnett G. Sedgewick, *Of Irony, Especially in Drama* (Toronto: University of Toronto Press, 1948), p. 13.
86. Frye, p. 223.
87. *Ibid.,* p. 224.
88. *Ibid.*
89. *Ibid.,* p. 223.
90. *Ibid.,* pp. 40–41.

becomes by the author's intellectual apprehension of real ironies coupled with his moral incentive for correction. Perhaps this explains Frye's comment that:

> Irony is consistent both with complete realism of content and with the supression of attitude on the part of the author. Satire demands at least a token fantasy, a content which the reader recognizes as grotesque, and at least an implicit moral standard, the latter being essential in a militant attitude to experience.[91]

Waugh's fiction, therefore, must, because it is generally satirical, be considered as belonging to the ironic mode and thus it may be expected to partake to some degree of the narrative, thematic and technical characteristics of that mode. It has been noted previously, however, that his fiction is not exclusively or rigidly satire and that during his career it becomes something more or less than satirical. It may be suggested at this point that this is true of his work because he freely explores the range offered by the ironic mode, its possibilities in both theme and technical methods beyond the strict limits of satire.

Thematic Possibilities of Mode. The mode of irony lends itself to a variety of thematic shadings and is best realized through certain characteristic techniques. It has been noted earlier that Waugh's themes are pervaded by a sense of both the comic and the tragic. This is possible because comedy and tragedy exist side-by-side in the ironic mode; emphasis on one or the other produces what may be called "tone" in the novel and this is derived through the technique.

Worcester, in speaking of *Gulliver's Travels,* observes that it is "tragic and comic at the same time; as ironical works are apt to be."[92] Then, in a rather lengthy dis-

---

91. *Ibid.,* p. 224.
92. Worcester, p. 104. Maynard Mack in "The Muse of Satire," *Studies in the Literature of the Augustan Age,* Richard C. Boys, ed. (Chicago: University of Chicago Press, 1965), suggests that "tragedy and satire . . . are two ends of a literary spectrum," pp. 219–31.

cussion aimed at exploring the nature and relationship of comic and tragic elements, he comments on well-known but seldom well identified or described connections between the two. Noting that "if irony injects an element of comedy into tragedy, no less does it inject tragic feelings into comedy,"[93] he continues:

> Irony, then, is that common genius of tragedy and comedy which Alcibiades in the *Symposium* promised to explain, just before he collapsed under the table. Laughter and tears are reconciled in irony; it brings laughter to tragedy and tears to comedy .... More than any other form, the novel offers scope for the parallel development of tragic and comic themes.[94]

Frye finds a common basis of irony in both tragedy and comedy; when he speaks of "tragic irony"[95] and then of "ironic comedy"[96] he joins comedy and tragedy as counterparts of the ironic mode. In his discussion of irony and satire he arranges the satiric-ironic spectrum into five phases, and, basing his explanation on this structural device, he has described more lucidly than anyone else the relationship of tragedy and comedy and their paradoxical commingling in the ironic mode. He notes that "the first three are phases of satire, and correspond to the first three phases of comedy."[97] The first of these three phases is the phase of purely ironic comedy in which the comic is the paramount feature, even to the point of absurdity.

> The sense of absurdity about such a comedy arises as a kind of backfire or recall after the work has been seen or read. Once we have finished with it, deserts of futility open up on all sides, and we have, in spite of the humor, a sense of nightmare and close proximity to something demonic.[98]

93. *Ibid.*, p. 139.
94. *Ibid.*, p. 140. Johnson, who does not agree that satire must be comic, nevertheless points out the close relationship of comedy and tragedy in satire (p. 6).
95. Frye, p. 41.
96. *Ibid.*, p. 45.
97. *Ibid.*, p. 225.
98. *Ibid.*, p. 226.

He then proceeds to describe the second and third phases of satire, which are progressively less comic and more serious. The second phase corresponds to the "low mimetic mode" and thus forswears absurdity for realism and common experience.[99] With the third phase, the fiction becomes "satire of the high norm,"[100] at least reaching for the "high mimetic mode"[101] that characterizes "most epic and tragedy." Transition is made here from the comic to the tragic, for next, with the fourth phase, [the theme] moves around to the ironic aspect of tragedy, and satire begins to recede."[102] Frye observes that such fiction contains a type of irony that differs from satire in that no attempt to ridicule is made—the situation portrayed is "all too human."[103] The fifth phase corresponds to fatalistic tragedy in which the emphasis is on the natural cycle of the wheel of fate. This scheme of phases well explains earlier remarks that "satire is irony which is structurally close to the comic," and that "irony with little satire is the non-heroic residue of tragedy."

It is because of Frye's incisive distinctions that the comic and the tragic can be seen as they variously blend in satire, particularly in the second and third phases. Comedy is one extreme of the spectrum, tragedy the other —both based on ironic realities and both employing ironic devices in expression. These two modal possibilities and the tonal range thus made possible give satire its peculiar "attachment-detachment" appeal.[104] Thus, satire, though it will likely be close to the comic, is not likely ever to be "pure comedy" because, by virtue of its being in the ironic mode, there is always present the

---

99. *Ibid.*, p. 34.
100. *Ibid.*, p. 234.
101. *Ibid.*, p. 34.
102. *Ibid.*, p. 236.
103. *Ibid.*, p. 237.
104. Worcester discusses the affinity of tragedy and comedy briefly but incisively in *The Art of Satire*, pp. 138–41. See also, chapters on "Irony, the Ally of Comedy" and "Irony, the Ally of Tragedy."

shadow of the tragic. Likewise, when it reaches toward
tragic irony, there must be, if it is to remain satire, the
tug of comic incongruity. If satire moves outside the
ironic mode, it is no longer satire but becomes either
farce on the one hand, or melodrama on the other, because, as Worcester notes, "without irony tragedy degenerates into melodrama and comedy into farce."[105]
Maintaining the delicate balance between the possibilities
of farce and melodrama is the principal technical and
thematic problem of the satirist. It is this balance and
the phasal variations within the balance that give satire
either a comic or a tragic tone.[106]

Technical Exigencies of Mode. The satirist's fundamental
technique has to do with that of the novelist in general,
particularly—the second of Schorer's divisions of technique—that of point of view. But because the satirist
writes in the ironic mode the technique becomes a somewhat complex matter. Satire must be entered with the
possibility of two points of view being manifested in the
work: the one fictional and ironic, the other actual and
earnest; the first apparent, the second implied. Although
Kernan identifies both points of view with the "satirist,"[107] obviously they create different problems, for the
narrator or satirist in this kind of novel is usually sub-
ordinated in favor of the main character. However, the
narrator does control the degree of knowledge which the

105. Worcester, p. 139. Johnson similarly notes that "melodrama is
a treacherous force in satire precisely because it seizes control of the
satirist instead of being controlled by him" (p. 19).
106. Because satire cannot be "pure comedy" or "pure tragedy" (see
Worcester, pp. 37–38), but because it contains elements of both by
virtue of the ironic mode, its "tone" may be a reflection of the author's
comic vision or tragic vision. "Tone" in this sense is the recreating
of the mood or attitude of the author toward fictional characters, incidents, situations, in the mind of the reader by certain precise artistic
techniques (see Nichols, pp. 134–35).
107. Kernan, "A Theory of Satire," p. 67.

reader will have about the character and dictates by his comment the reader's attitude toward this character.

Irony, as it has been pointed out, is a mode which encourages the exit of the real author—it compels authorial detachment. As a result, the author may appear in the work only as a projection in a character often referred to as a "mask" or "persona" through whom the author implies his real norms. The persona in a genuine satirical work will more than likely uphold an attitude quite contrary to that of the real author, and the reader must be alert to certain guideposts and tones in the work itself in order to determine the actual beliefs of the author. Maynard Mack, who has focused a great deal of attention on this satirical technique, defines three basic character types of the persona: (1) the voice of the man (*ethos*) of plain living, high thinking; (2) the voice of the *naïf*, the *ingénu*, the simple heart; and (3) the voice of the public defender . . . the satirist as hero.[108]

Feinberg has suggested a further refinement which opens doors to greater complexity in technique. He ob-

---

108. Mack, pp. 88, 89. Although the satiric "mask" or "persona" is as old as satire itself (see Knox, pp. 162 ff) and is in perfect keeping with the demands of the essential detachment and objectivity of irony, recently at least one critic has questioned the validity of such a concept. In a commentary on personae, particularly as applied to Pope and Swift, Ehrenpreis ("Personae," *Restoration and Eighteenth-Century Literature*, C. Carroll Camden, ed. [Chicago: The University of Chicago Press, 1963], pp. 25–37), evidently overlooking the dramatic if not the artistic requirements of the ironic mode, suggests that the real author should somehow be inferred in everything the narrator says. This point of view is unpopular among most contemporary scholars. The Spring, 1966, edition of *Satire Newsletter* is given in large part to various rebuttals and discussions of Ehrenpreis's theory. Although it is impossible to review the dialogue here, most of the critics agree with William F. Cunningham, Jr., who suggests that "the moral and artistic justification of satire would seem to rest on some intermediary voice" ("A Concert of the Persona in Satire: A Symposium," *Satire Newsletter* 3 [Spring, 1966]: 93). Also, Wayne C. Booth, in writing of other than satirical works, introduces the concept of "implied author" and notes that "the art of constructing reliable narrators is largely that of mastering all of oneself in order to protect the persona, the second self, that really belongs in the book" (*The Rhetoric of Fiction* [Chicago: The University of Chicago Press, 1961], pp. 159, 160, 200).

serves that the author may assume the role of persona in at least three ways: (1) a first-person narrative in which the narrator is ostensibly the real author; (2) the first-person narrative in which the narrator is a character other than the real author by admission; and (3) a third-person narrative in which the narrator is unidentified and ambiguous, and the attention is centered on the major fictional character, who also serves as a kind of persona in satire.[109] This third method, according to Feinberg, is "the technique presumably furthest removed from direct author comment," but he notes that even this technique "is no guarantee of objectivity."[110]

The problem of technical analysis may be somewhat less difficult in a work in which the author uses either of the first-person methods, or what may be termed *personal narrative*. But, in the case of Waugh (except for one and one-half novels), the stories are told by an omniscient narrator who varies his detachment at will; such third-person narrations may be considered *dramatic narratives*. In novels of this kind, the reader must be concerned not only with the attitudes of the real author and the evanescent narrator-persona but also with that of the character-persona. It is a natural impulse for the reader to identify with the central character and at the same time to trust the narrator; the key, then, to successful thematic development and to evoking the proper response through the tonal effects lies in the relationship of the narrator-persona to the character-persona. Davis, quoted earlier,

109. Feinberg, "A Concert of the Persona in Satire: A Symposium," *Satire Newsletter* 3 (Spring, 1966) : 108–11.

110. *Ibid.*, p. 108. There is yet another distinction which could reasonably be made: that in which the narrator writes in first person and is involved in the action but not the central, and thereby not the thematic, character. For instance, *The Spectator Papers* are ostensibly written by an "observer" of human types and, although the characters move around him, he, unless voicing opinion in a sort of essay-like manner, is not the central character; he is merely a "recorder," yet what he records and the manner in which he records it dictates the readers' response to the characters.

implies that the essential technique of Waugh's early
novels at least was the use of the "neutral voice of the
detached author"[111] or the author's assumption of the
"role of detached analyst."[112] He notes further that because of this basic technique Waugh is able to create
effects by clever manipulation of incidents, dialogue, and
commentary not otherwise possible. He surmises that
"The thematic or rhetorical effect . . . is made possible
because his style as omniscient author is clearly differen-
tiated from that of his characters."[113]

Yet, as suggested earlier, the narrator-persona is not
necessarily the most important device of thematic development; in third-person satire, great emphasis is placed upon
the central character as a narrative, thematic, and tonal
device. Reflecting recent trends in criticism, Frye has
noted that the novel's central figure is the one most influential factor in determining mode. Basing his observation on Aristotle's *Poetics*, he notes that "the differences
in works of fiction are caused by different elevations of
the characters in them."[114] Frye therefore bases his entire
scheme of fictional modes on the assumption that "fictions . . . may be classified by the hero's power of action."[115] And the phases of the irony-satire spectrum
already reviewed are based on the nature of the central
character in the work. For instance, in speaking of the
first phase of satire, he says:

> The satirist may employ a plain, common-sense, conventional
> person as a foil for the various *alazons* of society. Such a person
> may be the author himself or a narrator, and he corresponds to
> the plain dealer in comedy, or the blunt advisor in tragedy.
> When distinguished from the author, he is often a rustic with

111. Davis, p. 99.
112. *Ibid.*, p. 102.
113. *Ibid.*, p. 103.
114. Frye, p. 33.
115. *Ibid.*

pastoral affinities, illustrating the connection of his role with the *agroikos* type in comedy.[116]

In this regard, Kernan also notes that:

> Somehow the satirist seems always to come from a world of pastoral innocence and kindness: he is the prophet come down from the hills to the cities of the plain; the gawky farmboy, shepherd, or plowman come to the big city; and the scholar, nurtured at the university, abroad in the cruel world.[117]

Frye makes clear the connection between this type of hero and the ironic mode:

> The figure of the low-norm *eiron* is irony's substitute for the hero, and when he is removed from satire we can see more clearly that one of the central themes of the mythos [that is, satire and irony] is the disappearance of the heroic.[118]

Just before the progression of the phases in satire enters the sphere of the tragic, there is a type of satire which Frye identifies as the *ingénu* form:

> Here an outsider to the society . . . is the low norm: he has no dogmatic views of his own, but he grants none of the premises which make the absurdities look logical to those accustomed to them. He is really a pastoral figure, and like the pastoral, a form congenial to satire, he contrasts a set of simple standards with the complex rationalizations of society.[119]

Waugh's Personae Technique. Critics of Waugh who have said anything at all regarding the nature of his central characters are in agreement as to the essential personality of these "heroes." Although each of these will be examined carefully in the course of the study, it may be

---

116. *Ibid.*, pp. 226–27.
117. Kernan, "A Theory of Satire," p. 171.
118. Frye, pp. 228–29.
119. *Ibid.*, p. 232.

observed here that these characters are of a common
stripe. Kernan has noted that "great voids are gradually
opened up behind the foreheads and in the hearts of the
dramatis personae. They have no private minds, no intense feelings whatsoever; no personality, no individuality."[120] He continues in explanation:

> The use of type characters is, of course, common in satire, the
> satirist is never interested in explorations of human nature. His
> characters are merely personifications of the particular form of
> dullness to which he wishes to give visible shape.[121]

O'Faolain describes the central figure in Waugh's fiction
as resembling that of other modern satires—"groping,
puzzled, cross, mocking, frustrated, and isolated"; "he is
never able to see any Pattern in life and rarely its Destination."[122] Stopp sees the character as a "passive, rather
melancholy, and isolated" figure. Of course, the *ingénu*
motif is easily recognized in these descriptions. Greenblatt
suggests that:

> One of Waugh's favorite satiric devices is suddenly to catapult
> a totally naïve individual into a grotesque and uncontrollable
> world, for, with this technique he can expose both the corruption
> of society and the hopelessness of naïve goodness and simple-
> minded humanism.[123]

Benedict, finding a "Candide figure" in Waugh's novels,
after meticulously and convincingly comparing some of
Waugh's early figures with Candide, concludes that:

> He is at his best when he centers a novel around such a character.
> Many critics have said that, in the light of Waugh's strong con-
> servatism, this is not surprising, since a conservative finds so many

---

120. Kernan, "The Wall and the Jungle," p. 204.
121. *Ibid.*, p. 205.
122. O'Faolain, pp. 16–17.
123. Greenblatt, p. 8.

evils in the modern world against which to contrast a simple and good hero.[124]

He suggests, however, a possibility that will be noted later:

> Waugh's chief interest in his finest comic novels may be not supporting conservatism but merely exploiting the comic situation which can arise when a character comes face to face with something which his previous experience has not equipped him to deal with.[125]

Carens has also noticed the *ingénu* motif but slightly refocuses the interpretation thematically. He suggests that "throughout Waugh's novels, devotion to childhood innocence expresses itself in ingénu satire and in what may be spoken of as the return-to-the-nursery theme."[126] Although suggesting that "the innocent provides the satirist with a particularly effective means of exposing vice and folly,"[127] and that "Waugh has seized upon the ironic manner of *ingénu* satire to give the reader a means of evaluating the essential object of satire—not the *naïf* himself but the world which surrounds him,"[128] Carens comes to a rather ineffective and quite meaningless conclusion as to what real purpose this motif serves :

> The innocent, however, is undoubtedly something more than a satiric tactic; his persistence as a type in Waugh's novels indicates a fundamental orientation toward youthful innocence.[129]

Regarding the thematic significance of these characters, Dyson suggests that Waugh's central characters are "dis-

---

124. Stewart H. Benedict, "The Candide Figure in the Novels of Evelyn Waugh," *Papers of the Michigan Academy of Science, Arts, and Letters* 48 (1963) : 689.
125. *Ibid.*
126. Carens, p. 35.
127. *Ibid.*, pp. 35–36.
128. *Ibid.*, p. 37.
129. *Ibid.*

appearing heroes," and although they may be a "mechanism for social satire," are themselves "scarcely important."[130] However, others have suggested that possibly they
as characters are more important to theme. Rolo suggests
as much when he says:

> Broadly speaking, the leading (male) characters in Waugh's
> comedies are of two types. There are the dim decent ones who,
> in a stable, rigid society, would fruitfully live out their lives in
> their predistined niche, but who are doomed to be victims when
> circumstances project them into the jungle of the modern world.[131]

Kernan implies thematic significance of the characters
when he notes that "what in some satirists is an artistic
device for getting dullness out into the open by disen-
tangling it from the complexities of real character becomes in Waugh a realism of sorts."[132] And Carens, speaking of the "anti-hero" figure common in Waugh's fiction
suggests that this "is something more than a satirical
tactic, and amounts to a comment on the nature of man
in contemporary society, and particularly on the condition of man during the twenties and thirties of this century."[133]

There is another technical factor to be considered in
a third-person satirical narrative, a factor which not only
involves the narrative process and the thematic concern,
but affects particularly the tone of the work. It has been
noted earlier that satire, while neither pure comedy nor
pure tragedy in tone, may reach toward one or both; in
fact, in a single ironic or satirical situation, there may
be both comic and tragic possibilities. The question thus
arises as to how the proper emotion is transmitted by the
author and invoked in the reader. The previous discussions of thematic possibilities of mode and of the nature

---

130. Dyson, p. 191.
131. Rolo, p. xii.
132. Kernan, "The Wall and the Jungle," p. 205.
133. Carens, p. 47.

of the narrator-persona and character-persona suggest that
the tone of a satirical work is determined by the relationship between these personae, particularly the narrator's
implied or expressed feelings toward the character. Nichols
has noted that "tone establishes the standard of values
necessary for satiric attack," and that "tone is essentially
the projection of an attitude toward, a point of view
about, not only the characters of [the] novels but also as
a direct consequence of the world which they inhabit."[134]
He continues by saying:

> The tension between Waugh's *realistic appraisal* of what the
> modern world is like and his *romantic yearning* for a system of
> values he *knows* no longer works informs the tone and provides
> the satiric standard.[135]

It is precisely this tension, realistic appraisal versus romantic yearning, that characterizes the relationship of the
narrator-persona and the character-persona.

Thus, the degree to which the narrator identifies with
his malleable central character and the degree to which
he solicits sympathy for him determines the tone of the
novel.[136] For instance, if the narrator in a satirical work
is both emotionally and artistically detached, the product
is likely to be farcical; if he is emotionally interested in
the character but artistically detached, the work will be
comic; if emotionally sympathetic but artistically detached, tragic; if both emotionally and artistically involved, the result is usually melodramatic. Although a
single satiric work may be dominated by one tone, obviously one work will hardly maintain a consistent tone,
especially a novel, because of the medley nature of satire

134. Nichols, pp. 55–56.
135. *Ibid.*, p. 56.
136. Booth notes that authors exercise "careful control over the
reader's degree of involvement in or distance from the events of the
story, by insuring that the reader views the materials with the degree
of detachment or sympathy felt by the implied author," *The Rhetoric
of Fiction*, p. 200.

itself, nor can it, for it is the shifting tonal values that give satire its unique *satura* nature. It is consistent with this theory that a satirist might run the complete scale of tonal effects in one work, but likely one tone will dominate.

In a satirical novel of the dramatic narrative type, there are within the interplay of narrator-persona and character-persona all the basic technical necessities for the structuring of any ironic novel and for complete thematic expression.[137] This combination serves first as the *narrative center:* the narrator relates a story about his character; it is also the *thematic center:* the character is usually the embodiment of the theme and as the narrator controls his activities and comments and gives selected information about him—the theme is thus delineated and solidified; it is also the *tonal* center: the particular attitude which the narrator assumes in regard to the character determines the degree and nature of the irony and therefore whether the novel is comic, farcical, tragic, melodramatic, or any blend or combination of these.

It is the dominating presence of the character-persona, shaped and colored by the commentary or implied attitude of the narrator-persona who may reflect a range of possible views of the character, coupled with the comic and tragic possibilities of the ironic mode that explains the diversity of Waugh's fiction and reveals the manner

---

137. Waugh, writing in 1948 of a conventional novel by Graham Greene, implied the necessity of the character-persona and narrator-persona relationship in the formulation of a novel. He speaks of a relationship being "established between writer and reader," and of the reader's enjoying a "conversation with a third party (the narrator)"; moreover, he sees the necessity for there being "within the structure of the story an observer through whom the events are recorded and the emotions transmitted." "Felix Culpa?" *Commonweal* 48 (July 16, 1948), 323. Waugh's only other comment directly regarding the use of "personae" is in his review of *Chesterton: Man and Mask* ("Chesterton," *National Review* 10 (1961): 251). In this essay he acknowledges "persona" as "one of the cant terms of modern criticism"; but he is considering it not in its artistic or dramatic sense, rather as a "disguise deliberately adopted to conceal some fear or vice."

in which all his novels are progressively united in theme and artistry.

This study will demonstrate the thematic and technical unity and the consistent artistic and thematic development in Waugh's fiction by examining the special relationship of the narrator-persona and the character-persona and by establishing the centrality of this relationship in narrative, theme, and tone. As each novel is considered in the detail commensurate with its significance, an unmistakable pattern of development evolves through the ironic spectrum, from farce through comedy, near tragedy, almost pure melodrama, to finally a unique kind of realistic fiction in which Waugh achieves a congenial blend of refined artistry with a positive, but tempered, moral statement.

2
The Establishment of Mode

Waugh's first two novels often are considered together as representing the earliest period of his career as a novelist. This view is valid for several reasons, but primarily because both of these novels deal almost exclusively with the decadence of contemporary society. Here, however, these novels will be considered together for slightly different reasons. First, they demonstrate clearly all the factors of Waugh's basic satiric technique—a technique which seems to be remarkably well formulated even from the beginning; second, they begin to reveal the different thematic and tonal possibilities that occur when the same or similar material is handled with a variation in the basic technique.

It may be said that *Decline and Fall* evidences a definite artistic method; *Vile Bodies* begins experimentation. Although the technique of *Decline and Fall* is never wholly given up, variation in the technique begins immediately. In fact, although the novels are similar enough to be thought of as complementary, they are in many respects quite opposite in technique and, therefore, distinct in total effect. It is almost as though the author purposefully swung the pendulum from one extreme to the other, either to determine the range of the technique or to search for satisfactory balance in necessary technical factors conducive to a serious moral statement. The difference in these novels lies not within their basic narrative material, their plots, characters, or action, nor in the author's apparent purpose. Their dissimilarity arises out of variation in technique involving the narrative, thematic, and tonal factors.

Specifically, *Decline and Fall* relies upon a dominant character-persona; *Vile Bodies*, on a dominant narrator-persona. *Decline and Fall* concentrates on the plight of the individual in a hostile society; *Vile Bodies* emphasizes more the society itself. *Decline and Fall* is a comedy turned serious; *Vile Bodies* is near-tragedy made farce. Yet, despite the difference in technique and in overall effect, in these first two novels there are the germinal narrative processes, thematic concerns, and tonal possibilities found in all Waugh's fiction.

DECLINE AND FALL

Critics agree almost unanimously that in *Decline and Fall* Waugh, the author, is completely absent artistically;[1] if his attitudes or opinions are represented at all, they are implied primarily through the narrator's account of, his reaction to, and his interpretation of the experiences of the central character. In this novel, it is immediately obvious that the central character, Paul Pennyfeather, is to be the major technical means for both narrative continuity and thematic development; and, because it is natural for the reader to identify with this character, the degree to which the narrator solicits or denies interest in him determines the tone of the work, and to that extent the significance of the character in relation to theme.

The special relationship of narrator and character serves first as the narrative center; this is the basis of both thematic and tonal development. In *Decline and*

---

1. James W. Nichols, "Romantic and Realistic: The Tone of Evelyn Waugh's Early Novels," *College English* 24 (Spring, 1962) : 46, 51.

Fall, except for a few brief explanatory remarks and narrative connections, the narrator reports all the action either as seen or experienced by the hero. Paul, a theological student at Oxford is drawn, through no fault of his own, into a fantastic world which he cannot fully comprehend. The butt of a practical joke, he is sent down from Oxford for indecent behavior. Shortly thereafter, he is hired by the seedy, incompetent headmaster of Llanabba Castle, Dr. Fagan. Besides the mischievous students, numerous other unlikely characters inhabit the place: Fagan's daughters, Captain Grimes, Pendergrast, and Philbrick. While here, Paul is seduced by the mother of one of the students. He is about to marry Margot Beste-Chetwynde when he is arrested while unknowingly trying to arrange for her the transportation of a group of prostitutes. He is sentenced and imprisoned, only to fall victim of the ridiculous Lucas-Dockery experiments in criminal rehabilitation. From Blackstone Gaol he is rescued by Margot, who arranges a fake release and a change of identity for him. Finally, under this new name, he returns to college and resumes his studies. Stopp is correct in noting that Paul, possibly more than any other early hero, is the dramatic center of the action.

> Just as the author is the implicit mainspring of his world . . . so the innocent hero is the concealed fulcrum of the action. Not only is the action precipitated by his contact with the world, but many of the other characters derive their role from the fantasy which lies behind the external events, a fantasy having its origin in the hero's mind.[2]

Perhaps this use of Paul is intended as DeVitis has suggested, "to create a link between himself [the author] and the real world and to make offhand commentary on the actions of his sophisticated and depraved characters."[3]

2. Frederick J. Stopp, *Evelyn Waugh: Portrait of an Artist* (Boston: Little, Brown and Company, 1958), p. 197.
3. A. A. DeVitis, *Roman Holiday: The Catholic Novels of Evelyn Waugh* (New York: Bookman Associates, 1956), p. 20.

But more important, he is the technical device which organizes the diverse incidents into a semblance of plot and allows the development of thematic significance. Kernan has suggested that "the most striking quality of satire is the absence of plot." "We seem," he says, "at the conclusion to be always at very nearly the same point where we began."[4] In speaking particularly of Waugh's novels, he observes that they "like most satires . . . lack a conventional story intricately constructed and carefully followed."[5] Further, he notes the emphasis that in these novels is placed on the thematic development through controlled and directed shifting of scenes and episodes:

> The major portion of the satires is composed of a series of brief and apparently unrelated episodes which flash on the pages in a manner of scenes from a newsreel. A scene in a fashionable London restaurant will be followed by a meal in the African or Brazilian jungles; a business journey will be interrupted by a long, carefully reported conversation between two women—neither of whom we have ever seen before or see again—about a recent scandal at Ten Downing Street. Events at a boys' school will give way to a discussion of modern architecture by a professor Otto Silenus.[6]

This kind of confusion, however, is supposed to be undergirded by logical arrangement and aimed at thematic significance:

> It is the arrangement of incidents and the overall pattern of events —plot—which ultimately establish the "meaning" in Waugh's novels.[7]

Davis has applauded Waugh's ability to "select only the relevant details; to shift rapidly from scene to scene with-

4. Alvin B. Kernan, "A Theory of Satire," *Modern Satire*, Alvin B. Kernan, ed. (New York: Harcourt, Brace & World, Inc., 1962), p. 176.
5. Alvin B. Kernan, "The Wall and the Jungle: The Early Novels of Evelyn Waugh," *The Yale Review* 53 (Autumn, 1963): 206.
6. *Ibid.*, p. 207.
7. *Ibid.*, p. 206.

out formal transition" and to use "rapid and fragmentary action and dialogue" as a means of thematic development.[8] And Nichols suggests that Waugh implies his "point of view" through "the structure of the novel itself"; as an example he quotes from a "pair of contrasting scenes" which serve to define the theme.[9] But without some kind of central narrative device, center of interest, or "norm" the story may indeed become not a story at all but a panoramic view of "disorderly profusion."[10] As a result plot is likely to be nonexistent, circular movement obscured, and thematic concerns, although hinted at in a harum-scarum way, somewhat less than precise moral statements.

The "cinematic" method of *Decline and Fall* is effective only because of an identifiable and restrictive narrative center which provides the basis for thematic development, and, at the same time, informs the overall tone of the work. Paul serves the dramatic necessity of strict narrative center in at least three ways: he is witness to the medley of events and thereby a kind of focal point; he is a dramatic filter for other characters; and, he is, even *in absentia,* a means of tying together the threads of the major action and of concurrently giving unity and progression to the many subplots.

First, Paul is the single most important device in holding together the three otherwise unrelated worlds depicted in the novel. The story of Paul's experiences is the tenuous filament which undulates through the effete school systems at both Scone and Llanabba, the corrupt upper class-society of the Beste-Chetwyndes, and the pretentious and ineffective penal system represented by the archboob Lucas-Dockery. Structurally, the novel is geo-

---

8. Robert Murray Davis, "Evelyn Waugh's Early Work: The Formation of a Method," *Texas Studies in Literature and Language* 7 (Spring, 1965) : 100.
9. Nichols, p. 53.
10. Kernan, "A Theory of Satire," p. 167.

metrically arranged so that each of its three parts explores one of these segments of modern civilization. The prelude serves to impel Paul on his voyage through the diverse but commonly decadent societies; the epilogue reestablishes him in almost the same circumstance he originally enjoyed even though he has in the course of his adventures lost his original identity. Paul's story thus provides the narrator an overall structural device for exploring the several elements of modern society and representative characters while at the same time maintaining internal unity in the narrative.

Closely related to this use of Paul as a narrative technical device is the function of this character as a passive revealer of other characters and the sub-plots in which they are involved. The rapidly changing, contrasting scenes are peopled by an assortment of characters, original to the point of incredibility. None of them may be called "round" characters by Forster's definition;[11] for that matter, none is so fully developed as Paul, who in the final analysis is neither altogether "round" nor completely "flat." But there is in this novel a menagerie of significant minor characters, unrelated for the most part, brought together only through the experiences of Paul.

Although the narrator at times suggests or implies character traits or offers a brief historical résumé of the most important minor figures, for practical purposes all of the characters are revealed in one of three ways, or by a combination of these: first, through their own conversation with Paul; second, by the conversation of others with Paul; third, in the conversation of the characters themselves is the presence of Paul. The stories of Captain Grimes, who stays "in the soup" continually; Philbrick, the deranged imposter; Fagan and his imperturbable daughters, who live in insecurity on the outer fringes

---

11. E. M. Forster, *Aspects of the Novel* (New York: Harcourt, & World, Inc., 1927), p. 67.

of a faded tradition; Potts, the energetic young crusader and opportunist; Pendergrast, the pathetic, skeptical churchman; Silenus, the opaque philosopher; and the nameless mystical homicide, who thinks himself the death-angel, are all mingled together in a kind of harmonious cacaphony through the pervasive shadow of Paul.[12]

Finally, Paul as narrative center serves as the unifying device of the three societies not only progressively but also concurrently. This is accomplished in two ways. First, Paul is the recipient of letters from characters yet to appear in the story and in this way he prepares the reader for later action. For instance, Arthur Potts is introduced first as a correspondent of Paul's and until relatively late in the novel is known only by his letters. Second, through the same technique, Paul, even though removed from certain scenes and subplots, continues to serve as a unifying device, insuring that all fictional elements of the novel ultimately coalesce in a reasonable, relatively complete narrative. Late in the novel, after Paul has been away from Llanabba for quite some time and the action there almost forgotten by the reader, he receives a long letter from Fagan which continues in brief the stories of the characters met earlier. Similarly, while Paul is in prison, he receives a letter from Margot which continues information regarding that particular subplot. In both instances, the action of the former social area is carried over into the next through the experience of Paul, so, despite the diversity of activity, the plots are at least apparently interrelated.

Through the relationship of the character-persona and the narrator-persona Waugh has satisfied completely the "exit-author" requirement of the ironic mode, at least in narrative. He guarantees the continuation of the ironic stance throughout the novel by limiting the narrator

---

12. For a discussion of the characters of this novel see Stopp, pp. 64–69.

generally to observing and reporting the activity of the
character-persona. Although the central character is the
dominant narrative factor, the narrator reserves the right
to maintain control not only in the narrative process
itself by his relation of events but also by injecting, when-
ever he deems appropriate, his own description, reaction,
or evaluation of characters or events.

In this regard, Davis has noted that Waugh as narrator
frequently provides background information, analysis of
character, or summary of action. Sometimes the narrator
will address the character directly.[13] Specifically, the narrator may provide short comments to heighten the comedy of the situation by sharing with the reader privy
information:

> "Pennyfeather, did Beste-Chetwynde make that noise?"
> "No, I don't think so," said Paul, and Beste-Chetwynde gave
> him a friendly look, because, as a matter of fact, he had.[14]

He may suddenly drop this confidential attitude and
withdraw almost completely in disinterested reporting:

> Clearly Tangent was not going to win; he was sitting on the
> grass crying because he had been wounded in the foot by Mr.
> Pendergrast's bullet.
>
> "Am I going to die?" said Tangent, his mouth full of cake (80).

Or, he may rather straightforwardly supply historical
background information, such as the lengthy description
of King's Thursday (129–36).

More significantly, at several places in the narrative,
the narrator seems to stand outside the structure of the
novel, obviously directing its many parts toward some

---

13. Davis, p. 102.
14. Evelyn Waugh, *Decline and Fall* (London: Chapman & Hall,
1928), pp. 32–33. Quotations in this chapter from *Vile Bodies* also
taken from Chapman & Hall ed., 1930.

wholeness, narratively or thematically, much as the director of a symphony:

> Before this happened, however, a conversation took place which deserves the attention of all interested in the confused series of events of which Paul had become a part (180).

This passage indicates the stance of the narrator as teller of the tale, but there is also a hint of his personal evaluation of the events in Paul's life, however ironic these estimates may be.

The most remarkable example of this type of narrator commentary is the chapter "Interlude in Belgravia," in which the narrator pauses to comment directly to the reader, outside the narrative structure, on the character of Paul:

> For an evening at least the shadow that has flitted about this narrative under the name of Paul Pennyfeather materialized into the solid figure of an intelligent, well-educated, well-conducted young man, a man who could be trusted to use his vote at a general election with discretion and proper detachment. . . . This was the Paul Pennyfeather who had been developing in the placid years which preceded this story. In fact, the whole of this book is really an account of the mysterious disappearance of Paul Pennyfeather, so that readers must not complain if the shadow which took his name does not amply fill the important part of hero for which he was originally cast (138).

It seems that Waugh here has violated all contemporary novelistic theory and certainly the ironic mode which discourages authorial intrusions. Yet the total effect of this novel could not be achieved without the freedom of the narrator within or outside the structure of the narrative. By this special ironic relationship of narrator and character, Waugh is able not only to handle the fantastic narrative material in a logical manner, but also to direct attention to a specific thematic concern and to imply its serious nature.

One is tempted to draw the thematic significance of the novel solely from the cumulative portrait of society provided by Paul's excursions and his association with the host of unique characters. Indeed, it is easy to agree with Hollis that the major thematic contribution of this book is its "picture of a society of irremediable futility."[15] Especially encouraging to this way of thinking is the narrator's own comment that:

> Paul Pennyfeather would never have made a hero, and the only interest about him arises from the unusual series of events of which his shadow was witness (139).

Kernan's idea that meaning arises from the proper arrangement of scenes in satire is a valid critical concept and is nowhere more applicable, it seems, than in this novel. And the narrator himself, while remaining artistically detached, provides information regarding the episodes and scenes that in itself suggests thematic significance. For instance, there is implicit social commentary in descriptive passages such as this one:

> The explanation of this rather striking contrast is simple enough. At the time of the cotton famine in the 'sixties Llanabba House was the property of a prosperous Lancashire millowner. His wife could not bear to think of their men starving; in fact she and her daughters organized a little bazaar in their aid, though without any real very substantial results. Her husband had read the Liberal economists and could not think of paying without due return. Accordingly "enlightened self-interest" found a way. An encampment of mill-hands was settled in the park, and they were put to work walling the grounds and facing the house with great blocks of stone from a neighboring quarry. At the end of the American war they returned to their mills, and Llanabba House became Llanabba Castle after a great deal of work had been done very cheaply (26).

15. Christopher Hollis, *Evelyn Waugh* (London: Published for the British Council and the National Book League by Longmans, Green & Co., 1966), p. 5.

Similarly, the description of the other dominant house in the novel, King's Thursday, is handled in the same quasi-historical, obliquely satirical manner—"Modern democracy called for lifts and labour-saving devices, for hot-water taps and cold-water taps and (horrible innovation!) drinking water taps, for gas-rings and electric ovens" (131).

Furthermore, there are in each social area a variety of scenes and activities, which whether presented straightforwardly, humorously, or satirically, without question have thematic significance. Hence, Nichols suggests that Waugh is satirizing a number of things: "the beastliness of undergraduate societies and the leniency of college authorities toward wealthy and aristocratic members of such societies," "private preparatory schools," " 'modern' religion," " 'enlightened' prison reform," possibly the "national character and culture of Wales," but most of all "the morals and outlook of 'smart' society."[16]

Yet, the satiric attack on the manifold foibles of the various societies into which Paul is thrust may be only one thematic possibility. At the most, these elements cumulatively provide the central theme; at the least, they may serve as an environmental backdrop—a condition necessary for thematic development on another level. The crux of this problem lies in the function of Paul in regard to the theme of the novel, specifically, whether he is intended to be himself thematically significant or whether he is, as the narrator says, only a mechanical device allowing penetration into various areas and the necessary center for synthesizing the subsequent insights into contemporary society.

Critics who hold this latter view evidently consider Paul truly "someone of no importance" (17) and take seriously the statements by the narrator to this effect. As already pointed out, the narrator explains that "Paul

---

16. Nichols, pp. 51–52.

Pennyfeather would never have made a hero, and the only interest about him arises from the unusual series of events of which his shadow was witness" (139) . Dyson and others assume this to be the narrator's straight-forward estimation of Paul and a renunciation of any interest in him as a character, other than as a mere technical device.[17] Yet there are two things about this interpretation which do not agree with the totality of the novel. First, it is not necessarily Waugh commenting as reliable author; the narrator is a technical mask, essential to the ironic mode. Second, the relationship of the narrator with Paul and their increasing intimacy after this statement does not corroborate a sincere disclaimer of interest in Paul.

Regarding the first, the narrator's ironic stance, it is apparent throughout the novel that, even with the narrative centered on Paul, just over his shoulder are the glaring, laughing, perhaps scorning eyes of the narrator who freely admits his role and, if he has not arranged the whole affair and does not have a puppeteer's control over his characters, at least is aloof by virtue of his superior awareness of the total situation; with this overall view he can reveal by implication or direct comment (usually ironic) his own opinion of Paul and the events:

Little suspecting the incalculable consequences that the evening was to have for him, he bicycled happily back from a meeting of the League of Nations Union. There had been a most interesting paper about plebiscites in Poland. He thought of smoking a pipe and reading another chapter of the *Forsyte Saga* before going to bed. He knocked at the gate, was admitted, put away his bicycle, and diffidently, as always, made his way across the quad towards his rooms. What a lot of people there seemed to be about! Paul had no particular objection to drunkenness—he had read a rather daring paper to the Thomas More Society

17. A. E. Dyson, "Evelyn Waugh: And the Mysteriously Disappearing Hero," in *The Crazy Fabric: Essays in Irony* (New York: St. Martins Press, 1965) , p. 189.

on the subject—but he was consumedly shy of drunkards (15, 16).

Waugh here assumes the role of detached narrator which allows commentary on the characters and events. Davis has referred to this stance as that of "detached analyst," who makes no pretense to "total objectivity."[18] But, while this may be a valid observation concerning the narrator, it must be remembered that this narrator-persona must not be confused with the real author. In speaking of the narrator's comment on Margot, Carens seems to assume that the statement reflects Waugh's own personal opinion of her.

> On the other hand, Waugh is plainly enchanted by Margot; she appears in the novel, emerging from her limousine, "like the first breath of spring in the Champs Elysées."[19]

Carens does not seem to recognize the obvious irony in this statement; as anything other than irony this comment makes little sense in the context of the novel. Even the concluding sentence in the same description strongly suggests that this is oblique ridicule carried off quite well by a rather mischievous narrator—"two lizard-skin feet, silk legs, chinchilla body, a tight little black hat, pinned with platinum and diamonds, and the high invariable voice that may be heard in any Ritz Hotel from New York to Budapesth" (84).

With regard to the second point, the special intimacy of the narrator with Paul, there is demonstrated even in these passages a dramatic distance between the narrator and the character of Paul, but not so much as there is between the narrator and the other characters. It is the detachment of narrator from characters and events that gives *Decline and Fall* its madly comic tone—a tone which

---

18. Davis, p. 102.
19. James F. Carens, *The Satiric Art of Evelyn Waugh* (Seattle: University of Washington Press, 1966), p. 72.

is almost consistent throughout the work; yet is is the increasingly close identification of the narrator with Paul that causes the comedy to take on a rather serious aspect. Martin has observed that "as a narrator, Waugh is usually neutral, concealing his attitude behind a front of impersonal reporting,"[20] and, indeed, the narrator's ironic stance appears much as that of the child who looked at Paul with a "penetrating impersonal interest" (27), but the narrator's special identification with Paul causes the interest to become in the course of the novel somewhat more than impersonal curiosity. As a result, this novel is not only the finest early example of the tension between the objectivity of the detached narrator and his genuine interest in the character, but also of the tension between realistic appraisal by the narrator and the rather bland innocence of the character; this tension transmitted to the reader through the narrator-character relationship informs the tone necessary to the full realization of theme.

The tone of *Decline and Fall* is essentially comic, but, as pointed out in the discussion of the ironic mode, in satire the comic is only slightly removed from the serious or even tragic. Also, it has been suggested that the ironic mode necessitates complete objectivity on the part of the narrator and that the comic tone is marked specifically by the narrator's being detached artistically but interested emotionally, this interest being implied despite the ironic stance. O'Faolain has observed "the delicate balance [Waugh] strikes between his detachment from his characters which allows him to satirise them and his affection for them which allows him to pity them."[21] In *Decline and Fall* there is a distinct, special relationship between the narrator and the central character which grows in

20. Graham Martin, "Novelists of Three Decades: Evelyn Waugh, Graham Greene, C. P. Snow," *The Pelican Guide to English Literature* (Baltimore: Penguin Books, 1963), p. 396.

21. Sean O'Faolain, *The Vanishing Hero: Studies in Novelists of the Twenties* (London: Eyre & Spottieswood, 1956), p. 53.

intimacy as the novel progresses. Artistically, the narrator remains aloof, noncommittal; openly, he neither approves nor disapproves, praises nor condemns; nor can he, for to admit even the slightest interest is to violate the artistic stance. Yet, through subtle means within the limitations of his detached artistic stance, he implies more than passing concern with his hero. The chief manner in which he solicits interest in the central character is his own identification with him, by concentrating on the hero's plight, his action and motives, his secret contemplations.

Although Hollis has concluded that "the characters in his first two novels . . . are too wholly fantastic for any question of sympathy or antipathy to arise,"[22] others are not so quick to dismiss Paul simply as a two-dimensional satiric device. Spender considers him "among [Waugh's] few sympathetic portraits of characters not gentlemen";[23] and DeVitis frankly states that "Waugh's sympathy—and the reader's—is for Paul."[24] Even if there is not a "deep personal concern" manifested in this relationship, there is more than what Booth terms "a bland or mildly amused or merely curious detachment."[25]

As the novel progresses there is prolonged identification of the narrator with Paul; the occasion of the identification more and more becomes not action but private meditation. Although several examples of this could be cited, the most illustrative is Paul's mental debate over the question of honor:

> Paul sat back in the carriage for a long time looking at the photograph, while his companions played several hands of poker in reckless disregard of Standing Orders. In his six weeks of

22. Hollis, p. 6.
23. Stephen Spender, *The Creative Element* (New York: British Book Center, 1954), p. 160.
24. DeVitis, p. 21.
25. Wayne C. Booth, *The Rhetoric of Fiction* (Chicago: The University of Chicago Press, 1961), p. 158.

solitude and grave consideration he had failed to make up his mind about Margot Beste-Chetwynde; it was torn and distracted by two methods of thought (208).

There follows a lengthy argument pitting the "two methods of thought" against each other; finally the passage concludes:

> If some one had to suffer that the public might be discouraged from providing poor Mrs. Grimes with the only employment for which civilization had prepared her, then it had better be Paul than that other woman with Margot's name, for anyone who has been to an English public school will always feel comparatively at home in prison. It is the people brought up in the gay intimacy of the slums, Paul learned, who find prison so soul-destroying (209).

Even though a certain amount of irony and satire is detected, it is difficult to separate the narrator from Paul and even more difficult to think that the narrator's objectivity admits no interest.

Any ostensible withdrawal of the narrator from Paul must be ironic; that is, while denying any interest whatsoever in Paul, the narrator admits a concern for him; consequently, Paul becomes thematically meaningful. It is true that contemporary society is under attack, for it is because of his perverse society that "the Paul Pennyfeather who had been developing" in earlier years "mysteriously" disappears, why he "does not amply fill the part of hero for which he was originally cast" (138). Here again is irony, for Paul's disappearance is no more a mystery to the narrator than the reality of the society. Dyson correctly notes that the plight of Paul by easy transition may become representative of that of modern man:

> The hero who falls among Mayfair wolves is an average English gentlemen of his time. Good-natured, well-educated as theories of education go, an ordinand with an Anglican training and

background, placid rather than fiery in his dealings with the world, not very bright but by no means a half-wit, he is the born victim of a corrupt society which he is ill-equipped either to understand or to resist.[26]

Greenblatt has noted also the thematic significance of Paul:

One of Waugh's favorite satiric devices is suddenly to catapult a totally naive individual into a grotesque and uncontrollable world, for, with this technique, he can expose both the corruption of society and the hopelessness of naive goodness and simple-minded humanism.[27]

Other critics agree that Paul is indeed much more than a mechanical device. Kernan sees both sides of the theme as does Greenblatt, but he places the emphasis on the plight of the individual.

Leave man, individual man, to decide on his own values, throw him into a relativistic world in which nothing is certain, corrupt the traditional institutions and ways of doing things so that no honest man can believe in them, and the result will be, as Waugh regularly shows, confusion, self-defeat, the grotesque distortion of human nature, and frantic but meaningless activity.[28]

Carens suggests that Paul is "something more than a satirical tactic, and amounts to a comment on the nature of man in contemporary society, and particularly on the conditions of man during the twenties and thirties of this century."[29] Paul is the center of the dominant theme of the novel—the plight of the sensitive, intelligent individual in a world of "disorderly profusion." This is to be the single continuing and developing theme of Waugh's

26. Dyson, p. 188.
27. Stephen J. Greenblatt, *Three Modern Satirists: Waugh, Orwell, and Huxley* (New Haven: Yale University Press, 1965), p. 8.
28. Kernan, "The Wall and the Jungle," p. 206.
29. Carens, p. 47.

fiction; here is the essential conflict that is central to all his fiction.

Concern for the individual transcends in moral significance the decadent society and its implications. Especially from the "Interlude" on, Paul's personal difficulties are graphically before the reader although cloaked in the irony of an artistically detached narrator. Paul's particular circumstance is finally given specific dimensions by Professor Silenus's analogy. Critics who have remarked about the professor's use of the "big wheel at Luna Park" to "tell Paul of life" find it very much out of place in the context of the novel; Carens seems to think of it as a kind of makeshift moral hurriedly tacked on because many readers insist that a novel be a "moral fable."[30] Few critics take this analogy as a serious comment on the predicament of Paul; but it can hardly be anything else, even though it is ironically delivered by the foolish Silenus. Waugh has prepared for this particular thematic emphasis from the beginning of the novel.

Although Silenus's analogy may be rather crudely conceived and awkwardly pronounced, it does put into perspective the two thematic possibilities by calling attention to the "static" individual in a "dynamic" society.

"People don't see that when they say 'life' they mean two different things. They can mean simply existence, with its physiological implications of growth and organic change. They can't escape that—even by death, but because that's inevitable they think the other idea of life is too—the scrambling and excitement and bumps and the effort to get to the middle, and when we do get to the middle, it's as if we never started. It's so odd.

"Now you're a person who was clearly meant to stay in the seats and sit still and if you get bored watch the others. Somehow you got on to the wheel, and you got thrown off again at once with a hard bump. It's all right for Margot, who can cling on, and for me, at the centre, but you're static. Instead of this

30. *Ibid.*, p. 74.

absurd division into sexes they ought to class people as static and dynamic" (231–32).

Perhaps it is the "static" nature of Paul which is described earlier in the novel, not ironically, but as an attempt to identify him with the traditional settled order, the *ancien régime,* in education, morals, and manners. From the time he is introduced riding his bicycle through the streets toward the gates of Scone, he is all this and more. When the narrator stops to comment specifically on him, he is "well-educated," "well-conducted," and competently knowledgeable of affairs of gentle life. Such a personality is unprepared to face the violent disorder portrayed throughout the novel. It is the overwhelming confusion into which he is thrust that causes him to appear as the innocent *ingénu.* His past experience and training, however admirable and complete, have not prepared him for the kind of world he is confronted with; therefore, he quite easily falls into the role of scapegoat or victim, helpless against overpowering odds. Dyson observes that "in no real sense is he guilty, but neither in himself, nor in his associates, not in the powers-that-be is there a will to establish this."[31] Perhaps the chaplain to whom Potts refers in his letter to Paul is correct—"great sensibility usually leads to enervation of will" (51).

Carens well describes the role of Paul:

> Although Evelyn Waugh's Paul Pennyfeather has little in common with the simpleton of the American naturalistic novel, the fact remains that he, as innocent, also plays a significant role in the pervasive negativism of the novel. As the only represented "good" in *Decline and Fall,* Paul is so passive that he is incapable not only of deliberate action but also of distinction between the apparent and the real, and so blank that he can be acted upon by vice and become a part of folly.[32]

31. Dyson, p. 188.
32. Carens, pp. 70–71.

Significantly, Paul, despite the fact that he is surrounded by a circus of activity and characters, is isolated throughout the novel. At the beginning of the novel he is alone amidst wild confusion and this condition becomes characteristic of the entire novel. As the book progresses, the isolation increases in intensity. Early in the novel the boys at Llanabba greet Paul by opening his door, looking in, and giggling at him (28). Later, in the Rue de Reynarde, after Paul realizes where he is:

> All the street seemed to be laughing at him. He hesitated; and then, forsaking, in a moment of panic, both his black hat and his self-possession, he turned and fled for the broad streets and the tram lines where, he knew at heart, was his spiritual home (171).

Yet there is another side of Paul—a positive, even somewhat aggressive nature that except on rare occasions remains totally submerged below the surface timidity. Paul shows some pluck when he bids farewell to Scone with "God damn and blast them all to hell" (18), although the narrator quickly adds that he said this "meekly to himself." Later he boldly refuses to marry the daughter of Dr. Fagan and even seems to take a fiendish delight in caning the pupils at Llanabba. He openly evidences disgust with the sham of Llanabba, although for the most part his dissatisfaction is kept within his own mind. In his relationship with Margot, at least at first, he does not seem to be the same weak, completely passive character of the first part, although it is true that Morgot is the dominating partner of this liaison.

Closely associated with this underlying vitality, Paul seems to recognize his own plight, even though he cannot fully understand it or arrive at a satisfactory solution. He is not, as Carens has suggested, oblivious to "what is happening to him."[33] It is true that Paul does not find a

---

33. *Ibid.*, p. 75.

solution because, indeed, there is none, but it does not necessarily hold that "Nothing that has happened has had any effect on him";[34] nor can the reader be sure that "Paul learns nothing from his experience."[35] In fact, his recognition of his plight and his awkward grappling with his own personal code of honor seems to be evidence to the contrary. Paul frequently contemplates his situation and on one occasion admits that his problem is "a test case of the durability of ideals" (52). Although at this particular time, with gentle prodding from Grimes, he acquiesces and feels rather content to have forsaken his ideals, he continues to be bothered by the problem of honor; his concept of virtue is never quite so sharp as it was originally nor his conscience so forbidding. When Margot asks him "Would you be happy if you were rich . . . ?" Paul replies, "Well, it depends how I got the money." But, when pressed to explain, he can only stammer:

> "No, I don't quite mean that. What I mean is that I think there's only one thing that could make me really happy, and if I got that I should be happy too, but it wouldn't matter being rich, you see, because, however rich I was, and I hadn't got what would make me happy, I shouldn't be happy, you see" (152).

Immediately after this faltering defense, he accepts Margot as a lover and the next day the engagement is announced.

Still later in the novel, after embarrassing experiences arising out of his relationship with Margot and after he has "honorably" but unjustly assumed all the guilt and the ensuing punishment, Paul has even graver doubts about the "code of ready-made honour." Yet even after "six weeks of solitude and grave consideration he had

---

34. *Ibid.,* p. 11.
35. Stopp, p. 199.

failed to make up his mind"; still his mind "was torn
and distracted by two conflicting methods of thought":

> On the one side was the dead weight of precept, inherited from
> generations of schoolmasters and divines. According to these, the
> problem was difficult but not insoluble. He had "done the right
> thing" in shielding the woman: so much was clear, but Margot
> had not quite filled the place assigned to her, for in this case
> she was grossly culpable, and he was shielding her, not from
> misfortune nor injustice, but from the consequence of her crimes.
> . . . On the other hand was the undeniable cogency of Peter
> Beste-Chetwynde's "You can't see Mamma in prison, can you?"
> The more Paul considered this, the more he perceived it to be the
> statement of a natural law (208).

It is this stalemate which throughout the novel has
been essential to thematic development; there is no
reconciliation of the two traditions. Yet, there seems to
be at least a tentative solution suggested: for Paul the
answer is the rejection of the dynamic society and the
return to the sheltered society he has known earlier.
Here there are moral codes, standards of value, traditional beliefs, however irrelevant, faded, and effete. Paul
is comfortably secure at last in the confidence that the
heretical "bishop in Bithynia" (who had "denied the
Divinity of Christ, the immortality of the soul, the existence of good," and several other orthodox notions)
should have certainly been condemned, and that the "as-
cetic Ebionites" (who "used to turn towards Jerusalem
when they prayed") were quite properly suppressed.

It is not fagging perceptivity that causes the latter part
of this novel to seem less poignantly satirical than the
first, for by gradually increasing serious identification
with the hero, the narrator, while maintaining his ironic
stance, has shifted the emphasis on Paul from an almost
strictly narrative device in the first part to that of near-
victim in the second. By the end of the novel, because
of the increasing identification with Paul, the reader is

too close to him to laugh for long. Perhaps Alastair's remark summarizes the strappado effect: "Good God, how
damned funny! At least it would be at any other time"
(176). *Decline and Fall* is predominantly a comic novel,
but it is permeated by an underlying sense of seriousness; just when the reader is laughing loudest, he is
struck with an awareness of a reality which portends a
tragedy of human proportions.

VILE BODIES

Vile Bodies (1930), while perhaps the most difficult of
all of Waugh's works to evaluate, offers as does no other
early novel insights into his artistic development, for,
when considered in light of the first novel, it provides
a lucid demonstration of both the complexity and flexibility of the primary technique employed by the author
throughout his career. Here the technical factors are
combined in a manner very much unlike his other
novels; but, even more significant, this novel is transitional, reflecting earlier technical achievement, and introducing technical difficulties that are overcome only in
the later works. In fact, *Vile Bodies* offers such variation
in the technique of the narrator-persona and character-
persona relationship that it is recognized as "experimental."[36]
The crux of the distinctive nature of *Vile Bodies* is
the diminished role of the character-persona and the increased dramatic importance of the narrator. As in *Decline and Fall,* the relationship of these personae determines the narrative method, thematic concerns, and tonal
control, but in this novel, the character-persona does not
function as the controlling figure in the progression of
the narrative, and consequently does not function in
either the discovery of theme or the establishment of

36. Greenblatt, p. 13.

tone. The action is generally related to Adam Fenwick-Symes; but from the beginning paragraphs, it is obvious that Waugh has chosen to minimize the narrative role of the hero and to put the burden of narration and the responsibility of thematic development and tonal control on the narrator, who functions freely and independently of the central character. The narrator is free to shift his view from scene to scene and his interest in one minor character to another and to observe and comment as omniscient. The central character in this novel does not have the important function of organizational device; although he is important to theme, the major thematic development occurs because of the narrator's interpretation of events; yet, the central character is essential to the tone.

First, regarding the narrative, Adam's role is less than vital to the continuity of the story and certainly provides within itself little plot. Adam, returning from Paris with a manuscript of his autobiography ready for the publisher, and intent on marrying Nina Blount, encounters during the voyage a curious group of characters including Mrs. Melrose Ape, her angels, and Father Rothschild, who figure slightly in the subsequent activity. Arriving at the customs check-point, Adam has his manuscript taken into custody and then destroyed by officials who think the material salacious. Thus with his source of income and "identity" lost, he rejoins the Bright Young Things whom he had known before his trip abroad; however, Adam is older now and seems never really to adapt to the adolescent's role. Because he has no immediate prospects of marying Nina, his subsequent adventures generally center on acquiring enough money to effect this happy union, but there is little direction or consistency in any of the activities. The diversity and rapidity of Adam's adventures give the novel its "patchwork" impression: wild parties throughout London, even at the

Prime Minister's house; nights of pseudo-serious love making with Nina; devil-may-care weekend trips to the race track with friends such as Archie Schwert and Lottie Crump; interviews with Colonel Blount, Nina's quite absent-minded father, who is in the process of making a movie of John Wesley's life; fleeting glimpses of an unidentified drunk major—all these incongruous activities are precariously held together by the love affair of Nina and Adam, but plot or unity is all but absent.

Because the narrator is unquestionably pulling the strings, Adam, although functioning in the central capacity like Paul, is obviously less important to the making of the story, and the plot lacks the unified thrust characteristic of *Decline and Fall*. *Vile Bodies* is the "scene of satire," as Kernan says—"disorderly and crowded, packed to the very point of bursting"[37]—made a reality; here, without the stabilizing influence of a Paul Pennyfeather, the novel does not fall apart, but only because it never comes together. It has been noted that "the picaresque convention, much transformed, provides the skeleton of the structure,"[38] but Stopp hardly finds even this degree of unity.

> Into the lightest of narratives, or rather into a kaleidoscope of scenes loosely associated with Adam's efforts to earn, borrow or win by chance, skill or sleight of hand, enough money to redeem honourably his engagement to marry Nina Blount, Mr. Waugh has woven certain contemporary phenomena, and some minor themes representing his own preoccupations at the time.[39]

Even though Adam is associated with most of the action, one gets the idea that the action does not revolve around him, but would go on just as well in his absence. The result is a scenic, "cinematic" presentation which trusts to the jumbled scenes for "meaning." These scenes,

---

37. Kernan, "A Theory of Satire," p. 167.
38. Carens, p. 74.
39. Stopp, p. 73.

"gathered loosely around the engagement of Adam Fenwick-Symes and Nina Blount,"[40] produce what Stopp refers to as "a patchwork impression which conceals the cunning with which the pasteboard figures have been mounted."[41] "The total effect," he says, "is one of crazy inconsequence."[42] Three scenes placed strategically near the end of the novel hammer home this effect: Nina's confused view of the earth from the plane (192–93); Miss Runcible's realistic nightmare (193); and Colonel Blount's fantastic film of the life of Wesley (203). The confusion of these scenes and of the whole novel is central to the thematic meaning of *Vile Bodies;* it is the authorial or narrator detachment demonstrated in these scenes that is essential to the particular tone.

As a narrative device, Adam is the only character who enters every major social area of the novel and who is associated with all of the other characters. Adam moves through several otherwise unrelated realms of contemporary society: there is the boat trip and the host of fantastic characters aboard; there are the customs officials, the book publisher, the "Bright Young Things"; comedy and satire are blended in the description of activities of the upper classes, the mad world of Colonel Blount, the madder world of the automobile racing buffs, the unmilitary confusion of the "biggest battlefield in the history of the world." Yet, the character of Adam is constantly overshadowed by the events themselves; it is as though he is merely a part of the fantastic panorama.

If Paul is an observing participant, Adam is a participant observed. Adam's subordinate role in the narrative is set from the beginning; in the first chapter the narrator backs into the introduction of Adam, so it is not exactly clear from his mildly ironic description that this

---

40. Kernan, "The Wall and the Jungle," p. 212.
41. Stopp, p. 73.
42. *Ibid.*

is the character to watch and with whom to identify:

> Two minutes before the advertised time of departure, while
> the first admonitory whistling and shouting was going on, a young
> man came on board carrying his bag. There was nothing par-
> ticularly remarkable about his appearance. He looked exactly
> as young men like him do look; he was carrying his own bag,
> which was disagreeably heavy, because he had no money left in
> francs and very little left in anything else. He had been two
> months in Paris writing a book and was coming home because,
> in the course of his correspondence, he had got engaged to be
> married. His name was Adam Fenwick-Symes (13).

Evidence of Adam's dubious centrality in the narrative
and acknowledgment of his less important role as character comes at the beginning of chapter 2, in which is
related the fracas at the customs checkpoint and his later
joining the *jeunesse dorée*.

In the action which follows, Adam serves the narrator
not as a focal point from which to observe but as a point
of reference in each area that the novel touches. For instance, it is only after association with Adam that Miss
Runcible suffers her degradation; the Benfleet episode, although involving Adam, is described not through him
but by the narrator; the transition to the high-society
"party generation" is made by "Adam got into the car-
riage with the Younger Set" (27), but the attention is
directed not toward Adam or even the influence of these
rowdies on him, but upon the Young Set as seen and as
presented by the narrator. With Chapter 5, Adam's role
becomes clearly defined; starting with this chapter, he is
the narrative device for initiating each chapter and its
activity, but, with the exception of this chapter, each subsequent chapter, while beginning with Adam as narrative center, gradually shifts to the detached narrator. The
effect is one of irregular circularity; the narrative wheel
has a flat side upon which it comes to rest momentarily
before beginning to move again. The narrator returns to

Adam, his reference point, each time before setting out to plumb other social areas.

The narrator provides the narrative continuity, necessary and unnecessary factual information, bits of analysis of character, the thoughts of the characters, and, above all, ironic commentary. It was noted that in *Decline and Fall* the narrator violated his typical stance at least once, to speak outside the narration as the arranger of the story to reflect on his major thematic character. In *Vile Bodies* outside commentary is the rule. The reader is aware throughout the novel that it is the narrator who, like the drunk major, is "spinning this yarn" (165); the narrator is frequently explicit about this fact. He continually manifests an awareness of the "novelist's point of view" (11), and the necessities of "the purposes of the narrative" (34). In fact, he seems to address the reader directly as old acquaintance, in a manner quite similar to that of the "mock-oral" tradition:

> (As a matter of fact, all you are likely to find in your room at Lottie's is an empty champagne bottle or two and a crumpled camisole.) (35).

Or, the narrator may stop the narrative completely to deliver his views on a certain aspect of modern culture:

> The truth is that motor cars offer a very happy illustration of the metaphysical distinction between "being" and "becoming." Some cars, mere vehicles with no purpose above bare locomotion, mechanical drudges such as Lady Metroland's Hispano Suiza, or Mrs. Mouse's Rolls Royce, or Lady Circumference's 1912 Daimler, or the "gentle reader's" Austin Seven, these have definite "being" just as much as their occupants. . . . Not so the *real* cars, that become masters of men (155).

The narrator is a freewheeler; in two pages, the scene changes nine times, without transition (20, 21). He is not only *coulissenmaler* but also *coulissenschieber*. And

as already suggested, the narrator is not confined to the
adventures of Adam. The narrator is free to wander also
into the minds of even minor characters, something done
only once in the previous novel:

> The angels crowded together disconsolately. It was awful when
> Mrs. Ape was like this. My, how they would pinch Chastity and
> Creative Endeavor when they got them alone in their nightshirts.
> It was bad enough their going to be sick without that they had
> Mrs. Ape pitching into them too (10).

> Poor Mr. Outrage, thought Mr. Outrage; poor, poor old Outrage,
> always just on the verge of revelation, of some sublime and trans-
> figuring experience; always frustrated. . . . Just Prime Minister,
> nothing more, bullied by his colleagues, a source of income to
> low caricaturists. Was Mr. Outrage an immortal soul, thought Mr.
> Outrage; had he wings, was he free and unconfined, was he born
> for eternity? He sipped his champagne, fingered his ribbon of
> the Order of Merit, and resigned himself to the dust (125) .

In these passages there is a noticeable change in the narrator from observer and reporter of facts to recorder of
even the most soul-searching contemplations of his characters, even to the point of capturing the thought-
language of the characters. Even so, there is an obvious
irony which guarantees artistic detachment and an implicit disgust which prevents sympathy.

One of the most obvious, and most awkward, narrator
devices—a device which in itself guarantees artistic detachment and, in this novel, emotional detachment—is
the abundant use of punctuation, specifically, parentheses
and dashes, to isolate certain information from the narrator:

> (It was a small suitcase of imitation crocodile hide. The initials
> stamped on it in Gothic characters were not Father Rothschild's,
> for he had borrowed it that morning from the *valet-de-chambre*
> of his hotel. It contained some rudimentary underclothes, six
> important new books in six languages, a false beard and a school
> atlas and gazetteer heavily annotated.) (9) .

In some cases the comments themselves, even without an artificial aside stance, would be obviously ironic:

> (When they spoke about him to each other they called him "the Right Honourable Rape," but that was more by way of being a pun about his name than a criticism of the conduct of his love affairs, in which, if the truth were known, he displayed a notable diffidence and the liability to panic.) (11).

The most sustained use of this device is in the episode in which Colonel Blount previews his film on John Wesley for an unreceptive audience; seven times in two pages necessary dialogue is included in parentheses, once in both dashes and parentheses (202–3). With this kind of side comment constantly before him, the reader cannot identify long with the character until he is reminded that the character is only to be observed, not felt.

Yet the narrator is not always so obvious in his manipulation of the reader's response; in some cases, he inserts his own commentary into the narrative without separating it from the rest of the text by punctuation. For instance, the first sentence in the book is clearly the narrator's own appraisal arising out of superior knowledge: "It was clearly going to be a bad crossing." Later, the narrator says, "Urged on by the taunts of the social editress, Adam brought new enterprise and humanity into this sorry column" (106). Sometimes, his intrusion takes the form of comments almost in the thought-language of the characters: *"Rapture"* (54); "and at last they all went to bed, very tired, but fairly contented, and oh, how they were bitten by bugs all that night" (151). One representative passage finds the narrator at once providing descriptive and historical information, narrator interpretation, mocking child's-language, and assessment of character:

> Sometimes the ship pitched and sometimes she rolled and sometimes she stood quite still and shivered all over, poised above

an abyss of dark water; then she would go swooping down like a scenic railway train into a windless hollow and up again with a rush into the gale; sometimes she would burrow her path, with convulsive nosings and scrambling like a terrier in a rabbit hole; and sometimes she would drop dead like a lift. It was this last movement that caused the most havoc among the passengers.

"Oh," said the Bright Young People, "Oh, oh, oh."

"It's just exactly like being inside a cocktail shaker," said Miles Malpractice. "Darling, your face—eau de Nil."

"Too, too sick-making," said Miss Runcible, with one of her rare flashes of accuracy" (14).

One of the passages which best illustrates the technical ability of Waugh to blend the narrator into the dramatic necessities of the narrative deals with Lottie Crump:

She liked to feel like that about all her guests. Actually in this young man's case she was wrong. He happened to have all that money in his pocket because he had just sold out his few remaining securities to buy a new motor car. So next day he bought a secondhand motor bicycle instead (42).

Here the narrator freely describes Lottie's mental state, explains the fact of the matter which contradicts her suppositions, and then drops back into a continuation of the narrative—all so smoothly that the reader is scarcely aware that the narrator is present.

But each of these methods contributes to the overall detached stance of the narrator and collectively they seem to prevent reader involvement. If in *Decline and Fall* the reader is conscious of the narrator looking over Paul's shoulder, in *Vile Bodies* he is aware continually of the immediate presence of the loquacious, knowledgeable, cynical narrator, who evidently has detached himself from the events and their implications, as well as from the feelings of his characters. The narrator assumes in this novel what may accurately be described as the stance of "detached analyst."[43] Davis has noted that:

---

43. Davis, p. 102.

By analyzing the characters so objectively he detaches himself from them, and from this position he is able to regard them, or seem to regard them, as specimens rather than as sufferers.[44]

In this regard, Nichols suggests that "Waugh's own point of view is much more clearly revealed in *Vile Bodies* than in *Decline and Fall*,"[45] and he goes on to point out how this is controlled within the dramatic necessities of the novel, specifically, "points of reference," "structure of the novel," and "commentary of the characters themselves." Carens, likewise, notes the dominating presence of "authorial" voice and suggests that as a result there is not in *Vile Bodies* the "uncertainty or moral ambivalence" of *Decline and Fall*.[46] One cannot escape the fact that, although the narrator's opinions are undisguised even when cloaked in heavy irony, he remains, both artistically and emotionally, even more aloof from his characters than in *Decline and Fall*; therefore, he can indeed look upon them, as Davis suggests, "as specimens rather than as sufferers." There is a loss of objectivity and distance, but only in the relationship of the narrator with the reader, not with the characters.[47]

It is paradoxical, perhaps, but in keeping with the logical and dramatic requirements of the ironic mode that as the narrator becomes more explicitly ironical regarding the objects of satire (that is, the more he himself implies both appearance and reality), the less necessary it is for him dramatically to imply interest in or sympathy with a character from whom he must be at least artistically detached in order to maintain the tension characteristic of the ironic mode. As a result, the characters, even Adam, are as Bergonzi has described them, "puppets, caricatures, pasteboard figures, rather than fully

---

44. *Ibid.*, p. 104.
45. Nichols, p. 52.
46. Carens, p. 74.
47. Analogous, perhaps, is the relationship of the sermonizer with the characters in his exemplum.

rounded characters."[48] *Vile Bodies* is more essayistic than novelistic; Adam, more exemplificative than real.

As a result of narrator and reader detachment, there is less thematic emphasis on the plight of the innocent hero than on the conditions that bring about his predicament. In *Decline and Fall* the social conditions serve more as a background against which Paul's innocence and ideals are tested and in which he struggles for a kind of identity; in *Vile Bodies,* on the other hand, the similar plight of a similar character seems to be more of an exposé of the social conditions which surround him. It is as Carens has pointed out: "Waugh has aimed his satire far more precisely than he did in *Decline and Fall*; and the activities of the Bright Young People introduce us to the futility and rootlessness of life in the twenties."[49] Kernan has suggested that *Vile Bodies* is "a savage indictment of a civilization in the last stages of decline because the defenders have left the wall."[50]

Perhaps, then, the remarks of Rothschild have real thematic significance and are not, as some critics suppose, artless moralizing:

> "Don't you think," said Father Rothschild gently, "that perhaps it is all in some way historical? I don't think people ever *want* to lose their faith either in religion or anything else. I know very few young people, but it seems to me that they are all possessed with an almost fatal hunger for permanence. . . . My Church has taught that in different words for centuries. But these young people have got hold of another end of the stick, and for all we know it may be the right one" (127).

In this regard, Hollis has suggested that:

> The part assigned to Father Rothschild in the novel shows

---

48. Bernard Bergonzi, "Evelyn Waugh's Gentlemen," *Critical Quarterly* 5 (Spring, 1963) : 24.
49. Carens, p. 74.
50. Alvin B. Kernan, *The Plot of Satire* (New Haven: Yale University Press, 1965) , p. 151.

clearly that he [Waugh] was beginning to feel that here were men who had something to say which the follies of the world neglected at their peril—here were men who had a secret, if only one could discover what it was.[51]

By shifting technique—specifically, by shifting *within* technique—Waugh in *Vile Bodies* explores the second thematic potential of the innocent in a hostile world— that of the corruption and decadence of the society itself.

However, Adam is potentially a serious if not tragic figure. Like Paul, he is isolated, even when with the Bright Young Things, and, like Paul, he recognizes that the world is somehow crazily mixed-up; but, unlike Paul, he joins in the chaos. When Adam returns from Paris, at the beginning of the book, he is a stranger; most of the people do not know him (26) and he does not re- member them (36–37). Throughout the novel, people continually "disappear" (180–181); and in the final scenes, Adam is still alone, this time on the "biggest battlefield in the history of the world" (212). The whole novel can be seen as Adam's attempt to gain some kind of identity in a world that by its very nature forbids individualism; Adam symbolically loses his identity with the burning of his autobiography at the beginning of the novel and never regains even a substitute. His plight is well depicted in the scene at the race track involving the drunk major:

> "I've been looking for you," shouted Adam. "I want some money."
> "Can't hear—what do you want?"
> "Money."
> "It's no good—these infernal things make too much noise. What's your name? Lottie had forgotten."
> "Adam Symes."
> "Can't hear."

---

51. Hollis, p. 8. (If the title "Vile Bodies" is an allusion to Philippians 3:20–21, then the implications of Rothschild's remarks are serious indeed.)

Archie turned off to the left. The drunk Major's car accelerated and swept away to the right.

"*I must know your name,*" he cried. All the drivers seemed to choose this moment to sound their horns; the woman cyclist at Adam's elbow rang her bell; the male cyclist tooted a little horn like a Paris taxi, and the programme boy yelled in his car, "Official programme—map of the course—all the drivers."

"Adam Symes" he shouted desperately, but the Major threw up his hands in despair and he disappeared in the crowd (158-59).

Adam is aware of his situation but does not have the strength of will to correct it. That he recognizes the vacuity in the flamboyant social life of the Bright Young Things is evidenced early by his almost plaintive response, "Oh, Nina, *what a lot of parties*" (118). He almost finds the moral strength to approach and overcome at least his own plight, but at the final moment lapses into "inervation of will":

"I don't know. . . . Nina, do you ever feel that things simply can't go on much longer?"

"What d'you mean by things—us or everything?"

"Everything."

"No—I wish I did."

"I dare say you're right . . . what are you looking for?"

"Clothes."

"Why?"

"Oh, Adam, what do you want . . . you're too impossible this evening."

"Don't let's talk anymore, Nina, d'you mind?"

Later he said: "I'd give anything in the world for something different."

But when pressed to explain what he means, Adam can only reply, "Nothing" (185).

These passages, and others similar to them, have been pointed out by critics as an indication of the real thematic significance of Adam and that the author, therefore, expects the reader to identify with Adam and in fact feel sympathy for him. Carens suggests that "the situation of Adam and Nina, however, is more pathetic than that of Pennyfeather, because they are conscious of what is happening to them."[52] Martin has supposed that Adam shares with Nina a "feeling toward which we are expected to be sympathetic."[53] DeVitis thinks that Adam is "wiser than Paul," and that he can see "the futility of an existence whose very worthlessness forms the basis of uncomfortably funny situations";[54] and Greenblatt classifies the novel as a "comedy haunted by an inexplicable sadness," portraying "the pathos of wasted lives."[55] But to take the gist of these comments as the final evaluation of the theme of this novel is to overlook the very carefully controlled and pervasive ironic tone.

Although there is assuredly the potentiality for sympathy in Adam's situation, the narrator does not seem to prepare the reader to look upon Adam as a character worthy of sympathy or, for that matter, very much interest. On the contrary, he has encouraged emotional detachment by the narration. As noted earlier, in *Decline and Fall* there is an obvious tension between the narrator's detached stance and his implicit interest in Paul; in *Vile Bodies,* the narrator who is artistically detached seems never to become emotionally involved in the affairs of Adam. It may well be that the complete detachment of the narrator artistically and emotionally is calculated to intensify the pathos inherent in Adam's situation. Davis suggests that:

Waugh uses his detachment to gain emotional emphasis by suddenly revealing the reality of the character's plight, as in the deaths of Lord Balcairn and Agatha Runcible or in the despond-

52. Carens, p. 75.
53. Martin, p. 399.
54. DeVitis, p. 29.
55. Greenblatt, pp. 12–13.

ent dialogue of Adam Fenwick-Symes and in Father Rothschild's speech on the younger generation's lack of respect.[56]

If this be the case, then Waugh has altered his technique of tonal control; the narrator's studied, almost contemptuous, emotional detachment from Adam is quite different from his implied benevolent attitude toward Paul.

The frankly incidental introduction of Adam at the beginning of the novel sets the tenor of the relationship of the narrator and Adam throughout the novel. The obvious shift from the character as narrative center and from monologue or lengthy description of his mental state to encourage the recognition of the character as thematic center is demonstrated in the complete emotional and artistic detachment with which the narrator backhandedly relates the particulars of Adam's experiences. Nor is there ever sympathetic brooding with him; rather, the narrator shuns even brief identification. In discussing the night in Arundel, Adam promises Nina, "You'll enjoy it more next time."

> Nina said, *"Next time,"* and told him that he took too much for granted.
> Adam said that that was a phrase which only prostitutes used.
> Then they started a real quarrel which lasted all through the film and all the way to Nina's flat and all the time she was cutting up a lemon and making a cocktail, until Adam said that if she didn't stop going on he would ravish her there and then on her own hearth rug.
> Then Nina went on.
> By the time that Adam went to dress she had climbed down enough to admit that perhaps love was a thing one could grow to be fond of after a time, like smoking a pipe. She still maintained that it made one feel very ill at first, and she doubted if it was worth it.
> They began to argue at the top of the lift about whether acquired tastes were ever worth acquiring. Adam said that it

---

56. Davis, p. 104.

was imitation, and that it was natural to man to be imitative, so that acquired tastes were natural.

But the presence of the lift boy stopped that argument coming to a solution as the other one had done (87–88).

Although there is in this scene and others like it potential dramatic revelation of character, fuller development of character, and involvement of the reader, the narrator chooses to stifle these possibilities. This detachment, coupled with the fact that the narrator makes no attempt whatsoever to explain Adam's action even though it contradicts his own beliefs, makes certain feints toward identification appear ridiculous. Statements such as "It hurt Adam deeply to think much about Nina" (178) seem absurd, for Adam is not capable of feeling. Savage, discussing the effect of *Decline and Fall,* comes closer to describing *Vile Bodies*:

> The world of human experience is held at such a distance as to preclude the possibility of its being taken seriously; at a distance at which persons become puppets and thereby appropriate objects of diversion.[57]

Several critics argue that Adam has the depth of a real character because he is able to reflect seriously upon the social scene and discover the implications. Carens particularly has called attention to the fact that "Adam reflects upon the feverish round of parties which are analogous to Miss Runcible's motor race":[58]

> (. . . Masked parties, Savage parties, Victorian parties, Greek parties, Wild West parties, Russian parties, Circus parties, parties where one had to dress as someone else, almost naked parties in St. John's Wood, parties in flats and studios and houses and ships and hotels and night clubs, in windmills and swimming baths,

57. D. S. Savage, "The Innocence of Evelyn Waugh," *Focus Four: The Novelist as Thinker,* B. Rajan, ed. (London, 1947), pp. 34–35, quoted by DeVitis, p. 22.
58. Carens, p. 75.

tea parties at school where one ate muffins and meringues and tinned crab, parties at Oxford where one drank brown sherry and smoked Turkish cigarettes, dull dancing in London and comic dances in Scotland and disgusting dances in Paris—all that succession and repetition of massed humanity. . . . Those vile bodies . . .) (118).

Carens has overlooked the fact, however, that this is not the interior monologue of Adam, but the inserted commentary of the narrator. Certainly, if the parentheses do not indicate that this is an aside, then the nature of the commentary itself does. In the first place, nowhere else does Adam seem to be capable of sustained thought on a limited subject; second, he never again is capable of such outright criticism of his society; third, it seems unlikely from the context that he has experienced every kind of party mentioned.

Spender has suggested that all of the Bright Young Things, including Adam, refuse sympathy:

What is really so attractive and seductive about the Bright Young Things is their refusal to be tragic. They are genuinely frivolous, real sneerers and jeerers who raise what is after all an important moral question: Is anything worth taking seriously? This question should only be answered in the negative by those who are able to treat love lightly, always maintain a certain gaiety, and never under any circumstances show the slightest trace of self-pity.[59]

Greenfield cannot take them seriously because they are, like so many characters in the early novels, "abstractions, reflections, counterfeits—sometimes no more than voices."[60] Stopp goes further by saying that *"Vile Bodies* is an account of young people who are disillusioned; but the author is disillusioned of their disillusion."[61] It is indeed this attitude which seems explicit in the narrator's

59. Spender, p. 164.
60. Meg Greenfield, "Half-People in a Double World," *Reporter* 18 (June 28, 1958) : 38.
61. Stopp, p. 195.

relationship to Adam as well as the other characters.

The narrator's lack of implicit interest in Adam robs the satire of *Vile Bodies* of any human sting and denies it the status of serious art. Because the reader cannot identify with the pasteboard character of Adam, any moral significance of the novel occurs to the reader only in retrospect—when he extends the possibilities of farce into a tragic reality involving the whole of contemporary society. It cannot be said, however, that the author encourages this extension. Yet, somehow there lingers with the reader the awareness that although the participants in the drama do not know it, and although the narrator neither admits the fact nor solicits sympathy for the characters, *Vile Bodies* portrays a human predicament that is closely akin to the tragic.

These two novels, then, despite their dissimilarities, first, place Waugh's fiction squarely in the satiric-ironic spectrum; second, they not only identify the mode but also pinpoint the basic technique; third, they demonstrate the intricacies of this technique and the technical variation possible. Fourth, there is here established the major theme of all the novels to follow; and, fifth, there are germinal suggestions of later innovations in both theme and technique.

3

Variation In Mode

If *Decline and Fall* and *Vile Bodies* establish the primary mode, identify the techniques, and suggest the dual theme of Waugh's fiction, the two subsequent novels, *Black Mischief* and *A Handful of Dust* demonstrate refinements and developments in artistry, in an expanding theme, and in deepening tone. Different as these two novels appear from the earlier novels, they evidence an unmistakable progression in both artistry and theme. Here again the theme is "disintegration social and moral," and the plight of the innocent in this overwhelming adversity. Again the technique is based on the relationship of the narrator-persona and the character-persona. Through the variations in this relationship, the author effects several significant innovations in narrative formulation, thematic development, and tonal control.

First, in narrative, these novels manifest a definite movement toward more complementary roles of narrator and character within the narrative itself. This means that the previous extreme ironic detachment is somewhat lessened; the narrator moves closer to the hero, at least in narrative process. Second, in theme, there seems to be a corresponding increase in the emphasis on the plight of the hero. Degenerate aspects of the society are satirized caustically enough, but more than before they directly work their ill on the hero; he becomes not primarily a device, camera-like, for observing, but a sensitive consciousness for experiencing. Finally, in tone, there is an increasing mélange of cruelty and outright barbarism, whose general tone becomes less comic and more tragic as the events gradually move from the realm of fantasy toward the real world.

BLACK MISCHIEF

Black Mischief (1932), seems at first to be an abrupt departure from *Decline and Fall* and *Vile Bodies,* but this novel is constructed from essentially the same narrative materials as the former novels and is ordered in such a way as to achieve a similar total effect. Whatever plot is apparent, the majority of the characters and the scenes are in some way extensions of the earlier fiction. The setting is not the Oxford quadrangle or a Mayfair townhouse, but Azania, a place described by Waugh as "a large, imaginary island off the East Coast of Africa, in character and history a combination of Zanzibar and Abyssinia";[1] yet the author is able to strike at the same general theme of the first two novels—barbarous modernity at its loudest, most irritable pitch and the discomforts it inflicts upon the alien.

The remote setting is, however, not the only feature which distinguishes this novel; the technique here attains a degree of refinement superior in many ways even to *Decline and Fall* but only indicative of the achievement of the later fiction. In *Black Mischief* Waugh introduces innovations in technique which demonstrate his growing skill in the craft of the novel; the result is a rather assured, if not altogether smooth, handling of a complexity of narrative material and thematic potential. *Black Mischief* is in many ways one of Waugh's most artistic works.

---

1. Frederick J. Stopp, *Evelyn Waugh: Portrait of an Artist* (Boston: Little, Brown and Company, 1958), p. 77.

When Spender refers to it as "poetic,"[2] it may be that he has in mind the rhapsodic passages that are interspersed throughout the novel, but he just as well could be describing the subtle and controlled technical factors which give this novel its own distinctive character. There is a balance in the related roles of narrator and character in the formulation of the narrative not found before. Corollary with this congenial function of narrator and character in narration is the positive identification of a dominant theme and the maintaining of a more definite if more complex tone within the novel.

Regarding the narrative, Waugh relies primarily on the narrator to satisfy the dramatic requirements of the story. Although he operates in close harmony with the central character, the narrator necessarily functions independently and often at length in providing essential information, historical and otherwise, or in presenting diverse scenes revolving around various significant characters; he is completely omniscient and directly provides information necessary for narrative continuity, atmospheric effects, and thematic interpretation.

The structure of the novel reflects both the flexibility of narrative method and the dominance of the narrator. There seems to be a programmed process of bringing together various societies and diverse characters to interact and so define one another; but once they are brought together, there begins a process of disintegration in which they are again separated and, with the exception of one character and his society, disappear. Stopp has noted that "the contrast and interaction of these [societies] is developed in eight concise and carefully balanced chapters . . . with the consistency of a dramatic action."[3] But he suggests further that the novel is char-

2. Stephen Spender, *The Creative Element* (New York: British Book Center, 1954) , p. 167.
3. Stopp, p. 80.

acterized, as are the previous works, by "a circular movement": conditions in Azania remain unchanged despite the flamboyant revolutions of Seth; Basil returns to London to continue playing the game of happy families with Alastair and Sonia.

The narrator, without the aid of any one character, presents the material in purposeful sequence. Chapter 1 reports both the past and present cultural, governmental, and social conditions of Azania and at the same time introduces Seth, the visionary emperor who is engaged in a ridiculous and hopeless attempt to modernize the country. Immediately after this, the scene shifts to the adolescent sexual activity of William and Prudence in the farcical world of the ineffectual foreign ministries. In chapter 2, more than any other, the strict narrative sequence is forgotten as the narrator presents a marvelous variety of incongruous incidents, circumstances, and descriptions which all together provide a genuinely realistic impression of the Westerners in Azania. Even when action is being related or dialogue reported, the reader is constantly aware of the narrator's dominating control over material if for no other reason than the rapidly changing scenes. For instance, the narrator interrupts a two-page, rather pointless, conversation to interject information pertaining to the civil war miles away:

> "More tea, Bishop. I'm sure you must be tired after your ride."
> Sixty miles southward in the Ukaka pass bloody bands of Sakuyu warriors played hide and seek among the rocks, chivvying the last fugitives of the Army of Seyid, while behind them down the gorge, from cave villages of incalculable antiquity, the women crept out to rob the dead.
> After tea the Consul looked in and invited Prudence and William over to play tennis (76).[4]

While certainly an effective narrative device, the strategic

---

4. Quotations taken from Little, Brown and Company ed., 1946.

insertion of this half-humorous account of front-line activities calls attention to the necessary function of the
narrator, first by its presence, second by its ironic tone.
Evidenced here are both the narrator's control over the
material as well as his detached stance as observer.

At the beginning of the next chapter, there is a sudden shift to the world of Basil Seal. Although the events
here are numerous and diverse, they are unified by the
character of Basil, but the narrative is not shackled to
the central figure as it was in *Decline and Fall* and, to
a great degree, in *Vile Bodies*. True, Basil is in some way
connected with all the characters and is somehow involved
in all the incidents contained in this chapter; generally
speaking, he is central to the action, yet the narrator is
free to describe scenes without him or to contribute information of which Basil himself has no knowledge.

It is not until chapter 4 that the reader is assured that
the cultures explored up to this point will come in contact with one another or that the various events are even
remotely connected; only here does it become clear that
their intermingling has been prepared for from the beginning of the novel:

> It thus happened that Basil Seal's arrival in Matodi coincided
> with the date fixed for Seth's triumphal return to Debra-Dowa
> (125).

After the societies and subplots are brought together and
their representatives identified and it seems that all major
interests and characters have been introduced, the narrator suddenly begins reporting directly the correspondence of a Dame Mildred Porch, an entirely new character, who not only becomes involved in the action, but
also serves the narrator as a device by which to comment
on the action. Her diary is directly transcribed, without
comment or introduction, into the text of the narrative;
more than this, it is she—not Basil, the central character

—who functions as the narrative device through which the fiasco of the birth control pageant is reported. Then, just as abruptly as she entered, this character disappears and the narrator returns to the generally omniscient presentation, sprinkled generously with wry, subtle observations. The final chapter also evidences the narrator's almost exclusive control of narrative in the meaningful ordering of scenes and the psychological states of Basil upon his return to London and the final sudden shifting away from Basil to the "lapping of the water along the sea wall" in Madodi.

However, despite the apparent disorder in narration, in this novel there is not the sense of fragmentation characteristic of *Vile Bodies,* even though the narrative material itself is probably more diverse. Waugh has learned to utilize effectively the omniscient narrator who does not have to depend on one central character for overall narrative perspective as in *Decline and Fall* or who, if he operates without such a character, is obvious as he roughly and awkwardly "spins the yarn" as in *Vile Bodies.*

Perhaps the relative mastery of the narrator's role within the ironic-satiric novel is nowhere better demonstrated than in the more subtle internal function of the narrator. Narration is generally carried out in one or a combination of six narrative methods—all reflecting the dominating influence of the narrator not only in narrative, but in theme and tone. First, the narrator may summarize action; this is not a new method, but here the style takes on a telegraphic crispness not common in the earlier works:

> The days passed rapturously for Mr. Youkoumian who had found in the stocking of the Museum work for which early training and all his natural instincts richly equipped him; he negotiated endlessly between the Earl of Ngumo and Viscount Boaz armed with orders for the dispossession of the lowest bidder; he brought and resold, haggled, flattered and depreciated, and ate

and slept in a clutter of dubious antiques. But on Basil the strain of modernity began to leave its traces. Brief rides with Prudence through the tinder-dry countryside, assignations furtively kept and interrupted at a moment's notice by some peremptory, crazy, summons to the Palace, alone broke the unquiet routine of his day (198–99).

One recognizes the presence of the narrator first in the overall ironic tone of the passage and second in the numerous interpretive words: "rapturously," "richly equipped," "crazy summons."

The second narrative method, the omniscient relation of information regarding the societies of the characters, calls attention to the narrator, but here he usually is not so obvious as in the summaries. In the lengthy initial discussion of Azania (11–21), although the style is cool, unhurried, and ostensibly straightforward, the narrator's ironic stance becomes obvious in statements such as, "Amurath instituted other changes, less sensational than the railway, but nevertheless noteworthy" (16). And the irony need not depend always on rhetorical devices for its effect; many times merely the straightforward observation of the narrator captures the irony of actuality, and, in doing so, demonstrates his dramatic objective stance: "Several Foreign Office despatches were swept up and incinerated among the litter of envelopes and wrappings" (136).

The same kind of detached observation or superior knowledge is shown in the third narrative component involving the narrator's parenthetical explanatory statements. Here the narrator, while providing ironic information, calls attention to his controlling role in the narrative:

A foreign commercial agent was knifed in a disorderly house on the coast. Amurath hanged the culprit publicly in the square before the Anglican Cathedral—(and with them two or three witnesses whose evidence was held to be unsatisfactory) (17).

The Metropolitan Arch-bishop (who was working with the American attaché on a half-commission basis) . . . (66).

(This with a scowl towards the Bishop who was very quietly playing Pegity with Prudence in a corner of the drawing room.) (260).

While these three narrative methods by their nature call attention to the presence of the narrator, there are three other methods which rather seem to be attempts to remove the narrator as much as possible. The first of these is the extended medley of conversations suggesting rapidly shifting scenes; this device is used to full advantage only once, significantly just previous to the introduction of Basil:

"Any news in the paper to-night, dear?"
"No, dear, nothing of interest."

"Azania? That's part of Africa, ain't it?"
"Ask Lil, she was at school last."
"Lil, where's Azania?"
"I don't know, father."
"What do they teach you at school, I'd like to know."

"Only niggers."

"It came in a cross-word quite lately. Independent native principality. You would have it was Turkey."

After two pages of such disconnected dialogue (86–87), Basil is introduced: "Late in the afternoon Basil Seal read the news on the Imperial and Foreign page of *The Times.*"

The second of these more objective narrative methods is the almost dramatic descriptions of scenes; since these for the most part serve virtually the same purpose as stage directions, they are written in the same kind of elliptical style:

Croydon, le Bourget, Lyons, Marseilles; colourless, gusty

weather, cloud-spray dripping and trickling on the windows; late
in the afternoon, stillness from the roar of the propellers; sodden
turf; the road from the aerodrome to the harbour heavily scented
with damp shrub; wind-swept sheds on the quay; an Annamite
boy swabbing the decks; a surly steward, the ship does not sail
until tomorrow (116–17).

It must be pointed out here, however, that an interesting
thing happens with this method in the course of the
novel. As indicated in the impressionistic passage above,
the narrator has so removed himself that the experience
becomes one directly shared by the character and the
reader; the reader is aware of the "maker" only because
of the necessary imposition of language between himself
and the scenes.

Finally, the narrator negates himself in the narrative
process by frequently summarizing the mental states of
even the minor characters, evidently again in an attempt
to draw the reader into closer identification with them.
Plumbing the thoughts of Courteney in his bath, the narrator says:

Chance treats of this kind made or marred the happiness of the
Envoy's day. Soon he was rapt in a daydream about the Pleistocene
age, where among mists and vast, unpeopled crags, schools of
deep-sea monsters splashed and sported; oh, happy fifth day of
creation, thought the Envoy Extraordinary, oh, radiant sun, newly
weaned from the breasts of darkness, oh rich steam of the soggy
continents, oh, jolly whales and sea-serpents frisking in new
brine . . . Knocks at the door. William's voice outside (81–82).

Again, he pauses briefly to recount the thoughts of the
equerries at the grand ball:

The equerries behind his chair despaired of permission to dance.
If only His Majesty would go home, then they could slip back
before the fun was all over (145).

But, even though the narrator is emphasizing the character's state of mind and is himself artistically detached, the language of these passages usually is sufficient evidence of the ever-present ironic narrator. Thus, the reader approaches the characters only through the coloring mists of the narrator's comments.

Since in the earlier novels the narrator had scarcely dipped into the mind of even the central character, to say nothing of those less important, the effect here is quite noticeable. DeVitis correctly observes that in *Black Mischief* the narrator's "ties with the real world are closer than they had been in the preceding books,"[5] that here he is closer to the objects of satire, and less detached from the scenes. "It becomes apparent that he [the narrator] is still looking at his universe from an 'altitude,' but the 'altitude' is not as high as it had been before."[6] While this may be true, and while the narrator's intimacy with a host of characters gives that impression, still even here the narrator remains completely artistically aloof, reporting congenially from his detached observation post. He has, however, lost the harsh, scornful attitude of *Vile Bodies* and seems more compassionate toward the minor characters. Yet he is still able to appraise objectively the activities and is quite as willing to ridicule as to sympathize. Possibly no better example of this is found in the account of Lady Seal's interview with Sir Joseph Mannering, which ends on a note characteristic of the narrator's stance throughout the entire episode:

> The old boy bounced back in his taxicab to St. James and Lady Seal ascended the stairs to her room; both warm at heart and aglow from their fire-lit nursery game of "let's pretend" (109).

This discussion of the narrator's role may seem to imply that the narrator overshadows every other technical

5. A. A. DeVitis, *Roman Holiday: The Catholic Novels of Evelyn Waugh* (New York: Bookman Associates, 1956), p. 29.
6. *Ibid.*, p. 30.

aspect of the narrative continuity and that he is the center of reader interest and thematic development. This, however, is not the case. In fact, in casually reading the novel, one is not particularly aware of the narrator's presence because attention is expertly focused on the characters of the novel—especially Basil Seal. Basil does not appear in the first one-third of the novel; there arise before his introduction at least three temporary narrative centers in characters who are later relegated to their own particular realm of the story. From the first it appears that Seth is the heir to the Pennyworth tradition and is accordingly the "hero" of this novel; there are two other slight possibilities in the characters of William and Prudence, whose love story commands some interest for a while, and Courteney, whose bungling antics are a story within themselves. Yet all of these are predestined to serve minor roles. When Basil is brought into the novel, it becomes apparent that here is the character who will be the narrative center of the story.

Within this novel there are four societies which Waugh explores by bringing them into conflict; Basil is the only figure to enter into all four areas of civilization. Through Basil the reader explores first the decadent, effete upper class society of London; then, the foolish attempts of both the Azanian emperor to Westernize his primitive people and the leading figure of the opposing forces that make this acculturation impossible. The comic possibilities are more fully explored in this area than in the others: the shrewd business shenannigans of Youkoumian and his less than compassionate treatment of his stupid wife; the conflict between Basil and Connolly over the issuance of boots and the resolution of this problem ("They ate the boots"); and the "culture through sterilization" campaign go a long way in ameliorating the pathetic disgust evoked by Seth's vain dreams of grandeur. At the same time, Basil involves the reader in the adolescent world of the English Legation and its residents: Courteney, with his toy sea-serpent; Lady Courteney and her flower garden; Prudence and the "Panorama of Life" provide sufficient grounds for thematic significance, but only as they are put into relief by contact with the other societies. Finally, Basil is the only character to enter and leave the land of the Wanda— the realm of ultimate barbarism and cruelty, necessary for the thematic development of the novel. Basil's experiences are essentially the "story" of the novel, if not the "plot." Action in which he is not involved appears of interest only as it directly or indirectly contributes to his experience. Even the initial chapters, dealing with Azania, may be seen as a kind of prologue to the adventures of Basil.

There is in this novel what to this point is probably the most successful blending of the functions of both narrator and central character in the formulation of narrative; the narrator is quite independent and mature in handling novelistic necessities; the character is dominant enough to be the principal unifying factor and also the chief thematic figure. Because of the particular functions of character and narrator in the narrative, the tonal possibilities are increased to the point where it is difficult to determine with certainty the overall tone of the novel. In fact, one may likely conclude that there are at least two equally strong tones competing throughout the novel, but closer observation will reveal that both are carefully controlled to achieve a masterful ironic effect.

While it is true that there is a great deal of disagreement over the precise tone of *Black Mischief,* much of the confusion is caused by preconceived notions regarding the central theme. Here, as in Waugh's other works, the way to thematic discovery is through proper apprehension of the tonal qualities of the novel. Carens, as well as others, emphasizing the conflict of cultures, sees *Black*

Mischief as "bitter,"[7] and "entirely pessimistic,"[8] a book full of "savage irony."[9] However, others, such as Benedict, still emphasizing the conflict of cultures, would consider this emphasis on the cruelty and savagery a bit unwarranted, for it may be that the author is "merely exploiting the comic situation which can arise when a character comes face to face with something for which his previous experience had not equipped him to deal with."[10] *Black Mischief* is probably the funniest book that Waugh ever wrote. Yet equally true is the observation that he never before or after approached the cruelty of action of this novel. Probably Greenblatt best describes the tone of *Black Mischief* as one of "comic cruelty," noting by way of explanation the "recurring references, quite hilarious in their context, to starving children, executed men, and mutilated bodies."[11]

In *Black Mischief,* although both comedy and savagery reach an intensity found only intermittently in the earlier novels, it cannot be said that either dominates the tone. The author is able to keep the comic and the cruel in perfect balance through the relationship of the narrator and the central character. This method allows the reader an ironic perspective within the novel itself; as a result, the comic is immediately made serious, and the cruel, comic. Not only does Basil guarantee ironic perspective, but as the reader is drawn into sympathy with him, his own personal dilemma takes on serious overtones.

The narrator goes to great trouble to establish reader identity with Basil by introducing him in a rather shock-

7. James F. Carens, *The Satiric Art of Evelyn Waugh* (Seattle: University of Washington Press, 1966) , p. 144.

8. *Ibid.*, p. 140.

9. *Ibid.*, p. 139.

10. Stewart H. Benedict, "The Candide Figure in the Novels of Evelyn Waugh," *Papers of the Michigan Academy of Sciences, Arts, and Letters* 48 (1963) : 689.

11. Stephen Jay Greenblatt, *Three Modern Satirists: Waugh, Orwell, and Huxley* (New Haven: Yale University Press, 1965) , p. 20.

ing manner; the effect of the abrupt narrative shift to Basil is quite striking, but the specific introduction demands that even more attention be focused on Basil:

> Late in the afternoon Basil Seal read the news on the Imperial and Foreign page of *The Times* as he stopped at his club on the way to Lady Metroland's to cash a bad check.
> For the last four days Basil had been on a racket. He had woken up an hour ago on the sofa of a totally strange flat. There was a gramophone playing. A lady in a dressing jacket sat in an armchair by the gas fire, eating sardines from the tin with a shoe horn. An unknown man in shirtsleeves was shaving, the glass propped on the chimney-piece (87–88).

As the chapter continues, Basil is developed by at least two methods into what is to this point Waugh's roundest character. First the narrator gives his own descriptions of Basil, although they are rather more limited than those of Paul and Adam; however, it is clearly apparent that the narrator himself is fascinated with Basil:[12]

> He stood in the doorway, a glass of whiskey in one hand, looking insolently round the room, his head back, chin forward, shoulders rounded, dark hair over his forehead, contemptuous grey eyes over grey pouches, a proud rather childish mouth, a scar on one cheek.
> "My word, he is a corker," remarked one of the girls (94).

Second, Basil's portrait is drawn primarily by the reactions and comments of others and by his own reaction to situations. Remarks or reported meditations of several assorted characters together construct the reader's impression of Basil. The reaction of Arthur, attendant at the club (90); the self-consoling eulogy of the elderly gentlemen (90–91); the conversation of the girls at Lady Metroland's party (92–94); and the confessions of his mother (106–7) are sufficient to establish very quickly Basil as one who deserves the reader's attention. Coupled with these comments are Basil's own actions which even

---

12. Carens, p. 79.

more strongly solicit the reader's involvement with Basil:
the initial "racket" (88); his intrusion at Lady Metroland's party (91); his interruption of Monomark's conversation and the subsequent proposal (95–96); his affair
with Angela (115–16); his theft of his mother's bracelet
(116); his cosmopolitan attitude aboard ship (116–19).
By the end of the chapter the reader is also fascinated
with Basil to the point that the comedy inherent in the
various activities is rendered many times quite serious
because of his reaction, and the cruel is in the same way
made comic.

As an example of the first, when Seth presents Basil
with the Vitamin menu which in itself is riotously funny,
Basil's rather heavy reaction drains the scene of its comic
potential:

> Basil looked at the card. A month ago he might have suggested
> emendations. To-day he was tired (218).

But the cruel can be made rather comic through Basil.
Scenes such as the interview with the captain in front
of the gallows on which hangs his cousin have obvious
comic overtones. Even the scene of ultimate savagery is
brought off in a high comic fashion:

> "Where did you get that?"
> "Pretty."
> "Where did you get it?"
> "Pretty hat. It came in the great bird. The white woman wore
> it. On her head like this." He giggled weakly and pulled it
> askew over his glistening pate.
> "But the white woman. Where is she?"
> The headman was lapsing into coma. He said "Pretty" again
> and turned up sightless eyes.
> Basil shook him violently. "Speak, you old fool. Where is the
> white woman?"
> The headman grunted and stirred; then a flicker of conscious-
> ness revived him. He raised his head. "The white woman? Why,
> here," he patted his distended paunch. "You and I and the big
> chiefs—we have just eaten her."

Then he fell forward into a sound sleep (301–2).

The narrator throughout the novel is detached in an artistic stance suited to whatever ironic commentary necessary to the desired comic effect, but he is close enough to Basil emotionally to guarantee serious interest in him. The result of the relationship is a balanced tone in which there is distance enough to appreciate the comedy inherent in the various situations, however cruel or savage; yet, there is constantly before the reader what is probably the most serious commentary on modern civilization and the effects upon the individual that Waugh has achieved to this point in his career.

The theme of *Black Mischief* is an unsettled matter among critics. Hollis thinks that the novel is "the study of the politics of an Abyssinia-like African island whose emperor Seth attempts to impose on his barbarous subjects what he conceives to be the customs of 'modern progress' ";[13] this basic story, he admits, "is enlivened by the sub-plots."[14] Later, still emphasizing the Azanian turmoil, he suggests that *"Black Mischief* [is] concerned with how Africans behave when they come in contact with the superficial pattern of European culture."[15] De-Vitis takes this idea a step further and asserts that:

> *Black Mischief,* in picturing the life of a remote African principality, makes its appeal primarily on the basis of snobbery: the white man's racial superiority is the bias that cuts across the novel's action.[16]

Even Carens is influenced by this way of thinking:

> The satirical irony of *Black Mischief* is thus entirely pessimistic

---

13. Christopher Hollis, *Evelyn Waugh* (London: Published for the British Council and the National Book League by Longmans, Green and Co., 1966) , p. 8.
14. *Ibid.*
15. *Ibid.,* p. 12.
16. DeVitis, p. 29.

—it suggests not only that Seth's reforms were foolish but also that the primitive African country is entirely impervious to civilization.[17]

Yet, Carens recognizes other, possibly more universal, implications in the conflict of cultures:

> The irony of *Black Mischief* is multiple; it is directed not only at the primitive mind but also at the follies of progressive thought, which, as Waugh regards it, so often does not take into account the intransigent irrationality of man.[18]

Stopp, while also seeing the novel as a "portrayal of a conflict of cultures," goes on to describe it more analytically: "To a ground of primitive savagery, with a superimposed veneer of rootless Western culture, is added a study in Western civilized futility."[19] Similarly, Spender speaks of the "decadent life of an over-civilized society falling into unreality that resembles the cannibalism of savages";[20] and Greenblatt notes the "shabbiness of Western culture, the decline and fall of institutions, the savagery underlying society."[21] It is Kernan, however, who summarizes best this view of thematic significance:

> Most readers have considered, wrongly, that *Black Mischief* is a brutal and unjustified satire on the stupidity of the black races and their comical mangling of Western ideas and institutions. Some elements of racial chauvinism can undoubtedly be found, but the main thrust of the satire is against Western liberals who believe that life can be utterly reformed, anywhere, by increased control over the nature and the change of social institutions. Waugh makes this point very cleverly and consistently, by juxtaposing similar scenes in Africa and England, showing the same forces at work in both places.[22]

---

17. Carens, p. 140.
18. *Ibid.*, p. 143.
19. Stopp, pp. 77, 79.
20. Spender, p. 166.
21. Greenblatt, p. 16.
22. Alvin B. Kernan, *The Plot of Satire* (New Haven: Yale University Press, 1965), p. 161.

Black Mischief is not a caricature of a savage and ludicrous African kingdom but a grotesque image of Western civilization in the twentieth century.[23]

But to see this novel solely as a satirical commentary on the Negro, Western civilization, or progressive thought generally, is to overlook a serious, perhaps the central, concern of the book; that is, the manner in which modern decadence is reflected in individual human histories and particularly the influence that the modern age has on the individual who is somehow spiritually alienated from it. It has been suggested that in *Decline and Fall* the thematic emphasis seems to be on the plight of Paul—the innocent mauled by the toying, clumsy, and whimsical paws of modernity; again, in *Vile Bodies* it was noted that although there is a shifting of thematic emphasis, there still remains a lingering interest in the individual. In *Black Mischief*, the theme is centered on personal dilemmas arising not just from the conflict of societies but also from the conflicts between the individual and society.

In fact, in this novel there are as many as four possible characters that are thematically significant in this way, but only one who can be considered central to the theme. First, Seth seems to be patterned directly after the character of Paul; Greenblatt, reflecting the thoughts of other critics observes:

Seth serves the artistic purpose of a Paul Pennyfeather: he is a naive outsider who, in his contact with an alien society, is the means of satirizing that society.[24]

But this appraisal of Seth will not hold up throughout the novel, or, for that matter, even through the first chapter. Seth is not in an alien society; he has departed

---

23. *Ibid.*, p. 162.
24. Greenblatt, p. 17.

from his native culture, not it from him. He does not serve as a means of satirizing his society; he is rather "proved plain fool at last" by his society. He is not presented with the same interest as Paul; the narrator in no way solicits sympathy for him; even the ironical combination of royal rhetoric and back-alley slang in the first paragraph invites ridicule of Seth's visionary bombast:

> "We, Seth, Emperor of Azania, Chief of the Chiefs of Sakuyu, Lord of Wanda and Tyrant of the Seas, Bachelor of the Arts of Oxford University, being in this the twenty-fourth year of our life, summoned by the wisdom of Almighty God and the unanimous voice of our people to the throne of our ancestors, do hereby proclaim . . ." Seth paused in his dictation and gazed out across the harbour where in the fresh breeze of early morning the last dhow was setting sail for the open sea. "Rats," he said; "stinking curs. They are all running away" (9).

Many times, the narrator slyly mocks Seth. He overstates Seth's loneliness (41–43); describes with relish Seth's humiliation at the train station (132–33); finds him innocently foolish at the party celebrating his victory (145–50). Possibly the most mocking passage, and one of the most humorous, is Basil's eulogy of Seth:

> "Peace be among you. I bring you the body of the Great Chief, who has gone to rejoin Amurath and the spirits of his glorious ancestors. It is right for us to remember Seth. He was a great Emperor and all the peoples of the world vied with each other to do him homage. In his own island, among the peoples of Sakuyu and the Arabs, across the great waters to the mainland, far beyond in the cold lands of the North, Seth's name was a name of terror. Seyid rose against him and is no more. Achon also. They are gone before him to prepare suitable lodging among the fields of his ancestors. Thousands fell by his right hand. The words of his mouth were like thunder in the hills. Weep, women of Azania, for your royal lover is torn from your arms. His virility was inexhaustible, his progeny numerous beyond human computation. His staff was a grown palm tree. Weep, warriors of Azania. When he led you to battle there was no retreating.

In council the most guileful, in justice the most terrible, Seth the magnificent is dead" (298–99).

Although Carens possibly exaggerates the viciousness of the narrator, he is essentially correct when he says that:

Throughout the novel, savage irony slashes into the mock-heroic posturing of Seth; his inflated pretensions are constantly deflated by the realities of barbarism.[25]

Seth is a victim not just of a crudely ravenous society; he is a victim of himself.

Because of their relatively important roles in the narrative, two other characters seem to be at least briefly thematic possibilities. Courteney and Prudence, degenerate products of a like society are hopelessly condemned to vague, purposeless puttering at life and love. While there is a great deal of comedy in their activities, there is possibly even more pathos than in the case of Seth, for they are not only hopeless but unaware. He, because of a personality ill-suited for contemporary politics, has been relegated to a completely useless diplomatic position; she, in her vain attempts to give meaning to life through discovering the reality of love, which has in a sense fallen victim to a cannibalistic society, fittingly becomes a victim of real-life cannibals. Yet, for these characters there can be only little sympathy, for the narrator seems always to keep them at more than arm's distance; they appear as clowns in miniature, performing a well-rehearsed routine in the last act of a tragedy.

The central character of the novel, although he is somewhat different from the heroes of the earlier works, serves essentially the same dramatic function as his predecessors. Basil Seal is central to the thematic development because it is he who synthesizes all the experiences of the other characters into his own personal search for

---

25. Carens, p. 139.

something more meaningful than London's society. Basil's own plight in many ways is similar to that of Seth, Courteney, and Prudence, and the utter hopelessness of their absurd situations lends an air of gravity to that of Basil; for this reason, only Basil takes on near-human proportions. In this role, Basil seems at first a departure from the *ingénu* of the earlier novels, but he is a perfectly logical development of the two previous heroes. If Paul is innocent and Adam half-aware but passive, Basil completes the scheme: he is both partially aware and aggressive. Several critics have noted that Basil is merely an outgrowth of the innocent. Greenblatt connects him with the earlier characters because he is both "innocent and corrupt."[26] DeVitis suggests that in this novel "the innocence that characterized Paul Pennyfeather and Adam Symes finds a strange expression in the character of Basil Seal."[27] He further explains:

> In him Waugh prefers to examine the qualities of childhood which are boisterous, cruel and often sadistic. . . . In presenting through Basil Seal the exuberant, impetuous activity of youth without direction, Waugh creates in effect the portrait of a bounder.[28]

But to refer to Basil as innocent, with whatever qualifying stipulations, is possibly to place too much emphasis on the nature of the early adolescent activity in which he is involved—the "racket," or the conversation with the old gentleman at the club. Basil's later actions, even from his crashing Lady Metroland's party, are calculated with the coolness and effected with the savoir faire of a cosmopolitan cad. Basil is not another Paul. Unlike the innocent who passively accepts or at best reacts to the barbs of his society, Basil recognizes the hostility and

26. Greenblatt, p. 19.
27. DeVitis, p. 29.
28. *Ibid.*

emptiness of civilization, and actively attempts somehow to retaliate. His own experiences, although for the most part superficially comic, grow in seriousness as the activities of the characters around him increase in futility, absurdity, and cruelty. Basil is not, like the earlier heroes, impelled against his wishes into a hostile society, nor is he passively discontented with the condition of his surroundings; he is, rather, actively engaged in a search for something quite undefined even to himself. The object seems to be a personal satisfaction not available in the "too bogus" upper-class society of London. Although a devil-may-care cad, he must be considered, in the light of Paul and Adam, if not a quester, at least one who is willing to pursue solutions.

Thus, in this novel there is a clear identification of a specific thematic motif which, although hinted at in the earlier novels, begins to take the shape it will have in subsequent novels, in which it will provide not only the basic narrative structure but also the thematic center; that is, the doomed personal quest for meaning or identity in the jungle of modern civilization. Although here the quest motif is not central to the narrative progression, it must be noted that the hero foreshadows the visionaries of the later novels, particularly Tony Last and Helena, even Guy Crouchback. Spender's comment that "the underlying seriousness of Waugh's novels lies . . . in their narration of a *search*"[29] begins to be meaningful in this novel. Although some critics argue that the quest motif, which is central to Waugh's later works, begins with the next novel, *A Handful of Dust*, it seems to have its real origin in this novel; even if the treatment here is only half-serious, there is a serious, even tragic potential:

"You see I'm fed up with London and English politics. I want

29. Spender, p. 162.

to get away, Azania is the obvious place. . . . Every year or so there's *one* place on the globe worth going to where things are happening. The secret is to find out where and be on the spot in time" (112).

It is interesting to note in passing that here, as with all the later visionaries, there is closely allied with the search an attitude of escapism; yet, the search is not wholly negative. When Basil returns from his adventures, it is clear that his journey has not been prompted by escapist longings nor by love of mere excitement. The entire last chapter is characterized by a note of sadness arising not because Basil has failed in his attempt to get away from "London and English politics," but because he has failed to find any real spiritual values anywhere. His failure is intensified when he learns that the false bottom of gaiety and comfortable gentility, precariously held up by a declining upper class for so long, has suddenly dropped out. When Basil asks about Angela, Sonia replies:

> "Just the same. She's the only one who doesn't seem to have lost money. Margot's shut up her house and is spending the winter in America. There was a general election and a crisis—something about the gold standard" (304).

That Basil achieves some degree of moral awareness through his experiences is indicated by Sonia's remark: "D'you know, deep down in my heart I've got a tiny fear that Basil is going to turn serious on us too" (305–6). There is more at work in this novel than the picaro convention, and more thematic significance than the "tragic-comic conflict of cultures."

A HANDFUL OF DUST

Waugh's fourth novel, *A Handful of Dust* (1934), must be considered as the cumulative development of the artistic methods and thematic concerns which appear in the earlier novels. As Greenblatt says, *A Handful of Dust* is a "terrifying and bitter examination of humanism and modern society, which is the culmination of his art."[30] Yet, at the same time, the novel is the beginning of a new phase of Waugh's career and is, in this respect, "transitional," as Hollis has called it.[31] Viewing *A Handful of Dust* in light of both the earlier works and those of the later period, one finds identifiable and progressive developments in artistry and thematic concerns which, although present *ab ovo*, do not mature until the Crouchback trilogy. Even though Waugh in this novel has reshaped and reemphasized many of the narrative, thematic, and tonal elements of *Decline and Fall, Vile Bodies,* and *Black Mischief,* the total effect is unique in his works. Although a few critics consider it a "failure,"[32] it is generally recognized as a "minor classic,"[33] possibly the highest achievement of Waugh. Reflecting the view of a large number of readers, Carens says:

> Of the early, predominantly negative novels, *A Handful of Dust* is the masterpiece and perhaps also the finest of all Waugh's works.[34]

Narrative material similar to that of the earlier novels makes up the basic story of *A Handful of Dust*. Here again attention is focused on the innocent individual in an adverse society; in essence, this struggle constitutes the story. The corrupt society founded on materialism and amorality and the declining effete aristocracy in this

30. Greenblatt, p. 22.
31. Hollis, p. 6.
32. D. S. Savage, quoted by Robert Murry Davis, "Evelyn Waugh on The Art of Fiction," *Papers on Language and Literature* 2 (Summer, 1966) : 251.
33. Graham Martin, "Novelists of Three Decades: Evelyn Waugh, Graham Greene, C. P. Snow," *The Pelican Guide to English Literature* (Baltimore: Penguin Books, 1963), p. 400.
34. Carens, p. 81.

novel are identical to the upper-class decadence described in the first two novels; the Brazilian jungle with its diversity of terrors and confusion suggests the chaotic governmental conditions of Azania as well as duplicates precisely the physical background of that country in which savagery and brutality are the norm.

Moreover, the general thematic development of this novel is closely related to that of the other novels; again Waugh writes of the decay of tradition, order, even civilization itself in the wake of the "new regime" (127).[35] The central character of this novel is a logical extension of Paul and demonstrates also a close kinship to both Adam and Basil. More poignantly than in any of the previous novels, attention is focused on the plight of the alien spirit in a society which seems bent on destroying everything he stands for; the quest motif is here fully developed.

Perhaps the unique feature of this novel and the one thing that identifies it as serious art is the tonal control which guarantees that the universal human proportions of Tony's plight are fully realized. Here, as before, the tone results from the relationship of the narrator and the central character. Although this special relationship places the novel in the ironic mode, there is a significant shift in the attitude of the narrator toward the character; here he seems even closer to him than in *Black Mischief*. Specifically, there is emotional attachment to the character, even though artistic detachment is maintained throughout; as a result of this identification, there is a movement toward the tragic end of the ironic spectrum. This particular tone is established not only by the narrator's sympathetic reaction to Tony Last, but also by an increased emphasis on the hero in both the narrative formulation and thematic development.

Regarding particularly the narrative, it has been sug-

35. All quotations taken from Little, Brown and Company ed., 1934.

gested that Waugh manipulates the narrative center in various ways and that, because this technical necessity provides in any novel the basis of all thematic potential and determines largely the tonal emphasis, it becomes in a sense the principal influential factor of the novel. In *A Handful of Dust* neither the narrator nor the central character is dominant; the technical necessities of sequential and logical narrative are not unnaturally forced into the experience of one character, nor does the narrator take it upon himself to relate the action or arrange his own commentary dramatically independent of the central character. In this novel, while still working within the ironic mode and with implied double vision and artistic detachment of the narrator, Waugh achieves near perfection in the third-person narrative process through the blended, precisely complementary roles of narrator and character, and, as a result, seems to depart from the satiric mode, which demands a distinct separation of narrator's views from character experience.

The narrator appears as one much more refined artistically; he does not intrude awkwardly with information or interpretation; he does not keep up a constant barrage of side comments to influence the reader's response; rather, he is so involved in the presentation of the story itself that he is much less obvious as a necessary technical factor. The reader recognizes almost no narrator comment—even though it is hardly less present —because it is so inseparable from the activity and response of the central character himself. As a result of this close identification of narrator with character in narration, there is fuller development of the character. The narrator is no longer open to the charge of puppeteering; nor is he irritatingly voluble regarding the total situation involving the hero, but he becomes more than a detached recorder of fact, more even than a benevolent onlooker; he becomes an interested observer who seems capable of vicariously participating in the character's experiences.

This is not to say that the narrator has no important separate dramatic function in the formulation of the narrative, because even a casual reading of the novel will reveal narrative methods similar to those of *Black Mischief*. *A Handful of Dust* is begun and ended by the narrator's relation of events which although ultimately connected with Tony do not immediately involve him. In the first section of the novel, he has not yet appeared; in the last, he has disappeared. "Du Côté de Chez Beaver" by indirection moves to the main story; "English Gothic III" unnecessarily rounds out the story and suggests the continuation of the innocent's struggle with modernity.[36] Narrator control is also obvious in the adroit juxtaposition of contrasting scenes in rapid succession even though there is no narrator summary or transition (54–55; 170–71). Even when continuity is offered by the narrator, it is usually elliptically brief— "Next Morning" (170). This sort of shifting is similar to that in *Vile Bodies*, but the striking thing about it in this novel is that the scenes seem to coalesce more perfectly into a kind of logical as well as progressive unity rather than remaining scattered fragments. The narrator moves abruptly from one scene to another, yet with purpose.

> These scenes of domestic playfulness had been more or less continuous in Tony and Brenda's life for seven years.

> Outside, it was soft English weather; mist in the hollows and pale sunshine on the hills; the coverts had ceased dripping, for there were no leaves to hold the recent rain. . . .

> John Andrews sat on his pony and stiff as a life-guard, while

---

36. Here again is the circular movement which Kernan finds characteristic of satire.

Ben fixed the jump. Thunderclap had been a present on his sixth birthday from Uncle Reggie (19–20).

In one way or another all such arrangements of scenes contribute to the central plot and theme involving Tony and are not introduced merely as specifically directed ridicule. Particularly impressive is the manner in which the scenes, in the chapter "In Search of a City," build to a crescendo of madness and end in teeming vacuity: "The city is served" (279–81).

As in the other novels, the narrator is also a real factor in much of the strict narration. Some of the best narrative Waugh ever wrote is found in this novel, and in it all, especially in that which does not deal directly with Tony, there is the overwhelming presence of the old familiar detached narrator who half-humorously, half-cynically relates the incidents without comment but with comic, possibly tragic, innuendo. Most impressive are the crisp passages dealing with death, particularly that of Dr. Messinger:

> Dr. Messinger began to steer for the bank. The current was running strongly and he exerted his full strength; ten yards from the beginning of his rapids his bow ran in under the bank. There was a dense growth of thorn here, overhanging the river; the canoe slid under them and bit into the beach; very cautiously Dr. Messinger knelt forward in his place and stretched up to a bough over his head. It was at that moment he came to grief; the stern swung out downstream and as he snatched at the paddle the craft was swept broadside into the troubled waters; there it adopted an eccentric course, spinning and tumbling to the falls. Dr. Messinger was tipped into the water; it was quite shallow in places and he caught at the rocks but they were worn smooth as ivory and afforded no hold for his hands; he rolled over twice, found himself in deep water and attempted to swim, found himself among boulders again and attempted to grapple with them. Then he reached the falls.
>
> They were unspectacular as falls in that country go—a drop of ten feet or less—but they were enough for Dr. Messinger. At their foot the foam subsided into a great pool, almost still, and

strewn with blossoms from the forest trees that encircled it. Dr.
Messinger's hat floated very slowly towards the Amazon and the
water closed over his bald head (273–74) .

The narrator influences the reader's response to narrative in several other ways. As in all the earlier novels,
the narrator provides both necessary and unnecessary
information, but, although traces of the roughness of
the former novels remain, his commentary is handled
quite smoothly, with more aplomb and grace. For example, the narrator employs asides, usually indicated
with parentheses, to give additional information, to em-
phasize certain bits of knowledge, or to report conversations not in line with the current narrative, but there
is not the monotonous, ironic use made of these asides
that is characteristic of *Vile Bodies*. Related to this more
straightforward approach is the near absence of elliptical
pictorial descriptions which are so abundant in *Black
Mischief*. In fact, only three such passages occur (166,
167, 224) , despite the fact that many other potentially
impressionistic descriptions are accomplished with unhurried, full syntactical structure.

Also, the narrator functions as a source of special information; in this role he is quite knowledgeable even
of the minute details of the events, and is flexible in his
manner of presentation. He may note almost in passing
that "she had insisted on a modern bed" (16) , or that
"it was a way she had" (49) . Or, he may break completely away from the narrative stream at length and
offer background information, the style of which is usually light and free compared to passages describing
Tony's activities.

> It is not uncommon at Brat's Club, between nine and ten in
> the evening, to find men in white ties and tail coats sitting by
> themselves and eating, in evident low spirits, large and extrava-
> gant dinners. They are those who have been abandoned at the
> last minute by their women. For twenty minutes or so they have

sat in the foyer of some restaurant, gazing expectantly towards
the revolving doors and alternately taking out their watches and
ordering cocktails, until at length a telephone message has been
brought them that their guests are unable to come. Then they
go to Brat's half hoping to find friends but, more often than not,
taking a melancholy satisfaction in finding the club deserted or
peopled by strangers (84).

Sometimes he incorporates informative statements
with implicit light irony into the texture of the narrative:

Tony invariably wore a dark suit on Sundays and a stiff white
collar. He went to church, where he sat in a large pitch pine
pew, put in by his great-grandfather at the time of rebuilding
the house, furnished with very high crimson hassocks and a fire-
place, complete with iron grate and a little poker which his
father used to rattle when any point in the sermon attracted
his disapproval. Since his father's day a fire had not been laid
there; Tony had it in mind to revive the practice next winter. On
Christmas Day and Harvest Thanksgiving Tony read the lessons
from the back of the brass eagle (35).

Or, he may at length interfuse narrative progression and
information (sprinkled with ironic potential), as in the
initial description of Hetton (43–44).
Also, the narrator is allowed to offer direct ironic
commentary concerning the action:

What with Brenda's pretty ways and Tony's good sense, it was
not surprising that their friends pointed to them as a pair who
were pre-eminently successful in solving the problem of getting
along well together (28).

She was more solid than Brenda (48).

He is also used to point out explicitly the irony in much
of the goings-on:

They were awkward when Marjorie left, for in the week that
they had been apart, each had, in thought, grown more intimate

with the other than any actual occurrence warranted. Had Beaver been more experienced, he might have crossed to where Brenda was sitting on the arm of a chair, and made love to her at once; and probably he would have got away with it (58).

Despite the varied and influential role of the narrator in the formulation of the narrative, there is never the notion that here is a narrator who is the director of the events and therefore conspicuously withdrawn from the characters. In fact, it must be noted that most of the examples of strong narrator influence quoted above are taken from the first half of the book. As the narration progresses, less emphasis is placed on the narrator and the various information he has to offer and more on Tony and his immediate response to the activities. The first one-third of the novel prepares for the entrance of Tony both as narrative and thematic center, but it is not until one-third of the way through chapter 3 that he fully assumes this role. The close identification in narrative of the narrator with Tony in the last paragraph of Part I of "Hard Cheese on Tony" prepares the reader for the major thematic part this hero is to play throughout the remainder of the novel. This identification with Tony increases until the narrator is practically obliterated in the chapter titled "In Search of A City." Only the last chapter, anti-climactic as it is, reintroduces the narrator as the primary unifying device.

Since as the novel progresses more and more emphasis is placed on Tony as a unifying narrative factor, Waugh does not rely on the narrator to tie together the various subplots or to point out the relation of one society to another as he did in *Black Mischief.* It is true that this novel does not at first seem so complex in narrative material as the former novel, but closer investigation reveals that it is more complex, only less diverse. The greater degree of unity in this novel is achieved through the expert use of Tony as the central narrative device.

The personality here and his function are similar to those of Paul Pennyfeather; he is vital both as a progressive and unifying factor. Yet there is a difference between the role of Paul and that of Tony as narrative device: Tony, like Paul, is an observer, but here the narrative emphasis (as also the thematic) is definitely not on the various scenes to which "his shadow is witness" but unmistakably upon the hero. He is not as Dyson suggests, a "mechanism for social satire."[37] Hence, while there is not so much involvement of the hero in fantastic situations as in the earlier novels, there is an amazing degree of realism even in the most farfetched incidents. Perhaps it is the definite progression of more realistic events that has prompted Kernan to speak of an "illusion of a developing plot" in this novel.[38]

This is not to say, however, that the predominant narrative emphasis on Tony's individual plight precludes at least indirect sorties into general conditions of contemporary society as well as certain specific customs and character types. Since the hero alone connects the various segments of society, his story allows the author opportunity to vent his indignation on at least four different aspects of contemporary civilization. The foremost recipient of the rather blunt satire is the world of the Beavers, Margie, and company, or what may be called modern high-fashioned amorality (74–76). Second, Tony's own world of Gothic splendor and the ineffectuality of the aristocracy with its age-worn trappings is slyly ridiculed: specifically, the effete, malpracticed religion; time-honored genteel customs, such as the fox hunt; and even Hetton itself. Third, there is a real though humorous blow leveled at the courts and the

---

37. A. E. Dyson, "Evelyn Waugh: And the Mysteriously Disappearing Hero," *The Crazy Fabric: Essays in Irony* (New York: St. Martins Press, 1965), p. 191.
38. Alvin B. Kernan, "The Wall and the Jungle: The Early Novels of Evelyn Waugh," *Yale Review* 53 (Winter, 1963), 216.

legal system in the farcical "arrangement" by which
Tony is to provide Brenda grounds for divorce. Fourth,
there is a kind of incidental ridicule of professional ex-
plorers, specifically in the persons of Reggie St. Cloud
and Messinger.

As in previous novels a host of characters representative of some kind of corruption revolve around the central character. In this case he is not generally the instrument by which their personalities are defined; possibly
Miss Rattery is the exception. He does, however, serve
as the unifying device, for he is the only character to
come in contact with every other significant character.
Through him the characters of Beaver, Lady Beaver,
Brenda, John, the detectives, Molly, Messinger, St.
Cloud, Todd, and others are revealed. In toto, the characters as well as the events bring to the novel an atmosphere of jumbled confusion and each has his destructive
effect on Tony Last.

As the narrative centers primarily on Tony, so does
the theme. In this novel, themes which in the previous
works were suffused in a complexity of events, relationships, and activity recur; but here Waugh's chief thematic concern—that to which the earlier novels pointed
and which is central to the later ones—in finally identified. It is not merely a condemnation of the corrupt
conditions of modern civilization; nor is it the comic
potential of the *ingénu* thrown into relief against the
urbane savagery of contemporary society. Rather, the
primary theme of this novel seems to be very close to
the suggestion made by Carens that the "anti-hero" figure in Waugh's fiction "amounts to a comment on the
nature of man in contemporary society."[39]

If it is difficult in the earlier novels to separate for
analysis the narrative, theme, and tone, in this novel the
task is rendered all but impossible owing to the closely

39. Carens, p. 47.

woven fabric in which there is an almost perfect mesh-ing of the three. Particularly is the distinction between theme and tone difficult to make, for here as never before in Waugh's works they coalesce in a manner which removes the novel from the realm of strict satire. Although the ironic double vision[40] is maintained by the artistically detached narrator, there is a new serious-ness which is achieved by what seems to be more straightforward presentation and implicit sympathy with the hero.

Concerning the theme specifically, on the surface the novel seems to consist of a "simple story of the failure of marriage."[41] DeVitis agrees that "the central theme of the novel is one of infidelity";[42] Greenblatt also notes that the story is essentially that of "a typical bedroom farce—the stupid country squire with the beautiful wife is cuckolded by a young man from the city."[43] These estimates would make the novel quite unimpressive—at best, comic; at worst, boring. However, Waugh, himself, writing in 1945, suggested rather serious purpose and an equally serious theme:

> *A Handful of Dust* . . . began at the end. I had written a short story about a man trapped in the jungle, ending his days reading Dickens aloud. . . . Then, after the short story was written and published, the idea kept working in my mind. I wanted to dis-cover how the prisoner got there, and eventually the thing grew into a study of other sorts of savage at home and the civilized man's helpless plight among them.[44]

Nichols considers the novel as:

> An unforgettable picture of a brilliant, but sick, society whose decadence [Waugh] emphasizes not only by choosing both his

40. Greenblatt, p. 26.
41. *Ibid.,* p. 22.
42. DeVitis, p. 31.
43. Greenblatt, p. 26.
44. Evelyn Waugh, "Fan-Fare," *Life* (April 8, 1946), p. 60.

title and his motto from *The Waste Land* but also by echoing Proust in two of his chapter titles.[45]

One critic, Wasson, labors to prove that this novel is not to be read as a "satirical commentary on English society in the late twenties and thirties," but as a "critique of Victorianism,"[46] meaning evidently that Waugh is satirizing those, like Tony Last, who hold Victorian values in a modern society. Although the narrator is capable of mildly satirizing Tony or at least ironically viewing his activities, the book is not an attack on his values; rather, there is an inherent sympathy for him and a strong denunciation of modernity. Stopp, noting another of Waugh's comments about the novel, concludes:

> Of this book, Mr. Waugh said, many years later, '*A Handful of Dust* . . . dealt entirely with behaviour. It was humanist and contained all I had to say about humanism.' All Mr. Waugh had to say about humanism in 1934 was that it was helpless in the face of modern savagery. Decency, humanity and devotion have failed, civilized life has degenerated into the 'all-encompassing chaos that shriek about his ears'; jolliness, respectability, and a brittle modernity cannot touch the problem.[47]

One does not have to look deeply into the novel to discover the nature of the central thematic figure nor his plight. Here again, as in Frye's observation noted in chapter 1 of this study, the central character is the primary determining factor in theme. Critics agree that Tony Last is the culmination of the innocent-cad figure and the beginning of a new kind of hero fully developed only in the later novels. Stopp suggests that:

> Simple, trusting, loving, innocent, and above all boring, is how

45. James W. Nichols, "Romantic and Realistic: The Tone of Evelyn Waugh's Early Novels," *College English* 24 (October, 1962) : 53.
46. Richard Wasson, "*A Handful of Dust:* Critique of Victorianism," *Modern Fiction Studies* 7 (Winter, 1962–62) : 327.
47. Stopp, pp. 99–100.

at first we see the character of Tony Last. He is, surely, another Innocent's Progress through the World of Chaos; a Paul Penny-feather, perhaps, in the world of Margot Metroland, followed by a trip to Azania. Another Adam Fenwick-Symes trying in-effectually to make sense of the world. . . .[48]

DeVitis, while noting distinctions between Tony and the others, likewise sees him as "much the same innocent that Paul Pennyfeather and Adam Symes had been"; the main difference is that "he is overcome by the decadent world he refuses to understand."[49] Like the earlier he-roes, Tony is innocent to the point of being a genuine boob; he is the victim of an overwhelming isolation; he lives in a dream world characterized by the idea of ro-mantic quest.

But there is a seriousness in Tony's plight and search that is not found in the others. Perhaps this is because Waugh is dealing not with fantastic extravanganzas but with problems of real life—common human experience and emotions. Stopp notes that:

This is the real world, not a world of fantasy. Tony Last is the innocent who, by sheer selflessness and dedication to a principle, has become the instrument of a moral judgment.[50]

DeVitis suggests that "the novel, dealing as it does with marriage, brings Waugh quite near to the world of real men."[51] And yet, although the novel does deal primarily with marriage, as DeVitis points out, it does so only because this institution is part of a larger concern. The divorce is not tragic in itself. Yet, when it becomes sym-bolic of the decay of traditional order spiritually and socially, and when the reader is allowed to share the disillusioning experiences of Tony, the implications become tragic.

48. *Ibid.*, p. 91.
49. DeVitis, p. 31.
50. Stopp, p. 92.
51. DeVitis, p. 31.

That the theme is more than divorce or even the decay of family integrity is suggested by the deterioration of *everything* around Tony. John is corrupted by Ben (he begins "cursing like a stable boy"); Brenda succumbs to the amorality of the Beaver clan. Gradually, the relationship of Brenda and Beaver grows until there is a complete break in her relation to Tony; John is killed as a result of Ben's advice, but "it is no one's fault." Then, there is the threat of losing Hetton to finance Brenda's marriage to Beaver; next, the separation from Hetton; finally, Tony's complete destruction in the Brazilian jungles. Everything in the experience of Tony leads to what Dyson describes as "exuberantly audacious annihilation."[52]

Some critics, however, despite the reality of his experience, have found Tony himself quite an unsuitable character for a serious novel. Savage, while reluctantly approving of the early "comedies," dismisses *A Handful of Dust* because it lacks depth; Brenda and Tony are, in his view, "two-dimensional figures" incapable of serious motivation or any emotion.[53] Bergonzi tends to agree with Martin that "we are manipulated into accepting as 'real' characterizations and substantial moral involvements people and a story that are scarcely there at all."[54] Bergonzi notes further:

> In its essential method it doesn't greatly differ from the early farces . . . the characters are puppets, caricatures, pasteboard figures, rather than fully-rounded characters. There is rather more to him [Tony], more, perhaps to involve our sympathies, but he still remains a shadowy figure, the stylized embodiment of a number of predictable gestures.[55]

Greenblatt, however, sees more in the character of Tony:

52. Dyson, p. 191.
53. As quoted by Davis, p. 251.
54. Bernard Bergonzi, "Evelyn Waugh's Gentlemen," *Critical Quarterly* 5 (Spring, 1963) : 24.
55. *Ibid.*

Tony Last transcends a shallow characterization of a sap and becomes the complex symbol of a dying value system at once hopelessly naive and deeply sympathetic, unable to cope with society and yet the last spark of human decency in a vile world.[56]

No doubt, the disagreement over shadings of theme and the degree of Tony's thematic significance arises from the admittedly troublesome ambiguity in tone. Perhaps the most noteworthy feature about the artistry of this novel is the masterfully controlled tone, a delicate balance between parody and tragedy. It has been noted that Paul, Adam, and Basil are potentially tragic characters or, at least, representatives of a very serious human dilemma. But several factors keep them from reaching the humanity of Tony Last. The incidents in which they are involved, if not comical or farcical in themselves, are treated that way by the narrator; even though they may be granted the narrator's interest, they remain relatively undeveloped, even two-dimensional, personalities because of the narrator's refusal to enlarge them; they remain at best serio-comic because the author, even though allowing the narrator to appear interested in them, never quite allows him to break away from the ironic stance emotionally and show or directly elicit sympathy.

In *A Handful of Dust,* not only do the narrative circumstances themselves suggest the makings of a tragedy, but the narrator induces the reader's sympathy for the hero by constant and positive emotional identification with him. Yet, at the same time, the narrator can maintain his artistic ironic posture, making it possible for him to imply at times the comic in the tragic and to scorn from afar the sufferer for whom he feels the deepest sympathy.

There seems to be no narrator involvement with Tony

---

56. Greenblatt, p. 26.

and consequently no reader sympathy until the last two paragraphs in Part I of "Hard Cheese on Tony":

> Tony went and sat alone in front of the library fire. "Two men of thirty," he said to himself, "behaving as if they were up for the night from Sandhurst—getting drunk and ringing people up and dancing with tarts at the Sixty-four . . . And it makes it all the worse than Brenda was so nice about it." He dozed a little; then he went up to change. At dinner he said, "Ambrose, when I'm alone I think in future I'll have dinner at a table in the library." Afterwards he sat with a book in front of the fire, but he was unable to read. At ten o'clock he scattered the logs in the fireplace before going upstairs. He fastened the library windows and turned out the lights. That night he went into Brenda's empty room to sleep (102).

The close identification of the narrator with Tony in this passage not only shifts the narrative center to Tony but also for the first time evidences almost total absence of irony with regard to the narrator's view of Tony. There is nothing here to suggest anything but sympathy for the character. Although later the irony frequently reappears in various forms and degrees, for the most part the narrator's presentation is straightforward. Before this particular passage there has been narrator identification with Tony, especially in his introduction (13–15); there is, no doubt, a touch of irony even in this lengthy passage. But nothing before has seemed to elicit sympathy for Tony. As the narrative progresses, however, more emphasis is placed on Tony, on his personal dilemma, his state of mind, and hence the narrator is necessarily drawn closer to him and reader sympathy is quickened. One of the most illustrative passages is this penetrating account of Tony's mental frenzy.

> A change of clothes brought to both Tony and Milly a change of temper. She, in her best evening frock, backless and vermilion, her face newly done and her bleached curls brushed out, her feet in high red shoes, some bracelets on her wrists, a dab of scent

behind the large sham pearls in her ears, shook off the cares of domesticity and was once more in uniform, reporting for duty, a legionary ordered for active service after the enervating restraints of a winter in barracks; and Tony, filling his cigar case before the mirror, and slipping it into the pocket of his dinner jacket, reminded himself that phantasmagoric, and even gruesome as the situation might seem to him, he was nevertheless a host, so that he knocked at the communicating door and passed with a calm manner into his guest's room; for a month now he had lived in a world suddenly bereft of order; it was as though the whole reasonable and decent constitution of things, the sum of all he had experienced or learned to expect, were an inconspicuous, inconsiderable object mislaid somewhere on the dressing table; no outrageous circumstance in which he found himself, no new mad thing brought to his notice could add a jot to the all-encompassing chaos that shrieked about his ears (189).

Carens, therefore, suggests that "Last is perhaps the most sympathetic character in Waugh's entire canon."[57] Yet, because there is throughout the novel a great deal of irony, critics generally have not been able to agree on the exact tone of this novel—whether it is tragedy, parody, or farce.

Almost every critic of Waugh has noticed the peculiarly delicate tone of *A Handful of Dust*. Bergonzi says:

> The total effect of the book is certainly different from that of its two predecessors. The farce is very evident. . . . But the farce strangely co-exists with something very different, an intense pathos that would be tragic if the characters involved had a sufficient degree of humanity to support tragedy.[58]

Noticing still the kinship of this novel with the former ones, he observes further that "at the end of the novel farce deepens into horror" and that Tony Last embodies "the pathos of the wooden puppet that suddenly weeps real tears."[59] Even though he speaks consistently of "the

57. Carens, p. 57.
58. Bergonzi, pp. 24–25.
59. *Ibid.*, p. 25.

mixture of farce and seriousness," Bergonzi seems to
view the novel predominantly as farce, because he can
find no authorial or narrator emotional involvement
with the hero. Davis, agreeing that the characters "lack
sufficient humanity to be tragic," suggests that the whole
of *A Handful of Dust* demonstrates that "Waugh's technique enabled him to remain detached from his characters both emotionally and technically."[60] As the best
example of the narrator's emotional detachment, Davis
points out the conclusion of "In Search of a City":

> The conclusion of this section of the novel is a triumph for
> Waugh's external, objective method. As Tony sinks deeper into
> delirium, Brazil and England become mixed, and the people and
> events that have brought him where he is whirl about in a
> jumble of images and scraps of dialogue. Yet Waugh does not
> use the stream of consciousness method; he objectifies Tony's
> hallucinations so that he becomes a participant in the bizarre
> council meeting which passes sentence on him.[61]

He quotes the last paragraph in the chapter as evidence
of his conclusions:

> At last he came into the open. The gates were open before him
> and the trumpets were sounding along the walls, saluting his
> arrival; from bastion to bastion the message ran to the four
> points of the compass; petals of almond and apple blossom were
> in the air; they carpeted the way, as, after a summer storm, they
> lay in the orchards at Hetton. Gilded cupolas and spires of ala-
> baster shone in the sunlight.
>   Ambrose announced, "The City is served" (283).

Yet, one cannot be sure that the narrator is as detached as Davis suggests in this passage. In the first place,
this, while not stream-of-consciousness writing, is as near
as third-person omniscient narrative can come to it;
everything is presented as Tony sees it, and is in this

---

60. Davis, p. 108.
61. *Ibid.*

sense objective. But in these scenes there is not the implicit distance between Tony and the narrator as, say, in the scene involving Dr. Messinger's death; rather there seems to be no distance at all. The fact that the narrator does not imply an ironic view, or a double vision of Tony's predicament, and the fact that he is almost completely obliterated dramatically from the narrative in this passage, seems to imply a degree of identification with the hero sufficient to constitute sympathy; certainly not scorn, not even neutral observation.

Nichols is probably correct when he, in noting that *A Handful of Dust* "contains some of Waugh's finest tonal effects," points out the coexistence of artistic withdrawal and emotional attachment. Taking for example the scenes at Brighton, he says:

> The farcical tone of the incidents in which "evidence" for the divorce action is gathered is tempered by Waugh's compassion for Tony Last's real anguish. Thus he is able to imply a point of view—that modern marriage is hollow and farcical, although capable of causing deep distress to one who takes it seriously—which is never stated directly.[62]

He goes on to explain, interpreting the novel as an expression of Waugh's own personal sentiments:

> Tony belongs to, and to some extent represents, a tradition to which Waugh is strongly attached. D. S. Savage calls Tony's outlook "adolescent romanticism" and infers that this represents Waugh's *own* way of looking at the world. This is only part of the truth, I think. While Waugh can sympathize with Tony, he satirizes him as well. He comes to the conclusion that a man armed with only a traditional code of values is helpless in the modern world. He is no philosopher; he has no alternative to propose. But he *wishes* that Tony's values were not so completely outdated.[63]

However close the author's own sentiments are to those

62. Nichols, p. 55.
63. *Ibid.*, p. 56.

of the narrator, the tone results from the tension between the narrator's realistic appraisal of the modern
world and the character's romantic yearning for traditions long outworn, but in this case there is implicit
sympathy on the part of the narrator for the character.
The ironic method is never violated, for there is never
any explicit moral judgment; in this sense there is complete objectivity.

Frye seems to think that Tony Last has the sympathy
of the audience, but since he considers *A Handful of
Dust* as a novel characterized by "ironic comedy," it can
be at best "a parody of tragic irony."[64] He has earlier
defined tragic irony as:

> Tragic irony, then, becomes simply the study of tragic isolation
> as such, and it thereby drops out the element of the special case,
> which in some degree is in all other modes. Its hero does not
> necessarily have any tragic hamartia or pathetic obsession; he is
> only somebody who gets isolated from his society. Thus the cen-
> tral principle of tragic irony is that whatever exceptional happens
> to the hero should be causally out of line with his character.[65]

He further describes the typical figure of tragic irony:

> Thus the figure of a typical or random victim begins to crystallize
> in domestic tragedy as it deepens in ironic tone. We may call
> this typical victim the *pharmakos* or scapegoat. . . . The *pharmakos*
> is neither innocent nor guilty. He is innocent in the sense that
> what happens to him is far greater than anything he has done
> provokes, like the mountaineer whose shout brings down an ava-
> lanche. He is guilty in the sense that he a member of a guilty
> society, or living in a world where such injustices are an inescap-
> able part of existence.[66]

Both of these statements seem to correspond closely to
the nature of this novel and the central character; but

---

64. Northrop Frye, *Anatomy of Criticism* (Princeton: Princeton University Press, 1957) , p. 48.
65. *Ibid.,* p. 41.
66. *Ibid.*

there is at least one thing that prevents Tony from assuming the role of tragic hero. As Frye suggests, "discovery and recognition" are "essential to the tragic plot,"[67] and there does not seem to be this ingredient in the story of Tony. It may be for this reason that many have considered the hero shallow or the novel a failure; there are present in the circumstances all the makings of a tragedy, but the character does not meet the one essential requirement of a tragic hero. Perhaps this depthlessness of character is itself the tragedy.

Carens, who correctly observes that "little has been written about the relation between the irony of satire and the irony of tragedy, perhaps because there are variable and shifting borderlands which cannot easily be plotted,"[68] best describes the overall tonal and thematic effect of *A Handful of Dust*:

> The pervasive sense of tragicality or of terror which the reader feels in *A Handful of Dust* may perhaps be attributed to the approximation of its irony to the irony of tragedy. In themselves, the characters do not approach the tragic. Nor is the novel, of course, a tragedy. *A Handful of Dust* moves somehow in the direction of the tragic as the satirical impulse to criticize and ridicule shades into that irony ordinarily associated with non-satiric expression. Standing in the midst of the shifting borderlands between two modes of expression, it is, perhaps the best product of the whole satirical tendency in the modern novel.[69]

In the lingering hints of parody and in the directly satirical overtones, one detects the dominant tones of the early novels; yet, here, and now paramount, is the incipient tragedy which is present but suppressed in the previous works. Heretofore, Waugh has at best only implied tragic potential; inherent tragedy has been generally overshadowed by comic revelry or complete

---

67. *Ibid.*, p. 48.
68. Carens, p. 86.
69. *Ibid.*

emotional detachment. He has previously used the narrator-character relationship to induce various related dominant tones—comic, as in *Decline and Fall*; farcical, as in *Vile Bodies*; serio-comic, as in *Black Mischief*. Although in each of these there is an inherent implied seriousness, in *A Handful of Dust*, if the realm of tragic irony is not entered, the spectrum of the satiric-ironic mode is stretched taut in that direction.

A Handful of Dust is Waugh's most poignant expression of the terrifying nature of contemporary society and the irreversible fate of the cultured, traditionalistic, religious innocent. Yet, this novel, like the previous ones, attempts no more than a vivid portrayal of the corruption of society and the inevitable destruction of the individual; it is left to the subsequent novels to offer a positive solution.

4

Extension of Mode

In the three novels[1] immediately following *A Handful of Dust—Scoop* (1938); *Put Out More Flags* (1942); and *Brideshead Revisited* (1945) —there is a gradual but pronounced deepening in the seriousness of theme, at first within the context of comedy and, finally, in melodrama. In artistry, there is a continuing variation of technique toward a congenial blend of a positive moral statement with refined technical factors within the exigencies of the ironic mode.

Up to this point in his career, Waugh has consistently developed the narrative through what may be called a "narrative-plank"[2] technique, in which the narrator and character personae function complementarily in narrative progression and unity. In the novels which follow, Waugh continues to use the same basic narrative technique, but quite differently for different effects. One thing that is noticeable in these novels is that the narrator is more obvious than in any novel heretofore, with the exception of *Vile Bodies*. But in these novels he is not detached from his characters as in *Vile Bodies*; rather, his presence induces a new closeness between him and the characters, particularly the central character. In

---

1. A fourth work, unfinished, *Work Suspended* (1942), will be discussed in the next chapter along with *Brideshead Revisited*. Only *Scoop* and *Put Out More Flags*, novels that point the way to *Brideshead Revisited*, will be considered in the present chapter.

2. Franklin R. Rogers, *Mark Twain's Burlesque Patterns* (Dallas: Southern Methodist University Press, 1960).

Scoop his comments are insistent enough to allow him to serve as a kind of comic partner to the hero; in *Put Out More Flags,* the narrator is so pervasive in narrative and so knowledgeable of the characters, yet so personally independent, that he is able to voice his own opinions toward them and their representative philosophies. Gradually, there seems to be more narrator and less character in narrative formulation. Only in *Brideshead Revisited,* however, does this proclivity in narrative technique reach its culmination. Here the narrator *is* the hero, and, as a result, there is a lack of the narrative tension and intensity of tone characteristic of the earlier novels.

The tonal range of the character-narrator personae technique is evident in the variation among the first four novels. The designation of "comic" which La-France[3] and others would assign to Waugh's first six novels and the sharp distinction between these and the later "serious" novels do not sufficiently comprehend the complexities of tone even in the first four novels, nor does it take into consideration the deepening undertone of tragedy. In fact, LaFrance would suggest that these novels "lack both the tinge of bitterness" associated with irony, and the "moral indignation which usually accompanies satire."[4] Yet, *A Handful of Dust* alone offers ample testimony to the contrary, for this novel virtually vibrates with the intense ironic tension between the detached yet sympathetic narrator and the central character-persona.

In the next three novels, there seems to be a steady progression in tone similar to that in the first four, but not from farcical to tragic; here it is from the comic to the melodramatic, although elements of realism are in-

---

3. Marston LaFrance, "Context and Structure of Evelyn Waugh's *Brideshead Revisited," Twentieth Century Literature* 10 (April, 1964) : 12.
    4. *Ibid.*

troduced. One senses immediately, in the first novel after *A Handful of Dust,* a slackening in the narrator's severe detachment which is characteristic of the first novels. Even in the purely comic novel, *Scoop,* it seems that the narrator is closer to the character than even in *Decline and Fall,* but he is still not too close to generate genuine comedy from the events. Yet, this novel, by nature of the material dealt with, is not the real test of the narrator's objectivity; it is not until more serious material is introduced in *Put Out More Flags* that it becomes clear that the narrator is now more mellow in his attitude toward his characters and more apt to air his views freely and openly or admit his sympathy. Therefore, there is neither the tension in tone nor the severity of the earlier works. *Put Out More Flags* is, nevertheless, solidly within the ironic mode, and its irony lends itself at once to both satirical comedy and new dimensions in seriousness. Finally, in *Brideshead Revisited,* distance between narrator and character completely vanishes; the narrator becomes explicitly involved with the central character because he *is* the central character. The inherent seriousness of the narrative material and the loss of ironic perspective creates a mood in this novel that is very near the melodramatic.

The twofold theme of the previous four novels, that is, the conquest of civilization by modern-day barbarism and the plight of the alien in a world thus rendered hostile, is practically unchanged. In the next three novels, however, while the basic theme remains the same, the outcome in each is quite different from the earlier novels. Here, for the first time, the innocent hero-persona begins to emerge triumphant from the struggle. He first enjoys a mild victory over the chaos which surrounds him, ironically enough because of the chaos itself; even so, he still must remain an alien, isolated. But in the following novel, *Put Out More Flags,* the innocent-cad achieves a kind of integration with his society, not necessarily because he reforms, but more likely because a wartime society is more compatible with his own natural disposition. Finally, there is, what by now should not be a surprising development in theme, a quite sentimental affirmation of faith in a divine eternal purpose in the affairs of men and in the consequent perpetuation of human values and nobility despite overwhelming corruption. The hero, his traditions, his values, are at last victorious, if for no other reason than divine, and authorial, favor.

SCOOP

Because *Scoop,* like *Black Mischief,* is set for the most part in a culturally backward African country, and because it also deals with conflicting national traditions and personal interests, critics have found it appropriate to consider these two novels together. For instance, DeVitis finds a similarity between the two novels in that both "make a bald appeal to the white man's sense of racial superiority."[5] Martin sees both novels as offering "a contrast between types of social and political folly and a *relative* normality."[6] But it is Carens who most thoroughly explores the connection of these two novels. Both are, he says, "satires of empire, subtly different from such novels as E. M. Forster's *Passage to India* and George Orwell's *Burmese Days.*"[7] In both there is portrayed the conflict of civilization with savagery, a savagery which "can be neither extirpated nor reformed; it can, at best merely be contained."[8] But in both novels,

---

5. A. A. DeVitis, *Roman Holiday: The Catholic Novels of Evelyn Waugh* (New York: Bookman Associates, 1956), pp. 33–34.

6. Graham Martin, "Novelists of Three Decades: Evelyn Waugh, Graham Greene, C. P. Snow," *The Pelican Guide to English Literature* (Baltimore: Penguin Books, 1963), p. 398.

7. James F. Carens, *The Satiric Art of Evelyn Waugh* (Seattle: University of Washington Press, 1966), p. 138.

8. *Ibid.*

Carens notes, "chaos and disorder, provoked by modern political movements, are mastered and ordered."[9] Yet, there are certain distinctions to be made between the novels: *Scoop* is a "less bitter satire than *Black Mischief*," and it is also "more diffuse in structure and less incisive in its handling of the clash between political chaos and order."[10] Although each critic approaches the novels differently, the consensus seems to be succinctly stated by Hollis, who sees *Black Mischief* as a satire of Africans but *Scoop* as a comedy emphasizing the folly of Europeans in Africa.[11]

Yet, one cannot carefully read the two novels in succession and not be struck immediately with the notion that *Scoop* is somehow completely different from its counterpart. Not only is a slightly different theme pursued in *Scoop*, or the same theme from a different angle, but here the theme is realized in a manner quite distinct from that of *Black Mischief*, in fact, quite unlike any of the preceding novels. *Scoop* bears obvious similarities to the earlier novels, particularly in plot and thematic materials, but it is unique among Waugh's works in tone. This novel is of all Waugh's canon the only novel-length piece of fiction that can unreservedly be termed "funny."

In fact, the plot rather resembles a comedy of errors. William Boot, author of the *Daily Beast* column "Lush Places," is summoned by Lord Copper, through a mistake, from Boot Magna Hall into London and finally Ishmaelia as a war correspondent. After an unimpressive beginning, William arrives at Jacksonburg along with a host of other reporters. As the political situation becomes more complex and vague, William falls in love

9. *Ibid.*, p. 139.
10. *Ibid.*, p. 144.
11. Christopher Hollis, *Evelyn Waugh* (London: Published for The British Council and the National Book League by Longmans, Green & Co., 1966), p. 12.

with the deserted wife of a German soldier of fortune, meets an old school chum who has a rather important government position, and forms an unlikely friendship with a powerful French representative; through these circumstances, William naïvely "discovers" and reports to the *Daily Beast* a genuine scoop. Returning home a hero, he refuses even to attend the banquet in his honor, choosing rather to return to Boot Magna Hall and "Lush Places."

This is not to say, however, that for all its levity and good humor *Scoop* is not expertly brought off. It is true that critics have had little to say about *Scoop* and even less praise for its literary qualities. When it has been given attention, the commentary has not been particularly enthusiastic. For instance, DeVitis says that:

> *Scoop*, on the whole, is not a successful novel. It is hastily assembled and exhibits many of the characteristics of a potboiler. The love affair seems completely out of keeping with the main action, and often the scenes are too contrived to be funny. Often Waugh strains for his comic effect.[12]

While this assessment may be a bit severe, one would be hard pressed to defend *Scoop* as excellent Waugh; but, at the same time, there are many features in this novel worthy in themselves of at least mild acclaim and useful because of what they reveal about the development of the techniques and themes in Waugh's fiction.

Scoop evidences the same sure artistry of *A Handful of Dust,* only Waugh has chosen to deal with a less serious theme in an even less serious way. He has no visions of grandiose accomplishment in this novel; the nature of the events dealt with provide narrative material other than that essential to a truly great novel, and, if this were not enough, the tone of the novel removes

---

12. DeVitis, p. 35. (All quotes from *Scoop* taken from Little, Brown and Company ed., 1949).

all possibility of profundity. But, while the evident aims of *Scoop* are less noble than those of the other novels, Waugh's use of the special functions of the narrator-persona and the character-persona reflects a mature craftsman rather assured of his ability to handle deftly the narrative necessities in formulation of theme and to suffuse it all with a tone both indigenous to and interpretative of the narrative material. *Scoop's* singularity is accounted for by the combination of its peculiar narrative, thematic, and tonal features.

First, the narrative formulation. As in the two novels preceding, neither the narrator nor the character is dominant in narrative dramatic function; but here, quite differently from the earlier novels, they work in a tandem-like relationship in achieving not only the narrative progression and unity but also the theme and tone. This means that within the novel the pendulum swings abruptly from strict external narrator manipulation and comment to direct and intimate revelations of William's mental and emotional activity. There is never any doubt as to the narrator's controlling influence in narrative structure, because he continually interposes himself between the character and the reader, frequently reminding the latter that this novel is the account of one man's adventures related by a knowledgeable, chatty observer who has interests other than the mere adventures of the hero. The various sudden shifts in scene, which by now are familiar, demonstrate not only the narrator's objective omniscience, but also hint rather strongly at puppeteering on his part. The initial shifts, completely without transition, from the short episode involving John Boot (1–11) to that featuring Salter and his predicament (15) to the scenes and people at Boot Magna (20) remind the reader of the controlling presence of the narrator, but at the same time demonstrate the narrator's skill in dramatic presentation.

In addition there recurs an old technique, now somewhat refined—the cinematic method. First, there may be an omniscient cataloguing of scenes such as that found in the introduction to Jacksonburg and its inhabitants. Attention is directed from an outside, overall view of the town (111), into the streets of Jacksonburg (112), then into the hotel ruled by Mrs. Jackson (112), then into each of several rooms (113–14), and finally into the annex where Hitchcock sleeps (116); the last comment in this description zooms back to the larger perspective held at the beginning, "And the granite sky wept." Second, the narrator may record directly, without transition and with only brief parenthetical notes, the confusion of a press meeting (167–70). As further evidence of the narrator's externality in narrative formulation, only the omniscient narrator can and does neatly wrap up the "future of each of his characters at the end of the novel" (318–21).

There are other narrator functions within the novel, but functions still indicative of his externality, which keep his presence firmly in the mind of the reader. First the narrator is the independent source of information regarding the characters, places, and events. These matters of fact may be short incisive comments regarding the characters' circumstances.

> In other rooms about the house reposed: Nannie Price, ten years the junior of Nannie Bloggs, and bedridden from about the same age (she gave her wages to Chinese Missions and had little influence in the house) (23).

The narrator may offer incidental information regarding the action:

> Corker completed his purchase, haggled over the exchange from francs to rupees, was handsomely cheated, and drew up his elephant on a string (96).

Or, the narrator may provide incidental background information pertaining to the characters:

> A pious old darky named Mr. Samuel Smiles Jackson from Alabama was put in as the first president—a choice whose wisdom seemed to be confined by history, for, forty years later, a Mr. Rathbone Jackson held his grandfather's office in succession to his father Pankhurst, while the chief posts of the state were held by Messrs. Garnett Jackson, Mander Jackson, Huxley Jackson, his uncle and brothers, and by Mrs. "Teeny" Athol (*née* Jackson), his aunt (106–7).

Much in the same way, the narrator often indulges in rather lengthy historical sketches of locations, particularly of Boot Magna (20–24) and Ishmaelia (105–10).

These methods tend to remove the narrator from the characters, thus attesting to his ironic detachment. But there is within the narrator's range another technical privilege heretofore generally denied him which seems to signal a closer identification with all the characters; that is, here the narrator moves at will through the minds of his characters as dramatic necessities demand or as thematic potential presents itself. For instance, the narrator assumes the mental perspective of John Boot:

> Algernon Stitch was standing in the hall; his bowler hat was on his head; his right hand, grasping a crimson, royally emblazoned despatch case, emerged from the left sleeve of his overcoat. An umbrella under his left arm further inconvenienced him. He spoke indistinctly, for he was holding a folded copy of the morning paper between his teeth (4).

The narrator seems particularly drawn to Salter as a narrative device, for it is this character more than any other except, of course, William Boot, with whom the narrator collaborates in the formulation of the narrative (see pp. 15–16; 33; 285–86; 291–92); in fact, at times there seems to be a blending of the roles of narrator and character:

It was a familiar cry; during his fifteen years of service with the Megalopolitan Company Mr. Salter had heard it upon the lips of countless, distressed colleagues; upon his own. In a moment of compassion he remembered the morning when he had been called from his desk in *Clean Fun,* never to return to it. The post had been his delight and pride; one for which he believed he had a particular aptitude. . . . First he would open the morning mail and sort the jokes sent him by the private contributors (one man sent him thirty or forty a week) into those that were familiar, those that were indecent, and those that deserved the half-crown postal order payable upon publication (44).

Whatever the purposes or effects of these narrative methods, the point is that they demonstrate the dramatic agility and influence of the narrator both on the external formulation of the overall narrative and in the internal progressive development. He rather expertly manipulates the action, smoothly inserts his own varied commentary, and almost unnoticed moves in and out of characters to whatever end may be suggested by the circumstances at the moment. What this means is that the narrator is becoming a pronounced factor in narrative, and, consequently, in the development of theme and tone; yet, at the same time, he is learning to work effectively in a dual capacity—both outside and within the context of the novel—undisguised and convincingly.

The central character is no less important than the narrator as a unifying device of the narrative. The events, like those of *Decline and Fall,* are essentially unrelated except as they are tied together in the experiences of William Boot. Not only does the story of William's struggles provide the circular plot of the novel, but, in the course of his zany adventures, entrance is gained into several areas of society at which the author wishes to level some kind of criticism. This technique is reminiscent of the earlier novels, and the social areas explored here are likewise similar: upperclass or aristrocratic British society; the passing world of Boot Magna; Lord

Copper's fantastic and foolish newspaper empire; and the complexities and futility of African politics.

The narrator in Book I, chapter 1, moves as necessary from one character's point of view to another and remains wryly omniscient throughout; but, with chapter 2, although the narrator continues his flexible role, it becomes obvious that William is to be narrative center of the remainder of the book and that all preceding narrative was merely in preparation for his arrival on the scene—"It [a late newspaper] was a matter of great anxiety to William" (24), for he is at this time greatly concerned about a recent error in his column in the *Daily Beast*. After this, the reader through William first becomes acquainted with the eight righteous souls who share whatever safety that remains in a battered ark of effete aristrocracy. Next, William enters the city, where he is not only quickly assured of its hostility but straightway falls prey to its confusion and depersonalization (pp. 46–50). As part of this experience, he is introduced to the sanctum sanctorum of Lord Copper's newspaper empire (51; 54–55); and, later, to the more pedestrian aspects of the newspaper business. In fact, in this latter, his experience with the newspapermen, his assignment, the necessary newspaperish correspondence, his odd associates—all form further categories of events which William's experience fuses into one unified narrative. There are other segments of society explored in the narrative, namely, the African political scene replete with its ridiculous embassies in England and with corresponding European embassies in Ishmaelia (136; 140–41); the provincial life of Ishmaelia, particularly as seen in Jacksonburg (155–57); even the political underground, replete with shadowy, silent figures.

And the examination of these social groups is not without purpose; each offers tremendous thematic potential for Waugh's type of caustic satire, and he is quick to capitalize on this potential by having the detached narrator continually observe and comment on the activity. This technique has been used in all the novels so far, but seldom with more finesse than found here. In fact, there is in four of these social groups clearly a great deal of potential thematic significance. In the development of each there is also a demonstration of precision in the narrator-character personae technique: the central character is introduced into an area, plays the *ingénu,* while the narrator is continually making ironic observations from two major points of view, the character's and his own.

First, the novel may be taken as a quite laughable burlesque of the newspaper industry. Through the coalition of narrator and character the operations of big-time newspaper syndicates are held up for mild derision, all the way from Lord Copper's swank office to Corker and Pigge's surrey stranded somewhere in Ishmaelia. As Stopp says, "*Scoop* depicts some of the more incredible activities of the international group of journalists planted for the war in Addis Ababa by their respective employers."[13] There is a great deal of fun poked at the editors and policy makers. For example, Lord Copper says to William:

> "With regard to our Policy, I expect you already have your own views. I never hamper my correspondents in any way. What the British public wants first, last and all the time is News. Remember that the Patriots are in the right and going to win. The *Beast* stands for them foursquare. But they must win quickly. The British have no interest in a war which drags on indecisively. A few sharp victories, some conspicious acts of personal bravery on the Patriot side, and a colourful entry into the capital. That is the *Beast* policy for the war" (56) .

Much of the humor of this novel is in the narrator's ex-

13. Frederick J. Stopp, *Evelyn Waugh: Portrait of an Artist* (Boston: Little, Brown and Company, 1958) , p. 83.

aggerated accounts of newsmen in the field, particularly of Wenlock Jakes, who "scooped the world with an eye-witness story of the sinking of the *Lusitania* four hours before she was hit" (92) and who single-handedly created his own war in an erstwhile peaceful Balkan city simply because he overslept and got off at the wrong station. As a result of his spectacular but fabricated accounts of revolution,

> Government stocks dropped, financial panic, state of emergency declared, army mobilized, famine, mutiny—and in less than a week there was an honest to God revolution under way, just as Jakes had said. There's the power of the press for you (93).

Second, the book may be seen as a political spoof aimed at the absurd vacillations of the African governments. At least one critic sees *Scoop* as effecting "a curious transformation of the materials of Waugh in Abyssinia and of the Italian aggression against Haile Selassie's kingdom."[14] Whatever the source of the materials, there is an abundance of it, and it has been greatly transformed by the pervasive and satirical burlesque. The foolishly pretentious Consul-General to whom William first goes for a passport seems typical of the officials of both sides:

> "The patriotic cause in Ishmaelia," he said, "is the cause of the coloured man and of the proletariat throughout the world. . . . As that great Negro Karl Marx has so nobly written. . . ." He talked for about twenty minutes. The black-backed, pink-palmed, finlike hands beneath the violet cuffs flapped and slapped. "Who built the Pyramids?" he asked. "Who invented the circulation of the blood?" (68).

The "pseudo-consul" at the insolvent rival legation is equally absurd (69–71). Soon William comes to realize that the war and those supposedly engaged in the hostilities are as confusing as his first briefing:

---

14. Carens, p. 144.

"You see they are all Negroes. And the Fascists won't be called Black because of their racial pride, so they are called White after the White Russians. And the Bolshevists want to be called Black because of their racial pride. So when you say Black you mean Red, and when you mean Red you say White, and when the party who call themselves Blacks say Traitors they mean what we call Blacks, but what we mean when we say Traitors I really couldn't tell you. . . . But of course it's really a war between Russia and Germany and Italy and Japan who are all against one another on the patriotic side" (57–58).

Third, there is a blow struck at the declining aristocracy. The paragraph which begins a lengthy description of Boot Magna Hall and the remnants of aristocracy which still survive there sets the mood for all the author's dealings with the aristocratic class. The narrator himself notes that it is "decay, rather than change" that is "characteristic of the immediate prospect" (20), and everything else about Boot Magna bears this out:

> The immense trees which encircled Boot Magna Hall, shaded its drives and rides, and stood (tastefully disposed at the whim of some forgotten, provincial predecessor of Repton) singly and in groups about the park, had suffered, some from ivy, some from lightning, some from the various malignant disorders that vegetation is heir to, but all, principally, from old age. Some were supported with trusses and crutches of iron, some were filled with cement; some, even now, in June, could show only a handful of green leaves at their extremities. Sap ran thin and slow; a gusty night always brought a litter of dead timber (20).

Despite these three thematic possibilities, however, it is only the fourth that becomes the central theme. The social areas explored and the implied attitude of the narrator toward them, as well as any thematic significance derived therefrom, serve primarily as a necessary cumulative background for the story of the *"ingénu* hero's"[15] progress through strange, even hostile surroundings. In

15. *Ibid.,* p. 146.

Scoop particularly, the various experiences are only a springboard for narrator criticism, but possibly more important, they are a means of heightening the comic potential of the alien's face-to-face confrontation with modern civilization. Perhaps this is why DeVitis sees William as "a pawn in a comic drama of international intrigue."[16]

The hero is again one who is forced, through the blunderings of an incompetent *Daily Beast* staff, on an unwelcomed journey, the circumstances of which he cannot fully understand. In fact, it may be noted that the thematic motif thus arising, though noticeably different in tone, is somewhat reminiscent of both *Decline and Fall* and *A Handful of Dust;* there is both the forced entry into a chaotic circle of events and a similar, if strikingly less serious, idea of a quest in the alien's struggles to obtain or regain the permanence and security of age-worn tradition, represented here again by a once magnificent but now sadly decaying mansion.

> Like his predecessors William Boot lives in the nostalgic past, his happy days of childhood. All that he wants is at Boot Magna. And in the description of the house, Waugh obliquely makes reference to the great house as a bulwark of traditions in themselves valid, but outmoded in practice.[17]

The fact that William must be taken somehow as representative of the innocent fallen prey to modernity is abundantly clear throughout the novel. From the beginning of William's adventures, the viciousness of the city is sharply contrasted to the hero's temperament and experience:

> His spirits began to sink; the mood of defiance passed. It was always the way; the moment he left the confines of Boot Magna he found himself in a foreign and hostile world (29).

---

16. DeVitis, p. 35.
17. *Ibid.*

At seven he reached Paddington and the atrocious city was all around him (30).

That William's adventures are central to the theme is evident also because the narrator seems to identify especially with William throughout the novel. As the novel progresses, the identification increases, but ironic perspective is never wholly lost. This kind of identification begins early in the novel as William is lamenting Priscilla's playful substitution of "the great crested grebe" for "badger" in his last installment of "Lush Places":

> It had been exceedingly painful. All through the week-end William had awaited his dismissal but Monday and Tuesday passed without a word from the *Beast*. He composed and despatched a light dissertation on water voles and expected the worst. Perhaps the powers at the *Beast* were too much enraged even to send back his manuscript; when Wednesday's paper came he would find another tenant of *Lush Places*. It came. He hunted frantically for his half-column. It was there, a green oasis between Waffle Scramble and the bedtime pets. "Feather-footed through the plashy fen passes the questing vole . . ." It was all right. By some miracle Saturday's shame had been covered (25–26).

Later, the narrator seems to be even more closely identified with him, at least in narrative:

> Far away the trout were lying among the cool pebbles, nose upstream, meditative, hesitant, in the waters of his home; the barbed fly, unnaturally brilliant overhead; they were lying, blue-brown, scarred by the grill, with white-bead eyes, in chaste silver dishes. "Fresh green of the river bank; faded terra-cotta of the dining-room wallpaper, colours of distant Canaan, of deserted Eden," thought William—"are they still there? Shall I ever revisit those familiar places . . . ?" (83–84).

Yet, as indicated by the last passage, the close functional relationship of the narrator and character does not produce in this novel exactly the same tonal effect of the others; therefore, not the same degree of seriousness in theme. Carens has noted that:

> Waugh's satires, even at their most extravagant, generally do convince the reader that they reflect the realities of Waugh's time; but *Scoop's* wild improbabilities are too distant from the real world to ring true.[18]

But even if the circumstances in which the hero is involved were more serious within themselves, the tone of the entire novel would not allow more than the slightest note of genuine seriousness. The narrator refuses serious interest in William quite likely because nothing else in the novel is serious; instead, he allows himself to imply constantly the unseriousness of the events and in several ways himself heightens the comic potential. He becomes party to the comedy, functioning tandem-like with the central character especially in what appears to be a well-planned comic routine, complete with straight guy and fall guy, the roles being shared alternately by narrator and character. Although some of the scenes may be "too contrived to be funny," one gets the idea that the novel, like the map of Ishmaelia, is "a complete joke" (140). This overall comic effect is produced in a variety of ways throughout the novel, but all indicate a disposition of the narrator to move closer to his objects of ridicule, and, therefore, an increasing capacity for sympathy with the *ingénu* if the circumstances should more closely approximate their very serious counterparts in real life. First, the narrator's style reflects not only his ironic view of the events, but also the fact that he is up to something not entirely serious:

> "All right," said the chauffeur, and drove off at breakneck speed through the rain (133).

> The coon turned round in his seat and smiled (133).

---

18. Carens, p. 148.

He was a tough old warrior who passed his brief waking hours
in paring the soles of his feet with his dagger or buttering the
bolt of his ancient rifle (157).

When Lord Copper, a man of quick temper and ven-
geance, discovers the presence of Theodore Boot in lieu
of the real guest of honor, the omniscient narrator por-
tentously recalls images of another massacre: "Someone
had blundered" (314). When the traveler William arrives at the customs office on the continent, the narrator's
description of the officials' reaction is strictly a sally into
comic exaggeration:

> It was one of those rare occasions when the humdrum life of
> the douanier is exalted from the tedious traffic in vegetable silks
> and subversive literature, to realms of adventure; such an occa-
> sion as might have inspired the jungle scenes of Rousseau. Not
> since an Egyptian lady had been caught cosseting an artificial
> baby stuffed with hashish, had the custom officials of LeBorget
> had such a beano (74).

But some of the most brilliantly executed comic passages
deal with Ishmaelia and her people:

> Various courageous Europeans, in the seventies of the last
> century, came to Ishmaelia, or near it, furnished with suitable
> equipment of cuckoo clocks, phonographs, opera hats, draft-trea-
> ties and flags of the nations which they had been obliged to
> leave. They came as missionaries, ambassadors, tradesmen, pros-
> pectors, natural scientists. None returned. They were eaten,
> every one of them; some raw, others stewed and seasoned—accord-
> ing to local usage and the calendar (for the better sort of Ishmae-
> lites have been Christian for many centuries and will not publicly
> eat human flesh, uncooked, in Lent, without special and costly
> dispensation from their bishop) (105–106).

Of course, the narrator has a great deal of fun with the
names of his characters, even with the implications of
Ishmaelia; names like Corker, Pigge, Shumble, Salter,

Sister Sampson, or Smiles need little comment to suggest their comic potential.

But the highest form of comedy is realized in the relationship between the narrator and William: the narrator has the necessary ironic perspective and also is possessed of a keen wit; the author of "Lush Places" is a fall guy. William would be funny without the narrator, as evidenced by his ridiculous, chatty, and costly messages to the *Daily Beast*:

> NO NEWS AT PRESENT THANKS WARNING ABOUT CABLING PRICES BUT IVE PLENTY MONEY LEFT AND ANYWAY WHEN I OFFERED TO PAY WIRELESS MAN SAID IT WAS ALL RIGHT PAID OTHER END RAINING HARD HOPE ALL WELL IN ENGLAND WILL CABLE AGAIN IF ANY NEWS (173).

The narrator's good humor, often burlesque, plays to the fullest effect William's natural comic propensity:

> William, hesitating between polo sticks and hockey sticks, chose six of each; they were removed to the workshop. Then Miss Barton led him through the departments of the enormous store. By the time she had finished with him, William had acquired a well, perhaps rather over furnished tent, three months' rations, a collapsible canoe, a jointed flagstaff and Union Jack, a handpump and sterilizing plant, an astrolabe, six units of tropical linen and a sou'wester, a camp operating table and set of surgical instruments, a portable humidor, guaranteed to preserve cigars in condition in the Red Sea, and a Christmas hamper complete with Santa Claus costume and a tripod mistletoe stand, and a cane for whacking snakes (60).

The comic burlesque of William's ineptness gradually becomes out-and-out mock heroic in tone:

> William returned home with a mission; he was going to do down Benito. Dimly at first, then in vivid detail, he foresaw a spectacular, cinematographic consummation, when his country should rise chivalrously to arms: Bengal Lancers and kilted

Highlanders invested the heights of Jacksonburg; he at their head burst open the prison doors; with his own hands he grappled with Benito, shook him like a kitten and threw him choking out of his path; Katchen fluttered towards him like a wounded bird and he bore her in triumph to Boot Magna. . . . Love, patriotism, zeal for justice and personal spite flamed within him as he sat at his typewriter and began his message. One finger was not enough; he used both hands. The keys rose together like bristles on a porcupine, jammed, and were extricated; curious anagrams appeared on the paper before him; vulgar fractions and marks of punctuation mingled with the letters. Still he typed (221–222).

Yet the narrator is still close enough to William to serve as a comic partner within the narrative itself:

"This is a heavy one," she said, pointing to a worn leather bag. William attempted to lift it. It might have been full of stone. The girl opened it. It was full of stone (161).

As a result of these and other more subtle techniques, here, as in no other novel, Waugh realizes the light comic potential "which can arise when a character comes face to face with something which his previous experience has not equipped him to deal with."[19] Although *Scoop* is full of "wild improbabilities too distant from the real world to ring true" and, although the events of the narrative themselves appear to have no "serious relevance to the realities of modern political life,"[20] when considered in light of the deepening seriousness of the preceding novels and the overtly serious nature of the later novels, there emerges a significant development in Waugh's dominant theme. For the first time, the hero is given a choice; his accidental but no less astounding success as a journalist makes it possible for him to choose at last his own destiny. A true alien, he positively rejects

19. Stewart H. Benedict, "The Candide Figure in Waugh's Novels," *Papers of the Michigan Academy of Science, Arts, and Letters* 48 (1963): 689.
20. Carens, p. 148.

the chaotic hubbub of modern London and returns, quite satisfied, to the peace and tranquility of Boot Magna Hall. Although it may be true that "the alternatives are not particularly inspiring,"[21] and that "Boot's flight . . . is pure escapism,"[22] the fact remains that William retains his innocence at the novel's end "while beating the career-struck world at its own game";[23] moreover, "the fact that he prefers the eccentricities of his own home to the inane success of the world, indicates an optimistic note, a note that emerges dominant for the first time."[24] His return to Boot Magna is not just a return, as is Paul's to Scone Castle; it is really a kind of victory.

Thus in the disguise of comedy Waugh has begun to reach for some positive assertion of values through a sympathetic hero; perhaps this explains the sudden appearance of light humor in this novel as compared to the sardonic cynicism reflected in at least the preceding three novels. Carens has the idea that Waugh actually "presents positives" here, but through "mock-heroics and grotesquery."[25] *Scoop* may be viewed then as the first and, therefore, a germinative attempt at a positive serious moral statement, but before this can be achieved, reality must be grappled with and the dilemma of the alien translated into real, recognizable human experience. It is not surprising, therefore, to find Waugh entering the real world with the next novel.

PUT OUT MORE FLAGS

Put Out More Flags has received only slight critical attention mainly because it is overshadowed by both the preceding and subsequent novels, *A Handful of Dust* and

21. *Ibid.*
22. *Ibid.*
23. DeVitis, p. 36.
24. *Ibid.*
25. Carens, p. 148.

Brideshead Revisited. DeVitis unenthusiastically observes that:

> *Put Out More Flags* lacks the spontaneity of *Decline and Fall* and *Vile Bodies,* the ironic perspective of *A Handful of Dust.* Occasionally it rises to the comic heights of its predecessors.[26]

Carens suggests that *Put Out More Flags* makes no "artistic advance over its predecessors" and that the satire lacks "the resonance and the incisiveness of the other early novels."[27] Carens goes on to note that the author merely repeats "techniques and devices" which he has already mastered, pointing, however, "toward later developments in his career."[28] Yet, this novel is a respectable achievement in its own right artistically and thematically. It shows more than a slight development in technique, although it is perhaps no more an artistic achievement than one or two of the previous novels; there are no surprises in technique, but there are some definitely noticeable refinements which forecast particularly the specific thematic and tonal qualities of *Brideshead Revisited* and the Crouchback trilogy.

Perhaps the best clue to the nature of the novel is given by the author in the dedicatory letter to Major Randolph Churchill: the story deals "with a race of ghosts, the survivors of the world we both knew ten years ago," transported into that "odd period before the Churchillian renaissance, which people called at the time the Great Bore War."[29] As indicated by Waugh's comment, this novel stands between what may be called his early comedies or satires and the later romantic and realistic works. It is transitional particularly in the sense

---

26. DeVitis, p. 39.
27. Carens, p. 81.
28. *Ibid.*
29. "Dedicatory Letter to Major Randolph Churchill," *Put Out More Flags* (London: Chapman & Hall, 1942), p. 11. All quotations are taken from this edition.

that it concludes the activities of many of the characters introduced in the earlier novels and introduces a new social milieu to be peopled in Waugh's later fiction by genuinely human characters. With the change in characters and scene comes also a noticeable transition in time. This change is seen not so much in the continuing thematic motif of innocent versus hostile society as it is in the tone which results from a delineation of this conflict in more realistic terms and in the unmistakable, positive moral statement that is achieved.

Waugh's basic technique remains essentially the same as in the other novels; the relationship between the narrator-persona and character-persona continues to provide the centers of narrative formulation, thematic development, and tonal control. The narrative is again formulated through precise interaction of the detached narrator and the central character, but here the role of narrator becomes significant not only in narrative but also in theme. Again the innocent-cad Basil Seal figures as the central character; and again the story is primarily an account of his adventures. The theme deals principally with his experience in an incomprehensible society; and the tone, as far as centered on him, is rather comic, but it is a kind of reluctant comedy. As the narrator becomes more concerned with "minor" characters there is what seems to be an intentional expansion of theme not only through elaboration but also in realistically human proportions of both the characters and their problems. And, as the narrator, all the while artistically objective and detached, unquestionably implies sympathy for even the peripheral characters who are caught up in the terror and confusion of war, and as Basil himself becomes more involved in the tragedy, and apparently more capable of understanding it, the tone deepens into one of critical realism. The tonal effect is therefore quite distinct from that of any of the previous novels: the novel is basically critical, as are the early bitterly satirical works, yet there is a realism about it which, filtered through comedy, removes the bite and sting.

Regarding the formulation of narrative, the narrator achieves a technical maturity in this novel not consistently characteristic of any of the earlier novels. Again, it is he who obviously is in control of the progression of the narrative; he directs the arrangement of scenes, at times without transition, toward the total narrative and thematic effect. He is omniscient and quite detached, generally speaking, from the characters and events, but, although the detachment is sufficient for varying degrees of irony it is not so great as to exclude the implication of real interest in the characters. In fact, there is more narrator identification with the several minor characters than in any novel heretofore; hence, they become more thematically significant. The most outstanding thing about the narrator's role in this novel is that his honest interpretation of and reaction to certain of the most important events, or even what may be termed his "philosophy of life," become more apparent than before; yet, his intrusion into or his influence over the narrative material and thematic development, although considerable, is less noticeable than in the earlier works. Here, although the narrator is predominantly the influential factor in narrative, theme, and tone, he is woven rather inconspicuously into the fabric of the novel.

As narrative device, the narrator's continual presence is obvious because of his external manipulation of scenes, which are arranged for the best dramatic effect. From the opening pages, it is clear that the narrator is attempting a purposeful investigation of several characters and activities surrounding Basil and that, to accomplish this feat, he will shift at will to appropriate happenings or subjects. Accordingly, in the pages following, he methodically explores the worlds of Barbara Sothill, Lady Seal, and Angela Lyne; with this preparation for Basil and for other interesting experiences in the lives of these three women, he introduces Basil:

> Rubert Brooke, Old Bill, the Unknown Soldier—thus three fond women saw him, but Basil breakfasting late in Poppet Green's studio fell short and wide of all these ideals. He was not at his best that morning, both by reason of his heavy drinking with Poppet's friends the night before and the loss of face he was now suffering with Poppet in his attempts to explain his assertion that there would be no war (34).

From this point onward, through "Autumn," "Winter," and "Spring," the narrator utilizes a quite precise and progressive alternation between the action involving Basil Seal and Ambrose Silk, Jewish pansy, dipping in the meantime into the activities of the three ladies formerly introduced, the war at home and abroad, and anything else that strikes his fancy. That the detached narrator is in complete control of all dramatic effects is demonstrated best by his directing with the skill of a vaudeville *raconteur* the catastrophic conversation between Basil and Mr. Harkness as Basil attempts to con him into accepting the unbearable Connollies as wards:

> The moment for which Basil had been waiting was come. This was the time for the grenade he had been nursing ever since he opened the little, wrought-iron gate and put his hand to the wrought-iron bell-pull. "We pay eight shillings and sixpence a week," he said. That was the safety pin; the lever flew up, the spring struck home; within the serrated metal shell the primer spat and, invisibly, flame crept up the finger's-length of fuse. Count seven slowly, then throw. One, two, three, four . . . "Eight shillings and sixpence?" said Mr. Harkness. "I'm afraid there's been some misunderstanding."
> Five, six, seven. Here it comes. Bang! "Perhaps I should have told you at once. I am the billeting officer. I've three children for you in the car outside."
> It was magnificent. It was war. Basil was something of a specialist in shocks. He could not recall a better one (102).

After this scene, complete with the narrator's stage directions and critical comments, he revels in the elaborate details of Harkness's reaction—"First . . .," "Secondly . . .," "Thirdly . . .," he describes them omnisciently yet dramatically (102–3).

Although the narrator's role is quite similar to that in *Black Mischief, Put Out More Flags* is not so symmetrical as *Black Mischief* or *Decline and Fall*, probably because the action is all bound somehow to a historical background, that of the war, and therefore the story does not circle back on itself as do the previous novels, but progresses logically and naturally to an ending in every respect far removed from the beginning.

Other than these external functions, the narrator serves in several dramatically necessary roles more within the narrative itself. First, he is something of a historian, supplying information not only about particular characters and their relationship with others, but also about national political, economic, and military circumstances. He demonstrates very intimate knowledge of the characters, particularly the more central ones:

> Ambrose Silk was older than Poppet and her friends; he was, in fact, a contemporary of Basil's, with whom he had maintained a shadowy, mutually derisive acquaintance since they were undergraduates. In those days, the mid '20's at Oxford, when the last of the ex-service men had gone down and the first of the puritanical, politically minded had either not come up or, at any rate, had not made himself noticed . . . (39–40).

Moreover, he has a thorough knowledge of contemporary history:

> Poland was defeated; east and west the prisoners rolled away to slavery. English infantry cut trees and dug trenches along the Belgian frontier. Parties of distinguished visitors went to the Maginot Line and returned . . . . Russia invaded Finland and

the papers were full of tales of white robed armies scouting through the forests. English soldiers on leave brought back reports of the skill and daring of Nazi patrols and of how much better the blackout was managed in Paris. A number of people were saying quietly and firmly that Chamberlain must go (80).

Particularly impressive is the narrator's ability to blend the fictitiously personal with the real historical events:

> This was February 1940, in that strangely cosy interlude between peace and war, when there was leave every week-end and plenty to eat and drink and plenty to smoke, when France stood firm on the Maginot Line and the Finns stood firm in Finland, and everyone said what a cruel winter they must be having in Germany. During one of these week-ends Sonia conceived a child (116).

Second, the narrator provides descriptive information pertaining to places and characters. In this novel he usually describes through the agency of one of the other characters; in earlier novels, especially after *Decline and Fall,* the narrator is wont to describe outright, as omniscient observer. In the lengthy initial description of Angela Lyne, he sees her through the eyes of a hypothetical "stranger passing the open door of her compartment" who "might well have speculated on her nationality and place in the world and supposed her to be an American, the buyer perhaps for some important dress shop in New York" (29). Later in the passage, the narrator comes forward in his own person to reveal several "bare facts about this seemingly cosmopolitan, passionless, barren, civilized woman" (30).

Third, the narrator offers his own commentary regarding the characters and events. This more than anything else determines the reader's response in novels which depend for their satiric effect upon the sustained ironic view and the implicit or explicit attitude of the narrator. This function is less important in narrative formulation

in this novel, perhaps because the irony evidently is
not intended to be so intense as in the early works.
The narrator does, however, frequently interject a rather
light irony and thus displays his relatively external role
in the narrative:

> Had there been no other cause of offence; had Basil come to
> him with the most prepossessing appearance, the most glittering
> sporting record, a manner in which deference to age was most
> perfectly allied with social equality, had he been the lord of a
> thousand loyal tenants, had he been the nephew of the Colonel-
> in-Chief, the use by a civilian of such words as "stuffy" and
> "bogus" about the Brigade of Guards would have damned him
> utterly (63).

In the same manner, the narrator, through his frequently light and humorous style maintains throughout
the narrative a certain jocularity:

> Lady Seal devoted to this old booby a deep, personal fondness
> which was rare among his numerous friends (25).

> "Where can I go? It's the end of my painting. I've a good mind
> to follow Parsnip and Pimpernell" (two great poets of her ac-
> quaintance who had recently fled to New York) (36).

And he seems to relish recording laughable particulars
on every hand. For instance, the language of the troops:

> When the lecture was finished the compay fell out for twenty
> minutes; they smoked and ate chocolate and exchanged gossip,
> qualifying every noun, verb or adjective with the single, unvary-
> ing obscenity which punctuated all their speech like a hiccup;
> they stamped their feet and chaffed their hands.
> "What did the ——— company commander want?"
>   "He wanted to send me to a ——— O.C.T.U.," said Alastair.
>   "Well some ——— are ——— lucky. When are you off?"
>   "I'm staying here."
>   "Don't you want to be a ——— officer?"
>   "Not ——— likely," said Alastair (113).

Moreover, there is a particularly ironic detachment noticeable in some of his comments which are outside the narrative:

> London was full again. Those who had left in a hurry returned; those who had made arrangements to go after the first air raid remained. Margot Metroland shut her home and moved to the Ritz, opened her home and moved back; decided that after all she really preferred the Ritz and shut her home, this time, though she did not know it, for ever. No servant ever folded back the shutters from the long windows; they remained barred until late in the year when they were blown into Curzon Street; the furniture was still under dust sheets when it was splintered and burned.

Finally, regarding the narrator's role in narrative formulation, there is one narrator function in this novel that, while appearing in the earlier novels, is never before used with such effectiveness: that is, the narrator's direct revelation of the thoughts of the characters. While all the other narrative methods discussed thus far have the tendency to establish the narrator as the external "maker" of the novel, this method seems to draw the narrator into the narrative itself; as a result of the narrator's more internal role, the novel appears to be more organically developed than the previous ones. This type of narrator identification with character is seen primarily in two narrative methods: first, the narrator may merely summarize the mental states; or, second, the narrator may choose something close to an interior monologue:

> She was thinking: "Supposing Mr. Seal gets himself killed. Best thing really for all concerned."
> . . . Flaxman Greeks reclining in death among the rocks of Thermopylae; riddled scarecrows sprawling across the wire of no-man's land . . . Till death us do part . . . Through the haphazard trail of phrase and association, a single, unifying thought recurred, like the sentry posts at the side of the line, monotonously in Angela's mind. Death. "Death the Friend" of the six-

teenth-century woodcuts, who released the captive and bathed
the wounds of the fallen; Death in frock coat and whiskers, the
discreet undertaker, spreading his sable pall over all that was
rotten and unsightly; Death the macabre paramour in whose
embrace all earthly loves were forgotten; Death for Basil, that
Angela might live again . . . that was what she was thinking as
she sipped her Vichy water but no one, seeing the calm and
pensive mask of her face, could ever possibly have guessed (34) .

As a result of this narrator closeness to the various
characters in narrative, the characters seem more human;
hardly is there here a charge of "pasteboard" figures.
This development is completely in keeping with the
growing serious overtones. Although the narrator's techniques generally do not differ from the earlier basic
method, perhaps it is this one factor, the closeness of
the narrator to the several characters, that demonstrates
the continuing development toward a blending of refined artistry and serious moral themes.

The role of the central character in the formulation
of narrative is similar to that of *Black Mischief,* which
features the same hero, Basil Seal. Because the progression
is controlled by the narrator who arranges the scenes,
shifts them, and comments upon them, the central character's story does not become essential to the novel's
narrative progression. Yet the character is central to the
narrative in that it is he who serves as the unifying
factor of both narrative formulation and plot. Specifically, Basil allows entrance into the several areas of society
just as the earlier heroes do; through him the narrator
explores the several strata of British society and examines
the responses individually and collectively to the war.

But more important to the narrative unity and plot,
Basil is the narrator's device for entering and tying together the quite different worlds of the three women
introduced at the beginning of the novel; in the course
of the novel each of these initial acquaintances enlarges

to include a great deal of activity centered on Basil. The initial portrayal of Angela is extended logically not only into her continuing romance with Basil, but also into the thematically significant account of her husband's death; the initial interview with Lady Seal ultimately leads into the central portion of the narrative dealing with Basil's adventures with the Ministry of Information and to his later volunteering for military service; the introduction of Barbara logically develops into Basil's shameless comic ruses as billeting officer. In these narrative threads, several characters are introduced who become either background figures or characters of thematic significance, Alastair and Sonia, Peter Pastmaster, Susie, Mr. and Mrs. Harkness. There is another narrative strain, which seems strangely different from all the others, yet at the same time is bound up in all the others through the involvement of the central hero: this is the portion of the novel dealing with Ambrose Silk and his associates.

Although this rather panoramic view of English society and wartime activity seems quite fragmentary, it is masterfully unified by the pervading presence of the central character, who not only provides the basis for logical narrative unity but also is able finally to give realistic dimensions to the theme, a theme toward which all elements of the novel are directed. As the novel progresses, however, somehow the story of Basil does manage to get told, along with the several others. But it is only in light of the other characters and their stories that the experiences of Basil become thematically meaningful; likewise, it is only by being a part of Basil's experience that the others gain thematic relevance.

Basil is important not only to narrative unity but also to thematic unity as well. The specific theme is difficult to identify; perhaps that is why many critics are content to think of it merely as somehow "dealing with that odd, dead period before the Churchillian renaissance" and to

say that it offers little new in thematic development. A
search for thematic significance finds Waugh up to his old
tricks, having a hilarious time at the expense of various
segments of society and here and there at several pseudo-
intellectual politico-philosophical fads of the prewar
period. For instance, the author fires broadside at the
fumbling and confused upper-class reaction to the war
crisis, the ridiculous civilian war agencies, the befuddled
but sporting military organization, certain nebulous left
wing groups and their heretical ideas, and aesthetes in
general; he also delivers well-directed side blows at certain typical human characteristics embodied in exagger-
ated fictional characters: Captain Mayfield, Todhunter,
Poppet, Sir Joseph Mannering, Colonel Plum, Rampole,
and several other Dickensian figures. Therefore, if taken
on a rather superficial level, the novel may be considered
a kind of panoramic comedy in which these jocular,
sometimes sad, diversities all contribute to the central
comic activity, that is, Basil's exploitation of the landed
gentry with the formidable Connollies, and his impish
persecution of Ambrose Silk. At least one critic seems to
take this view:

> The bulk of the novel is concerned with Basil Seal's attempt
> to extract profit and amusement out of the war—profit by hawking
> round the countryside an impossibly odious family of slum chil-
> dren, called the Connollies, billeting them on unoffending house-
> holders and then taking money to remove them elsewhere; amuse-
> ment, by tricking his friend, Ambrose Silk, into writing what
> might pass for a Facist pamphlet and then denouncing him.[30]

It is true that much of the novel does seem to exist
only for the satiric or comic possibility it provides, but
to take these adventures as the exclusive or primary element of the theme is to underrate the author's quite
serious moral concern. Here for the first time in Waugh's

---

30. Hollis, p. 16.

fiction appear the realities of war between civilized peoples, and whatever the theme, it must necessarily be influenced if not dominated by this ever-present menace which in itself serves as a frightening commentary on the nature of man. The book is in large part concerned with an examination of British society, particularly as regards the personal and social demands of a people caught up together in an immediate national catastrophe; because of this one fact the theme must reflect the cruel realities of the time as well as the complexity of human reactions. And all of the personal emotions of war are faithfully and graphically recaptured, from the light comedy of Sir Joseph to the tragedy of Cedric's death.

Despite the varied elements in the narrative material and the opportunity it offers for a superficial reading, there is unity and seriousness of theme achieved primarily through the central character, Basil Seal. Basil is no stranger to readers familiar with *Black Mischief;* but what may be surprising is that he obviously has not, at least at the beginning of *Put Out More Flags,* "turn[ed] serious on us" as Sonia had predicted (*Black Mischief,* 306). He is reintroduced quite in his original character: a wastrel youth of the aristocracy:

> Four times in the last ten years Lady Seal had paid Basil's debts; once on condition of his living at home with her; once on condition of his living somewhere, anywhere, abroad; once on condition of his marrying; once on condition of refraining from his marriage. Twice he had been cut off with a penny; twice taken back to favour; once he had been set up in chambers in the Temple with an allowance of a thousand a year; several times a large lump sum of capital had been dangled before his eyes as the reward of his giving himself seriously to commerce; once he had been on the verge of becoming the recipient of a sisal farm in Kenya. . . . In the intervals of neglect and independence, Basil had fended for himself and had successively held all the jobs which were open to young men of his qualifications. He had never had much difficulty in getting jobs; the trouble had always

been in keeping them, for he regarded a potential employer as
his opponent in a game of skill (53).

He has the same male arrogance as before:

> Basil lay back on the divan and watched her with fascination.
> This was how he liked to see women behave in moments of
> alarm. He rejoiced, always, in the spectacle of women at a disad-
> vantage: thus he would watch, in the asparagus season, a dribble
> of melted butter on a woman's chin, marring her beauty and
> making her ridiculous, while she would still talk and turn her
> head, not knowing how she appeared to him (36).

Throughout the book each episode in which he is involved does nothing but solidify his reputation as a genuine cad: his complete disrespect during the interview
with the colonel; his mercenary tactics employing the
Connollies; his nonchalant yet connived betrayal of Ambrose; his lecherous flirtations with Susie; his adulterous
romance with Angela all serve to convince the reader
that here is decadence incarnate, although with enough
flair to make it attractive. But the story of Basil is not all
fun and games; all of Basil's activity is somehow predicated on the war and so there is always an underlying
seriousness even in his most humorous or fantastic behavior. The first hint of seriousness in Basil's affairs, and
thus in the nature of the theme, comes early in the novel,
in the initial "musings" of Lady Seal:

> The last war had cost her little; nothing, indeed, except a
> considerable holding of foreign investments and her brother
> Edward's reputation as a strategist. Now she had a son to offer
> her country. Tony had weak eyes and a career, Freddy was no
> blood of hers and was not cast in a heroic mould, but Basil,
> her wayward and graceless and grossly disappointing Basil, whose
> unaccountable taste for low company had led him into so many
> vexatious scrapes in the last ten years . . . ; Basil, his peculiari-
> ties merged in the manhood of England, at last was entering on
> his inheritance. She must ask Jo about getting him a commission
> in a decent regiment (24–25).

She later describes Basil's apparent unpreparedness to receive his "inheritance" of "the manhood of England" as "individuality"; here is the first suggestion of the novel's serious theme:

> Sometimes, lately, I've begun to doubt whether we shall even find the proper place for Basil. He's been a square peg in so many round holes. But this war seems to take the responsibility off our hands. There's room for everyone in war time, every *man*. It's always been Basil's *individuality* that's been wrong. You've said that often, Jo. In war time individuality doesn't matter any more. There are just *men,* aren't there?" (28)

Although Lady Seal is confident that the war will provide Basil the proper milieu for full and honorable expression of his many manly virtues, Basil, owing to his "individuality," finds the war quite foreign to his interest for the same reason that he earlier objected to the boredom of the Bright Young Things: "There are too many people in on the racket" (43). It is strangely ironic, yet typical of Waugh's observations, that the "respectable" world society has itself changed for the worst, has conformed to the cad's code of conduct; the hero-cad has not changed for the best. Basil himself suggests as much when he explains his lack of interest in the war:

> From time to time he disappeared from the civilized area and returned with tales to which no one attached much credence—of having worked for the secret police in Bolivia and advised the Emperor of Azania on the modernization of his country. Basil was in the habit, as it were, of conducting his own campaigns, issuing his own ultimatums, disseminating his own propaganda, erecting about himself his own blackout; he was an obstreperous minority of one in a world of otiose civilians. He was used, in his own life, to a system of push, appeasement, agitation and blackmail, which, except that it had no more distant aim than his own immediate amusement, ran parallel to Nazi diplomacy.
> Like Nazi diplomacy it postulated for success a peace-loving, orderly and honourable world in which to operate. In the new, busy, secretive, chaotic world which developed during the first

days of the war, Basil for the first time in his life felt himself
at a disadvantage. It was like being in Latin America at a time
of upheaval, and, instead of being an Englishman, being oneself
a Latin American (54–55).

Despite this antipathy toward the war, Basil suddenly
"reforms" at the end of the novel and goes off to fight
for his country; yet, one does not get the idea that he is
the "rake reformed," merely that he has accepted at least
a tentative alliance with society and on his own terms,
a society which because of its own decadence he finds
compatible. The theme, therefore, must have to do first
of all with the struggles of this hero to gain relative integration with his society and, second, with his final ironic
success, which serves also as a commentary on the nature
of the society. Here again is the shadow of the well-
established motif of the alien in hostile surroundings,
but in Basil there is the same character variation in this
motif that is found in *Black Mischief* (the hero-cad),
and the hostility of the society toward the hero is somewhat modified, but its decadence remains the same.

But Basil cannot be considered the only major thematic character in the novel; Ambrose Silk is also a key
figure in the development of theme. In the narrative,
Ambrose's story alternates with that of Basil and, therefore, must be of some thematic significance. In fact,
Waugh himself, in the prefatory letter suggests as much
when he admits that "I find much more food for thought
in the follies of Basil Seal and Ambrose Silk, than in the
sagacity of the higher command."[31] He verifies this interest in Ambrose by having the narrator spend almost as
much time delving into his affairs as in telling the adventures of Basil. Ambrose is in many ways a reflection
of the earlier passive heroes—Paul Pennyfeather, Adam
Fenwick-Symes, Seth, even Tony Last; he is in line of
direct descent from these *ingénus*, but his alienation is

---

31. "Dedicatory Letter."

more severely intense because Ambrose is the opposite
societal extreme from the preceding heroes:

> Nowadays Ambrose saw few of his old friends except Basil. He
> fancied that he had been dropped and sometimes in moments of
> vain glory, to the right audience, represented himself as a martyr
> to Art; as one who made no concessions to Mammon. "I can't
> come all the way with you," he said once to Parsnip and
> Pimpernell when they explained that only by becoming prole-
> tarian (an expression to which they attached no pedantic sug-
> gestion of childbearing; they meant that he should employ himself
> in some ill-paid, unskilled labour of a mechanical kind) could
> he hope to be a valuable writer, "I can't come all the way with
> you, dear Parsnip and Pimpernell. But at least you know I have
> never sold myself to the upper class." In this mood he saw
> himself as a figure in a dream, walking down an endless fash-
> ionable street; every door stood open and the waiting footmen
> cried, "Come in and join us; flatter our masters and we will feed
> you," but Ambrose always marched straight ahead unheeding. "I
> belong, hopelessly, to the age of the ivory tower," he said (40).

An introvert, Jewish, homosexual, left-wing aesthete,
Ambrose is haplessly out of step with traditional English
society and is therefore either more laughable or more
pathetic than the earlier tradition-bound Victorian
heroes:

> A pansy. An old queen. A habit of dress, a tone of voice, an
> elegant, humourous deportment that had been admired and imi-
> tated, a swift, epicene felicity of wit, the art of dazzling and con-
> fusing those he despised—these had been his, and now they were
> the current exchange of comedians; there were only a few
> restaurants, now, which he could frequent without fear of ridi-
> cule and there he was surrounded, as though by distorting mir-
> rors, with gross reflections and caricatures of himself. Was it
> thus that the rich passions of Greece and Arabia and the Renais-
> sance had worn themselves out? Did they simper when Leonardo
> passed and imitate with mincing grace the warriors of Sparta;
> was there a snigger across the sand outside the tents of Saladin?
> They burned the Knights Templar at the stake; their loves, at
> least, were monstrous and formidable, a thing to call down
> destruction from heaven if man neglected his duty of cruelty and

repression. Beddoes had died in solitude, by his own hand; Wilde had been driven into the shadows, tipsy and garrulous, but, to the end, a figure of tragedy looming big in his own twilight. But Ambrose, thought Ambrose, what of him? born after his time, in an age which made a type of him, a figure of farce; like mothers-in-law and kippers, the century's contribution to the national store of comic objects; akin with the chorus boys who tittered under the lamps of Shaftesbury Avenue (47).

Like Basil, however, for Ambrose the problem of life, specifically his alienation, results from his "individuality":

I should like to be one of them, he thought. I should like to go with them and drink beer and make rude noises at passing aesthetes. What does world revolution hold in store for *me*? Will it make me any nearer them? Shall I walk differently, speak differently, be less bored with Poppet Green and her friends? Here is the war, offering a new deal for everyone; I alone bear the weight of my singularity (67).

But with Ambrose this enigma transcends the personal and takes on the proportions of a national problem involving the perpetuation of the nation, especially politically and culturally, and the rights and responsibilities of individuals in relation to the national group. It seems that the whole novel is devoted to exploring this problem on a national, even universal, scale; Ambrose states the problem succinctly, if quite esoterically, as the conflict between the "conventual and the cenobitic":

"European scholarship has never lost its monastic character," he said. Chinese scholarship deals with taste and wisdom, not with the memorizing of facts. In China the man whom we make a don sat for the Imperial examinations and became a bureaucrat. Their scholars were lonely men of few books and fewer pupils, content with a single concubine, a pine tree and the prospect of a stream. European culture has become conventual; we must make it cenobitic" (186–187).

Because of their individuality neither Ambrose nor Basil

can accept the "conventual" nature of contemporary culture on the one hand, political order and national honor on the other.

For the first time, with the possible exception of *Black Mischief* in which Basil is contrasted briefly with Seth, Waugh brings together his two typical isolatoes, "victim" and "victimizer," and their representative philosophies, in what seems to be an attempt to evaluate them under conditions of real life. Heretofore, the novels have dealt with fantastic experiences and circumstances, but here the innocent and the cad are placed in the perspective of the real world; it seems clear that only one of the philosophies, maybe neither, will be able to stand the test of reality. In this way, *Put Out More Flags* is more than a final regrouping of several previous characters; it is in a sense a culmination of the seriousness of all the past novels. The real world is beginning to impinge on the world of the Bright Young Things and it must be met with a realistic view of life. It is as though Waugh purposefully brought together the two heroes, the one passive and ineffectual, the other active and virile, one an escapist, the other an exploiter in an effort to deduce a positive statement regarding the individual's moral responsibility to society, however chaotic that society might be. It is in this way that the novel is focused however humorously on a serious theme—the examination of personal values and group responsibilities. It is altogether logical historically and psychologically that the reality of World War II be the means of "forcing the moment to a crisis"; for this reason also it is understandable why a final solution is not reached until the postwar novels.

That the theme of the novel does deal primarily with the "conventual" versus the "cenobitic" is underscored by the late but emphatic introduction of Cedric Lyne. This character is mentioned in the narrator's interview with Angela, and several references throughout the book identify him as an ineffective, possibly tedious figure, a collector of grottos. However, thematic formulation demands that he become active in the narrative; and the circumstances surrounding his death provide the extension necessary to delineate emphatically the central theme. Cedric, like both Basil and Ambrose, is confronted with the problem of his own individuality:

> Cedric set out across the battlefield. . . . It was part of a crazy world where he was an interloper. It was nothing to do with him (222).

Even though he rather halfheartedly is serving, in his own way, the immediate needs of the corporate society, he echoes agreement with Ambrose's theory of the "conventual" versus the "cenobitic" and exults in his singularity:

> A reconnaissance plance came overhead. Cedric moved off the path but did not take cover, did not lie on his face or gaze into the earth and wonder if there was a rear gunner, as he would have done if he had been with headquarters. The great weapons of modern war did not count in single lives; it took a whole section to make a target worth a burst of machinegun fire; a platoon or a motor lorry to be worth a bomb. No one had anything against the individual; as long as he was alone he was free and safe; there's danger in numbers; divided we stand, united we fall, thought Cedric, striding happily towards the enemy, shaking from his boots all the frustration of corporate life. He did not know it, but he was thinking exactly what Ambrose had thought when he announced that culture must cease to be conventual and become cenobitic (220).

Before attempting to define specifically the theme of this novel, it is necessary to consider the tonal characteristics, for proper interpretation of theme depends upon recognition of the pervading tones and the way in which they influence the development of theme. First, regarding tone, as already suggested, the very actuality of the impending war just behind the comedy and general good fun consistently keeps before the reader a seriousness not found heretofore in Waugh's fiction. Much more than atmosphere is implied by the narrator's own terse reminders of the war situation:

> So the snows vanished and the weeks of winter melted away with them; presently, oblivious of the hazards of war, the swallows returned to their ancestral building grounds (144).

> There was no sign of Spring in this country. Everywhere the land lay frozen and dead, deep snow in the hills, thin ice in the valleys; the buds on the thorn were hard and small and black (216).

The chief method of tonal control is the narrator's specific relationship with the characters. As indicated earlier, this novel does not contain the biting satire nor even the consistent irony of the earlier works; the narrator generally seems to be less detached from at least the significant characters and quite willing to identify with them in narrative, even to sympathize with them. For instance, in the case of Angela Lyne, through the close narrative technique discussed earlier, the narrator is able to draw the reader into a genuine sympathy with her by his omniscient identification with her:

> Steam from the bath formed in a mist, and later in great beads of water, on the side of the glass. She finished her cocktail and felt the fumes rise inside her. She lay for a long time in the water, scarcely thinking, scarcely feeling anything except the warm water round her and the spirit within her. She called for her maid, from next door, to bring her a cigarette, smoked it slowly to the end, called for an ash tray and then for a towel. Presently she was ready to face the darkness, and the intense cold, and Margot Metroland's dinner party. She noticed in the last intense scrutiny before her mirrors that her mouth was beginning to droop a little at the corners. It was not the disappointed pout

that she knew in so many of her friends; it was as the droop
you sometimes saw in death masks, when the jaw had been set
and the face had stiffened in lines which told those waiting
round the bed that the will to live was gone (127–28).

Similarly, there seems to be a close narrator identification with other characters, such as Alastair:

"Who cares what *he* wants?" said Alastair. For him there was
no 'they.' England was at war; he, Alastair Trumpington, was at
war. It was not the business of any politician to tell him when
or how he should fight. But he could not put this into words;
not into words, anyway, which Basil would not make ridiculous,
so he walked on in silence behind Peter's martial figure until
Sonia decided to take a cab (52).

Although there is generally less distance between the
narrator and the characters, there is a peculiar relationship between the narrator and the hero, especially in
light of the narrator's relationship to Ambrose and Cedric, the other two thematically significant characters. In
short, despite Basil's major narrative role, the narrator
seems more withdrawn from Basil than from either of
the other two figures, especially Ambrose. The narrator
assumes always a strictly external method when describing Basil or his experiences, and, although the distance
is not great enough to be conducive to a satirical response, neither is it close enough for approval or for the
implication of genuine sympathy. In fact, Basil becomes
a rather depthless character, viewed somewhat clinically
by a hard-minded narrator. Never does the narrator
probe into the mind of Basil; there are no passages of
close identification; no interior monologues. The total
effect is that the reader is kept at a critical distance from
Basil throughout the novel. Perhaps this is because Basil
is an active character and actions are likely to demand
external dramatization, but more likely it is the result
of a concerted effort to prevent reader identification

with Basil and to turn any sympathy toward more responsible reactions to the war. This is the real war
period and Basil is too caddish to be seriously considered;
neither is there time to give consideration to comedians.
Hollis notes:

> The trouble with Basil Seal is that, if we consider him a real
> character, he is too odious to be funny. Had he been content to
> remain a character in one of Mr. Waugh's earlier novels, such
> as *Decline and Fall*—in a fantastic world of fantastic people—we
> would have laughed at him as a mere formula of villainy with-
> out any attempt to pass a moral judgement on a person. We can
> tolerate him even in Azania. But in a real world, alongside real
> and suffering people at a great crisis of our history, he is too
> horrible.[32]

In fact, he, of all the significant characters in the novel,
is the only one never to undergo any serious personal
crisis. He rather "skims over the surface of life" oblivious to or cynical toward those more noble who suffer
because of their acceptance of harsh realities and moral
responsibilities. Therefore, while the narrator may play
some scenes involving Basil to their full comic or satiric
effect, he appears to react coolly toward Basil's antics.
There is no implicit approval of the "complete amorality
and the irresponsible cruelty which permits him to vic-
timize others."[33]
On the other hand, there is identification with Ambrose. But this is not to say that the narrator fully sym-
pathizes with him. Just as the objective narrator finds
some comedy in Basil's irresponsibility, he also finds a
great deal of satirical potential in Ambrose's pathetic
isolation. Some think that this is Ambrose's sole function,
that is, to serve as the butt of satire, yet even those critics
who see Ambrose only as a satirical device admit that
there is a certain pathos in his situation:

---

32. Hollis, p. 17.
33. Carens, p. 51.

Ambrose Silk is made to seem thoroughly ridiculous in a way that the earlier victim antiheroes never were; though there is some pathos in the characterization, he is essentially the ludicrous figure of fun.[34]

As the narrative continues, the narrator allows more and more opportunities for reader identification with Ambrose, even for outright sympathy with him:

It is a curious thing, he thought, that every creed promises a paradise which will be absolutely uninhabitable for anyone of civilized taste. Nanny told me of a Heaven that was full of angels playing harps; the communists tell me of an earth full of leisured and contented factory hands. I don't see Basil getting past the gate of either. Religion is acceptable in its destructive phase; the desert monks carving up that humbug Hypatia; the anarchist gangs roasting the monks in Spain. Hellfire sermons in the chapels; soap-box orators screaming their envy of the rich. Hell is all right. The human mind is inspired enough when it comes to inventing horrors; it is when it tries to invent a Heaven that it shows itself cloddish. But Limbo is the place. In Limbo one has natural happiness without the beatific vision; no harps; no communal order; but wine and conversation and imperfect, various humanity. Limbo for the unbaptized, for the pious heathen, the sincere sceptic. Am I baptized into this modern world? At least I haven't taken a new name. All the rest of the left-wing writers have adopted plebeian monosyllables. Ambrose is irredeemably bourgeois. Parsnip often said so. Damn Parsnip, damn Pimpernell. Do these atrocious young people never discuss anything else? (66)

Even in quite humorous passages dealing with Ambrose, there is the recurring poignancy of alienation uncomprehended, overwhelming:

This is all that anyone talks about, thought Ambrose; jobs and the kind of war it is going to be. War in the air, war of attrition, tank war, war of nerves, war of propaganda, war of defence in depth, war of movement, people's war, total war, indivisible war,

---

34. *Ibid.,* p. 52.

war infinite, war incomprehensible, war of essence without accidents or attributes, metaphysical war, war in time-space, war eternal . . . all war is nonsense, thought Ambrose. I don't care about their war. It's got nothing on me. But if, thought Ambrose, I was one of these people, if I were not a cosmopolitan, Jewish pansy, if I were not all that the Nazis mean when they talk about 'degenerates,' if I were not a single, sane individual, if I were part of a herd, one of these people, normal and responsible for the welfare of my herd, Gawd strike me pink, thought Ambrose, I wouldn't sit around discussing what kind of war it was going to be. I'd make it my kind of war. I'd set about killing and stampeding the other herd as fast and as hard as I could. Lord love a duck, thought Ambrose, there wouldn't be any animals nosing about for suitable jobs in *my* herd (79).

Even if Ambrose is taken as a character with less than totally serious significance, his counterpart Cedric Lyne cannot be. Although the relationship of the narrator with Cedic is brief, there is enough implicit sympathy with him to establish him as a significant character in regard to theme. Cedric seems to be overshadowed from the beginning by an aura of respectable failure and doom. The chapter in which he is to play the star's role —the chapter in which he is killed—is pervaded from the beginning by a deepening tone of gloom; it is as though the narrator intensifies the tone and the significance of the episode by placing it immediately next to a typical exploit of Basil. So intense is this identification that the reader is shocked by the narrator's objective report of his death:

A Company were on the move now. As soon as they heard the firing, without waiting for orders, they were doing what the Colonel intended, edging up the opposing hillside among the boulders, getting into position where they could outflank the outflanking party. It did not matter now whether Cedric reached them. He never did; a bullet got him, killing him instantly while he was a quarter of a mile away (223).

In directing the reader's response to the two or three

major characters, the author is able to convey a positive moral statement regarding the conflict of the "conventual" and the "cenobitic," private morality and public responsibility. The narrator maintains a rather detached view of Basil, but a rather close relationship with Ambrose and Cedric as if to intensify the contrast between flagrant irresponsibility and honorable if mistaken and confused reactions to the demands and the terror of war. In this way he implies a rejection of Basil's attitude and, if not approval at least appreciation of Ambrose and Cedric's problem. For Ambrose and Cedric there is a degree of sympathy, yet not necessarily for the character or for the character's response but for the human problem thus represented. Interestingly, however, it is they who are destroyed and Basil who, "transformed," endures; as the author sees it, there can be no other way. Ultimately the philosophies of Ambrose and Cedric, the ineffectual, passive *ingénus,* as they must in contemporary society, prove woefully insufficient; but so also does Basil's original attitude. Thus, the author suggests that individual integrity matters but it is not all that matters, and that moral irresponsibility cannot be tolerated in modern civilization. Accordingly, Basil suddenly "reforms," accepts the reality of the war and his necessary and honorable role in the defense of his country. It is this positive view of responsibility that triumphs and not the irresponsibility of the cad. By this last stroke, the reformation of Basil, the author completes the examination of the "conventual" versus the "cenobitic."

In this novel he has presented three possible views, perhaps four, of the reality of conventual society and the impossibility of the cenobitic. For Ambrose, the thing is too real; he broods over his own individuality and the personal implications of the war until he is spiritually destroyed and physically exiled.

This is the country of Swift, Burke, Sheridan, Wellington, Wilde, T. E. Lawrence, he thought; this is the people who once lent fire to an imperial race, whose genius flashed through two stupendous centuries of culture and success, who are now quietly receding into their own mists, turning their backs on the world of effort and action. Fortunate islanders, thought Ambrose, happy, drab escapists, who have seen the gold lace and the candlelight and left the banquet before dawn revealed stained table linen and a tipsy buffoon!

But he knew it was not for him; the dark, nomadic strain in his blood, the long heritage of wandering and speculation allowed him no rest. Instead of Atlantic breakers he saw the camels swaying their heads resentfully against the lightening sky, as the caravan woke to another day's stage in the pilgrimage (230).

Cedric, on the other hand, denies reality; he fails even to recognize the reality of the war; he tries to participate in something he does not understand, in something that is quite "unreal" to him:

> Cedric set out across the little battlefield. All seemed quite unreal to him still.
> The bombers were not aiming at any particular target; they were plastering the ground in front of their cars, between battalion headquarters and the mouth of the valley where A Company were dug in. The noise was incessant and shattering. Still it did not seem real to Cedric. It was part of a crazy world where he was an interloper. It was nothing to do with him. A bomb came whistling down, it seemed from directly over his head. He fell on his face and it burst fifty yards away, bruising him with a shower of small stones (222).

Only Basil recognizes both the foolishness of war and the necessity for individual responsibility; he alone can accept reality and adapt to it. His final response to the war seems somehow even more noble than that of Alastair, who has joined the army earlier as a common soldier because he feels that he owes something to the world, for Basil's commitment, though less patriotic, seems all the more realistic. The novel thus becomes especially significant in the continuing thematic development of Waugh's fiction, for "the exile of Ambrose and the death of Lyne mark the disappearance of the entirely passive antihero from Waugh's fiction, as the transformation of Basil Seal into a commando marks the displacement of the rogue-hero."[35] For the first time, the hero joins the world. Basil's story epitomizes the growth of the innocent from the naïveté of childhood, through the roguery of adolescence, finally to awareness and participation in life. From now on in Waugh's fiction, "there's a new spirit abroad."

---

35. *Ibid.*

5
Mode Suspended-Brideshead Revisited

Marston LaFrance well describes the initial and continuing impact of *Brideshead Revisited* upon the criticism of Waugh's fiction in general when he says that:

> *Brideshead Revisited* . . . seems to have provided both the impetus and the focal point for most of the existing criticism of Evelyn Waugh's fiction.[1]

For most critics, and for most of the popular reading audience, this is the novel on which hangs Waugh's reputation as a novelist. This one book has influenced both public and critical opinion of Waugh more than any other and has gained for him both praise and condemnation. As an illustration of the wide diversity of opinion regarding the novel, at least one critic thinks that "it reveals the complete maturity of Evelyn Waugh as an artist";[2] another that it represents "not a development in which the artist's powers come to maturity, but a diminution."[3] But, whatever the final evaluation of this novel, it must be admitted at the outset that *Brideshead Revisited* is unique in Waugh's fiction, and, if it is

1. Marston LaFrance, "Context and Structure in Evelyn Waugh's *Brideshead Revisited,*" *Twentieth Century Literature* 10 (April, 1964) : 12.
2. A. A. DeVitis, *Roman Holiday:* The Catholic Novels of Evelyn Waugh (New York: Bookman Associates, 1956) , p. 52.
3. Frederick R. Karl, "The World of Evelyn Waugh: The Normally Insane," *The Contemporary English Novel* (New York: Farrar, Straus, and Cudahy, 1962) , p. 173.

not the consummation of his artistry, then, certainly, it is a decisive turning point in his development.

The novel is Charles Ryder's account of his coincidental return to Brideshead, which through the ravages of war has been all but destroyed; he returns a captain of an infantry company which is to bivouac in this once-magnificent center of culture. With a vision of the original splendor of the place, Ryder recalls his previous association with Brideshead and the Catholic family, the Marchmains, who once inhabited it. The main story is a lengthy flashback comprised of his "sacred and profane" memories. He tells of his early acquaintance with Sebastian, the Marchmain son, at Oxford, of the first visit to Brideshead, of his meeting Cordelia, the younger daughter, and Lady Marchmain, of his learning of the Byronic eccentricities of Lord Marchmain, and of his immediate attraction to Julia, the elder daughter. Ryder's relationship with Sebastian and Julia provides the stimulus for the action; in Book One, his friendship with Sebastian is the paramount interest, but as this section closes, Sebastian, who has become degenerate and dissipated, all but disappears from the novel. In this section Ryder grows from a state of bland innocence to a kind of adolescent awareness and cynicism, especially regarding Sebastian's religion. But counteracting this negative attitude is the beginning of the love affair with Julia. Book Two is primarily concerned with this very intense and rather tragic romance which begins in earnest ten years after they first meet. Even though Julia is willing at first to ignore the church's teaching on divorce and remarriage, she later refuses to "live in sin." Feeling the "twitch upon the thread," she finally chooses rather to deny herself happiness in this world as a kind of self-imposed penitence. Pervading the story and influencing every aspect of plot is the Catholic religion, which is embodied initially in the tyrannical Lady Marchmain, but later in Julia and then Ryder as they give themselves completely to the Church. Besides these thematic elements, throughout the novel there is a striking contrast of contemporary barbarism and traditional, aristocratic, in this case, Catholic culture. As the novel closes, Ryder, alone with happiness like the memories behind him, finds that the sanctuary lamp still burns in the chapel: the Church and culture still survive, if shedding a less than dazzling light.

Several features about this novel make it remarkably different from the earlier novels. The three most commonly noted are the first-person narration, the "romantic" tone, and the pronounced Catholic theme. Here the devices employed in the previous satirical novels are combined in such a way as to produce an effect quite different from the earlier novels which were formulated out of a satiric-ironic view of modernity. On the other hand, *Brideshead Revisited*, despite its singularity, is in every way the logical development, artistically and thematically, and even temperamentally, from the previous novels. Even Karl, who sees the novel as an absolute and abrupt break from the previous works, grants that, with certain stipulations accepted, "the reader can come to terms with the 'serious' *Brideshead Revisited* as a continuation, with variations, of early Waugh."[4] Recognizing similarities between this novel and previous ones that most other critics overlook in their rush to establish *Brideshead Revisited* as an aberration, LaFrance goes further than Karl and suggests that in both "thought and technique" there is "a remarkable amount of similarity between this novel and the earlier ones."[5] Although this critic does not greatly expand upon this observation, he does offer a convincing list of comparisons indicative of at least the superficial affinity that this

4. *Ibid.,* p. 175.
5. LaFrance, p. 13.

novel bears to the preceding ones, if not of progression
and development. The primary points of likeness are,
he says, the "great houses," representative of stability
and tradition; certain character types, specifically "waifs"
and "bosses"; many technical factors, especially the narrator's intrusion into the drama; and, finally the general
structure of the novel.[6] Although LaFrance ultimately
finds the primary weakness of the novel in the unhappy
combination of old methods with new materials and
purposes, he does establish two significant points: first,
that in the first seven novels there is a "progression away
from the comic and toward the conventional,"[7] and,
second, that *Brideshead Revisited* is not a "complete
escape from the earlier tradition."[8]

That *Brideshead Revisited* is legitimately descended
from the previous novels is witnessed by every aspect of
the novel, particularly narrative formulation, thematic
development, and tonal control. First, in narrative technique *Brideshead Revisited* resembles in many ways the
earlier novels. For example, the structure is similar to
that of the preceding works, particularly in that it is at
once both circular and progressive; and even the minute
elements of narration reflect strongly the previous narrative techniques. Thematically, *Brideshead Revisited* is
also closely related to the previous novels: if they have
been concerned with the plight of the alien in a hostile
society, this novel even more delves into the dilemma,
although here there is a slightly different type of hero,
more real circumstances, and a more positive affirmation
of the hero's code of values. Probably the thing that
separates this novel so sharply from its predecessors is
its introduction of a new dominant tone; yet, when this

6. *Ibid.*, pp. 12–15. LaFrance, like most critics, uses the original version of the novel. This study, also, will use the Little, Brown and Company edition of 1945 unless otherwise noted.
7. *Ibid.*, p. 12.
8. *Ibid.*

third aspect of the novel is viewed in light of the tonal techniques and the increasing seriousness of the earlier novels, it, too, becomes a logical development of the preceding fiction.

At the heart of the similarity of this novel to the earlier works lies the author's technique, a technique based on the exigencies of the ironic mode. As before, in *Brideshead Revisited* all the technical factors are formulated through the relationship of the narrator-persona and the character-persona; any distinctive quality of this novel can be accounted for primarily by the variation in the roles and relationships of these personae. The novel does not reflect either a sudden deterioration or abandonment of technique, but a logical, if somewhat unsuccessful, extension of technique and a realistic expansion of thematic concerns.

Although the circularity in narrative structure recalls previous works, *Brideshead Revisited* is unique because of the use in this novel of the first-person point of view. Karl finds what he calls "the change" in Waugh's fiction apparent in the second word of the novel, "I."[9] But the change may not be so real as it is apparent, at least in technique. A first-person point of view may well suggest that there can be no dramatic or emotional distinction between the narrator and the character; they become one and the same. But the particular narrative technique of this novel, even with the first-person point of view, allows a narrative formulation similar to that of the earlier novels; that is, the narrator tells the story of a character with whom he is not always completely identified. *Brideshead Revisited* is so arranged that the narrator actually does have narrative perspective on the character. This is true to some degree in all first-person narratives, for there is generally always a "tense" or time separation of the two personae, the "now I" narrator and

---

9. Karl, p. 173.

the "then I" character. For instance, the narrator Gulliver has a historic, even ironic, perspective of Gulliver the traveler. But in *Brideshead Revisited,* Waugh seems to attempt to gain the same kind of narrator perspective and control over the character that he has in the earlier novels by even further removing the narrator "I" from the character "I."

This is accomplished through the use of yet another "I" persona, an "intermediate I." The "now I" does not tell the story directly, but using a framing device, in this case somewhat reminiscent of the dream vision, allows an "intermediate I" to interpose himself between the "now I" and the "then I." Although Ryder, as the captain of infantry, is generally thought to be the narrator of the novel, this way of thinking overlooks the dramatic necessity of both a narrator and character in the prologue and epilogue. In these sections there is both a "now I" as narrator and a "then I" as the character, Captain Ryder; there is both time and tense separation. When the main story begins Captain Ryder is supposed to shift from the character of the prologue to the narrator of the main story, but this transition is not convincing either when it ostensibly occurs at the end of the prologue or in the course of the main story. The original "now I" narrator of the prologue refuses to relinquish the narrator's role. The result is that the omniscient narrator, the "now I," sees himself as a character, Captain Charles Ryder, remembering his own early adventures. This technique effects a kind of detached narration similar to the third-person narrative of the early novels. However, the memories about the "then I" supposedly arising within the "intermediate I" are often colored to such an extent by the "now I" that distinction between them is impossible. In fact, it is the "now I" who as narrator shapes and controls the entire novel, even to the point of interfusing "now" reactions to "then" activities and not always with the acknowledgment of time or dramatic distance. Yet it does seem that the author intended each persona to serve a specific function in the formulation of the novel. All three personae, their narrative distance, and their narrative roles are implied in one brief and unfortunate paragraph:

> That is the full account of my first brief visit to Brideshead; could I have known then that so small a thing, in other days, would be remembered with tears by a middle-aged captain of infantry (40).

The first clause identifies the narrator as the "now I"; the reference to the "visit to Brideshead . . . then" settles the identity of the hero as the "then I"; and the conspicuous mentioning of the middle-aged captain's remembrance of these events suggests not only the imposing of an "intermediate I" as narrative device but also something of the melodramatic tone. Although it is impossible to separate completely these entities, it might be suggested that in the make-up of the novel each distinct "I" has a definite function and is in at least one area the dominant factor: the "now I" is the primary narrative device; the "intermediate I," the chief tonal factor; and the "then I," the major thematic device. However, there is too much interfunctioning of the three personae to allow these otherwise convenient distinctions to be made sharply or consistently.

Nevertheless, in narrative the "now I" is the dominant persona despite the fact that it is the memories of the "intermediate I" which, according to the structure of the novel, are being related. Captain Ryder's memories are, of course, exactly those of the narrator, so in certain passages it is impossible to determine which is speaking:

> Looking back now, after twenty years, there is little I would have left undone or done otherwise (45).

The time implied in this passage is correlated with the "intermediate I," but the sentiment, viewed in context, can be that only of the "now I." One gets the idea that it is the narrator, the "now I," speaking continuously throughout the novel outside the "intermediate I" and that Captain Ryder has not actually taken over the narrative. That this is true is demonstrated particularly in those passages involving references to memory:

> He never declared his war aims, and I do not know to this day whether they were merely punitive . . . (72).

> On some days life kept pace with the gondola . . . ; it left a confused memory of fierce sunlight on the sands and cool, marble interiors (101).

> I was there twenty minutes before Rex. If I had to spend an evening with him, it should, at any rate, be in my own way. I remember that dinner well (171).

> Scraps of conversation come back to me with the memory of her room. I remember her saying . . . (126).

The ambiguity in point of view in these passages may be cleared up, however, by the recognition of the fact that, in most instances, it is quite obviously the "now I" who is the voice arranging and controlling all the narrative material; his personality influences the interpretation of the material. In fact, although this novel is written in first person, there is very little loss of the old omniscience of the narrator—this narrative freedom could hardly be granted to one already identified as a character. Perhaps this explains Churchill's observation that "In *Brideshead Revisited* Waugh abandoned the technique of omniscience (but not its spirit)."[10]

The narrator's omniscience is abundantly demon-

---

10. Thomas Churchill, "The Trouble with *Brideshead Revisited*," *Modern Language Quarterly* 28 (June, 1967): 225.

strated in narrative functions very similar to those of the earlier works, first in overall or external narrative formation and, second, in various functions within the narrative itself. Regarding the first, the narrator is identified as the "now I" and his complete control over the narrative is demonstrated by the framing device which gives the novel's structure its circularity. Both the prologue and the epilogue are on the same time plane, separated from the beginning of the main story by "more than twenty years"; although there is something of a plot developed in these portions, the body of the novel, comprising two books, contains the main story and is a self-contained unit within itself. The prologue and the epilogue serve the narrator not only as a narrative device for getting the story told, and in a way that promises to objectify the characters, but also as a means of interpreting the events retrospectively. Also, the narrator, as in the previous novels, demonstrates a degree of externality by his ability to shift scenes at will; but this freedom is explained here by the memory technique and is thus affiliated with Captain Ryder, the "intermediate I"; nevertheless, the narrator still admits to the role of external storyteller who is arranging the material to suit his purposes:

> It is time to speak of Julia, who till now has played an intermittent and somewhat enigmatic part in Sebastian's drama (178).

> It was ten years later that she said this to me in a storm in the Atlantic (200).

> Thus I come to the broken sentences which were the last words spoken between Julia and me, the last memories (339).

He even seems to pause at times to confide in the reader certain particulars about his narrative style, an externality similar to the narrator's direct commentary on Paul Pennyfeather:

1 have here compressed into a few sentences what, there, required many (157).

I must reduce to a few words a conversation which took us from Holywell to the Parks, through Mesopotamia, and over the ferry to North Oxford (142).

Second, the narrator's omniscience is evident in his several functions within the narrative itself. For instance, he is able to provide detailed historical information, particularly in regard to the backgrounds of characters. Of Anthony Blanche he says:

An attempt had been made in his childhood to make an Englishman out of him; he was two years at Eton; then in the middle of the war he had defied the submarines, rejoined his mother in the Argentine, and a clever and audacious schoolboy was added to the valet, the maid, the two chauffeurs, the Pekinese and the second husband. Criss-cross about the world he travelled with them, waxing in wickedness like a Hogarthian page-boy (46).

Of Lady Marchmain:

She appeared seldom in the books; she was older than the eldest of them by nine years and had married and left home while they were schoolboys; between her and them stood two other sisters; after the birth of the third daughter there had been pilgrimages and pious benefactions in request for a son, for theirs was a wide property and an ancient name (138).

Again, the narrator demonstrates his omniscience in the many descriptions of landscape and buildings:

It was an aesthetic education to live within those walls, to wander from room to room, from the Soanesque library to the Chinese drawing-room, adazzle with gilt pagodas and nodding mandarins, painted paper and Chippendale fret-work, from the Pompeian parlour to the great tapestry-hung hall which stood unchanged, as it had been designed two hundred and fifty years before; to sit, hour after hour, in the pillared shade looking out on the terrace (80).

Everywhere, on cobble and gravel and lawn, the leaves were falling and in the college gardens the smoke of the bonfires joined the wet river mist, drifting across grey walls; the flags were oily underfoot and as, one by one, the lamps were lit in the windows round the quad, the golden lights were diffuse and remote, like those of a foreign village seen from the slopes outside (104).

The narrator throughout the novel supplies incidental but helpful information outside the narrative through the use of parentheses, a device popular early in Waugh's fiction.

"Is *that* paid for?" (The box of a hundred cabinet Partagas on the sideboard.) "Or *those?*" (a dozen frivolous, new books on the table.) "Or those?" (A Lalique decanter and glasses.) "Or *that* peculiarly noisome object?" (A human skull lately purchased from the School of Medicine, which, resting in a bowl of roses, formed, at the moment, the chief decoration of my table. It bore the motto *Et in Arcadia ego* inscribed on its forehead.) (42).

Furthermore, the narrator serves as a kind of objective interpreter of certain of the events, indeed most of them:

Dinner was long and chosen, like the guests, in a spirit of careful mockery (71).

His year of anarchy had filled a deep, interior need of his, the escape from reality, and as he found himself increasingly hemmed in, where he once felt himself free, he became at times listless and morose, even with me (107).

Suggesting even more externality on the narrator's part than any of these, however, are the several comments outside the narrative relating to some event or circumstance in the narrative:

That was the cant phrase of the time, derived from heaven knows what misconception of popular science. "There's something chemical between them" was used to explain the overmastering

hate or love of any two people. It was the old concept of de-
terminism in a new form (129).

But perhaps the function of the narrator that best
both demonstrates his omniscience and identifies him as
a persona other than a character—the "now I," who of
dramatic necessity narrates the entire novel—is his ability to record precisely the mental activity of the characters, of Julia especially (180–83). This freedom is
explained, however, in a way that might quite logically
allow the character, or the "intermediate I," to have the
knowledge and therefore the ability to relate it:

> All this I learned about Julia, bit by bit, from the stories she
> told, from guesswork, knowing her, from what her friends said,
> from the odd expressions she now and then let slip, from occa-
> sional dreamy monologues of reminiscences . . . (183)

But this explanation fails to convince the reader that
the preceding several-page analysis of Julia's thoughts
does not come from an omniscient narrator; even the
explanation seems to be spoken by the "now I."

Thus, in narrative the "now I" is the chief factor,
much as the narrator-persona of the earlier third-person
novels. But this is not to say that the "now I" alone
formulates the narrative, for, like the character-personae
of previous novels, both the "intermediate I" and the
"then I" have important narrative roles. Captain Charles
Ryder, the intermediate persona, is of key dramatic
importance within the narrative because he provides the
structural unity. It is his return to Brideshead in 1943 as
a disillusioned captain of infantry that serves as the
springboard of the whole story; his "unexpected" arrival at the memorable site provides the narrative framework. The prologue and the epilogue are used to initiate
and to conclude rather neatly the activities of the main
story, told under the guise of his "memories." The fact

that the main story is made up of the memories of Captain Ryder allows the narrator objective distance, but the "now I" loses most of this by recording all of the adventures from a "now" perspective, so that there is no more distance between the narrator and the "then I" than between the narrator and the "intermediate I." Ryder, the captain, cannot be said to be, other than in the prologue and epilogue, central either to the progression or unity of the main narrative, even though the story is his meditations. Progression is handled by the "now I" and, while the intermediate may serve as a unifying device for the novel in totality, the unity of the main story, in narration and plot, is to be found only in the function of the "then I" persona.

The "then I" persona serves as the central narrative device within the main story. From "That day, too, I had come not knowing my destination" (21) to "Thus I come to the broken sentences which were the last words spoken between Julia and me, the last memories" (339), the main story features as the central narrative device the "then I." Not only does his activity become the central action of the progressive drama, but also he is the key factor in unifying the various narrative elements and characters in the novel. In this way he functions much like the previous heroes who serve as a pivot for all the novel's action. It is through him that all the events are entered, viewed, and commented upon and through him that all the characters are introduced into the drama; through him the narrator introduces Sebastian, Julia, Anthony, Lady Marchmain, and all other important "minor" characters. Although the "now I" as narrator interjects many omniscient comments regarding the characters, nevertheless he relies upon the "then I" for perspective within the narrative. In several instances information which could be easily and consistently presented by the omniscient process is introduced through the "then I." For example, much is revealed through the conversation of other characters with the "then" persona; especially illustrative is Anthony Blanche's lengthy disquisition on the Marchmain family (53–56); another example of this technique is the conversation of the "then I" with Rex (171–78); still another is the intimate revelations he receives from Julia (198–200). In addition to informative conversations, correspondence is reported through the "then I" (148, 170). This narrative technique provides not only information pertaining to the events, but it also serves as a unifying device within the narrative. Finally, the narrator, though omniscient at will, relies upon the sensibility of the "then I" for dramatic purposes; this is evidenced by the frequent use of the word "seemed" in reporting the activity. Although this factor, as will be pointed out later, is a key ingredient in the tonal control, attention should be given this technique here as it reflects dramatic perspective and not as it contributes to psychological identification. Dramatic identification attempting to capture the reality of the moment is seen in passages describing the "then" response of the "now I."

> At Sebastian's approach these grey figures seemed quietly to fade into the landscape (28).

> The sun was behind us as we drove, so that we seemed to be in pursuit of our own shadows (40).

> He cannot have been more than thirty at the time we met him, but he seemed very old to us in Oxford. Julia treated him, as she seemed to treat all the world, with mild disdain (111).

In these several ways the formulation of narrative is remarkably similar to that of the earlier novels. Yet, in the final analysis, *Brideshead Revisited* remains a first-person narrative and any number of technical innovations within this basic point of view will not remove the attending dangers, particularly the danger of too-close emotional identification of narrator with character. Perhaps it is in order here to clarify briefly what is meant by the "danger" of a first-person point of view. It has been noted earlier that the whole business of establishing a tone within a novel has to do with the relationship of character persona and narrator persona. It has been pointed out that the narrator's choice of both his emotional and artistic perspective produces the tone of the novel and, while this choice may be influenced by the nature of the narrative material, that is, whether it is inherently serious or comic, his attitude need not always be governed by it. In fact, it may be that nothing is inherently serious or comic, but that the response depends always upon perspective. Therefore, what may be rendered quite serious or even tragic by one author may be made comic by another merely by a slight shift of perspective, as Stendahl suggests.

It has been noted also that satire and tragedy, indeed all good art, demand a certain objectivity, which is achieved usually in the novel by the artistic and/or emotional detachment of the narrator from the character. Usually, as in the case of comedy, satire, or tragedy, detachment will be only in artistic stance, and the greatness of the work lies in the tension between the narrator's artistic detachment and his implied interest or genuine sympathy with the hero; tragedy emerges as the highest form of art by virtue of the intensity of the tension. As noted in *A Handful of Dust*, there is a fine line between satiric irony and tragic irony, but both are characterized by the detached stance of the narrator. Once the artistic detachment is dropped, however, the tragedy becomes melodrama; the comedy, romance. The ironic spectrum is broken. It is precisely for this reason that *Brideshead Revisited* is considered by most critics as an artistic failure.[11] Even though it possesses both comic and tragic potential, its loss of ironic perspective through the use of first person causes it to drift inevitably into melodrama.[12]

But it is not just the point of view that is to be blamed for any loss of detachment; the narrative technique demonstrates the ironic potential of the personae arrangement. The reason for the loss of irony seems primarily the disposition of the narrator, the "now I." One cannot say that first-person point of view always produces romance or melodrama, for the first-person point of view offers an infinite variety of relationships between the "now" narrator and the "then" hero. (On the other hand, melodramas in third person are not uncommon, but none is written by a detached narrator; yet, the classic satire *Candide,* is written in third person.) In fact, there are several highly artistic novels in which, although they are written in first-person point of view, the "narrator I" refrains from melodramatic association with the "character I": *Moby Dick* and *Huckleberry Finn,* for instance. Others become more "romantic" because of the unmistakable sympathy of the narrator with the character: *Farewell to Arms* is an example. Other works, the most ironic, appeal to a sort of burlesque melodrama or romance for their effect, *A Modest Proposal, Gulliver's Travels,* and Twain's "A Dog's Tale" are possible illustrations. Written in the first person, these works remain in the ironic spectrum because of the implied distance between the narrator I and the character I; if this distance were to be bridged by the present I's complete and honest sympathy, the ironic effect would be lost.

Briefly stated, then, third-person narration has inherently the benefit of artistic detachment by both person

---

11. See critical commentaries reviewed in chapter 1.
12. See discussion of tonal factors in chapter 1.

and time; emotional attachment must be implied. First-person narrative, on the other hand, has inherently only that little distance allowed by the time differential, and thus detachment, if there is any, must be consciously developed by the artist through the use of various narrative and tonal devices. Waugh has heretofore maintained artistic distance from the characters through the third-person approach and, although implying interest or sympathy in the heroes, he has sustained the dramatic tension required for good art. Yet in *Brideshead Revisited,* he abandons the third-person device and with it the ironic perspective in favor of the first person and a serious subjective mood. As a consequence the novel has received critical condemnation by those who find it "romantic," or lushly nostalgic[13] to the point of evidencing artistic deterioration. While there are comic elements in the novel which suggest at least some kind of ironic perspective, the comedy contrasts with the pervasive tone. As LaFrance suggests, Waugh has attempted to force a "serious frame of reference" upon the comic tradition and herein lies the flaw.[14] Carens, perhaps, best describes the tonal effect in this novel when he notes the "subordination of satire to sentiment":

> This fictional device [first person], whatever its merits, has also its dangers. Not only has the first person narrator contributed to the structural defect, but his presence has nearly banished from the novel the objective, ironic, satirical detachment which had hitherto distinguished Waugh's art.[15]

However, it is not as though *all* objectivity and irony are lost. Rather, the particular use of the first-person technique here itself suggests a kind of detachment. De-Vitis has noted in this regard:

---

13. James F. Carens, *The Satiric Art of Evelyn Waugh* (Seattle: University of Washington Press, 1966), p. 98.
14. LaFrance, p. 18.
15. Carens, p. 106.

> With the elimination of the satirical approach, Waugh had to devise another method of removing himself from the world of the Marchmains. He had to devise a method which would allow him to work with his delicate subject and yet afford him the distance necessary to manipulate his characters convincingly and according to the standards of the serious English novel. Yet he had to have a device which would allow him to make measured and cogent observations on the actions of the characters through whom he wished to portray the truth of his theme.[16]

While allowing certainly for a subjective thematic statement, this commentary assumes an objective method. If DeVitis is correct, perhaps what is demonstrated in *Brideshead Revisited* is not an accidental mishandling of artistic technique altogether, or an abandonment of the old technique, but an intentional and purposeful shift in the persona technique in an effort to achieve tonal qualities conducive to a more serious theme than before. One has only to reconsider the preceding works to realize that Waugh has been moving continuously toward a more serious handling of theme, if not a theme more serious in itself; and, corollary with this increasing seriousness, there has been a growing identification of the narrator with the character. One has only to recall the total artistic and emotional detachment of a novel like *Vile Bodies* or even *Black Mischief* and compare this to *A Handful of Dust, Put Out More Flags,* or even *Scoop* to be made aware of the gradual loss of total detachment and the increasing attachment of narrator with character.

Nor is *Brideshead Revisited* the first novel in which Waugh attempts identification, artistically and emotionally, with the hero. *Work Suspended,* an unfinished novel written before the publication of *Put Out More Flags,* utilizes the first-person point of view, but much less effectively than *Brideshead Revisited.* It is interesting that in this fragment the narrator, John Plant, a

---

16. DeVitis, pp. 45–46.

writer of detective novels, expresses a sentiment regarding narrative technique quite possibly reflecting Waugh's own ideas about this time:

> "I mean, I am in danger of becoming purely a technical expert. Take my father . . . . He spent his whole life perfecting his technique. It seems to me I am in danger of becoming mechanical, turning out year after year the kind of book I know I can write well. I feel I have got as good as I ever can be at this particular sort of writing. I need new worlds to conquer."[17]

Could it be that Waugh felt that he had done all he could within the satiric novel and because of the increasing positive nature of his themes felt that a less ironic, more conventional approach might be more congenial to a serious affirmation of values? At least Churchill seems to think this a valid supposition:

> He may have felt that he had gone as far as he could with the comic and satiric line, so that the change in the direction of seriousness and rhetorical pomp was as inevitable as it was necessary, considering that the writer must feel the need of doing something new and of doing it well.[18]

The first attempt in first person was unquestionably a technical failure. Perhaps Waugh's abandonment of the novel is mute testimony to his own dissatisfaction with the new technique. If so, it is quite understandable, for this novel fragment is the most "toneless" thing he ever wrote. One never knows quite how to have it, for the "narrator I" on the one hand seems too close to the "character I" for comedy, but, on the other hand, he does not seem involved enough emotionally with the character for him to be taken seriously; there is no real identification with the character. Despite the very pol-

---

17. *Work Suspended* (London: Chapman & Hall, 1949) , p. 167.
18. Churchill, p. 213.

ished style,[19] which may be Waugh's best writing up to this point, the novel is tedious at best, perhaps because all actions, even conversations, are filtered through the philosophic musings of the "narrator I" who never quite clarifies his attitude toward the "character I." But in *Brideshead Revisited* there are enough innovations in technique to indicate that Waugh is trying to overcome the shortcomings of the first attempt. In *Brideshead Revisited* the formulation of narrative is such—specifically, the three levels of the "I"—that there is made possible a kind of irony, even satire or tragedy. The "now I," because he is ostensibly twice removed from the "then I," is able frequently to imply an ironic view of this persona. Several passages indicate the ironic potential:

> It is easy, retrospectively, to endow one's youth with a false precocity or a false innocence; to tamper with the dates marking one's stature on the edge of the door (27).

> I was nineteen years old and completely ignorant of women. I could not with any certainty recognize a prostitute in the streets (100).

> How ungenerously later in life we disclaim the virtuous moods of our youth, living in restrospect long summer days of unreflecting dissipation, Dresden figures of pastoral gaiety! (62).

And in many more instances throughout the main narrative, even after the distancing effect of the "intermediate I" has long been forgotten, there seems to be abundant opportunity for viewing the "then I" ironically, even "anti-sympathetically."[20]

> But I had no mind for these smooth things; instead, fear worked like yeast in my thoughts, and the fermentation brought to the surface, in great gobs of scum, the images of disaster: a loaded

---

19. Waugh himself at the time thought that this novel represented his best writing.
20. Churchill, p. 226.

gun held carelessly at a stile, a horse rearing and rolling over, a shaded pool with a submerged stake, an elm bough falling suddenly on a still morning; a car at a blind corner; all the catalogue of threats to civilized life rose and haunted me; I even pictured a homicidal maniac mouthing in the shadows swinging a length of lead pipe (74).

It opened a prospect; the prospect one gained at the turn of the avenue, as I had first seen it with Sebastian, of the secluded valley, the lakes falling away one below the other, the old house in the foreground, the rest of the world abandoned and forgotten; a world of its own of peace and love and beauty . . . . Need I reproach myself if sometimes I was rapt in the vision (321–22).

However, even this ironic perspective is generally overshadowed by the positive and unabashed emotional identification of the "now I" with the "then I" despite the intermediate figure. As Captain Ryder, the "intermediate I," is absent from the main narrative, both in theme and tone, it becomes clear rather early that the "now I" is the voice of the novel. And he is straightforwardly sympathetic with the "then I"; in this way the ironic mode is violated. Irony requires that two things be present: first, a discrepancy between appearance and reality and, second, a center of consciousness for recognition. This recognition device is usually found within the narrative itself, that is, in a narrator who has necessary perspective on the character and imparts it to the reader. Perhaps the recognition may be found outside the novel, that is, only in the reader's apprehension of irony; if this is the desired end, the novelist will choose ways to imply irony: the organization of events; juxtaposing characters; a quick turn of events; or any number of tricks designed to make the reader conscious of the irony. But this novel's potential irony fails to materialize because Waugh's narrator first of all is in sympathy with the "then I" and, second, because the recognition of irony from a point outside the novel is discouraged.

As a result of the lack of detachment, whatever ironic potential the basic technique allows is obscured by sympathetic identification. There is virtually no irony regarding the hero and only little or light irony regarding other characters and events. But this is not to say that there are not ironic or satirical elements in the novel; in fact, both the "then I" and the "intermediate I" function as *devices* to discover the irony of the situation. For instance, the prologue-epilogue portion of the novel, that part which involves primarily the "intermediate I," has been called the novel's "most sustained satire."[21] The irony occurs here not because of the narrator's relationship to the intermediate figure, but because of the view that the combined personae offer of both the army and Hooper, the "new man." As Carens points out:

> The prologue and the epilogue are something more than a mechanical use of the frame technique; they are not merely a device for setting off the memories, but a means of expressing Waugh's emotional attitude toward the past and his satirical view of the present.[22]

Carens goes on to identify the particular butt of the satire as Hooper, who for the narrator becomes "a symbol of Young England" (9). However, one can hardly agree that the prologue is "bitterly ironic"[23] or the epilogue satirical, because the close sympathy of the "now I" with the intermediate persona somehow carries over into the view of Hooper and the contemporary world; the result is a more mellowed, wistfully tired critique of society, nothing at all like the caustic attack of the earlier novels.

Within the main story, the "then I" becomes an ironic device. The most demonstrative example of this func-

---

21. Carens, p. 102.
22. *Ibid.*, p. 103.
23. *Ibid.*, p. 102.

tion is the persona's cynical view of the Church and those who profess to be Catholics, specifically, the Marchmains. Through him several real weaknesses or flaws about their religion are laid bare even though it seems that he really does not intend this.

> "There were four of you," I said. "Cara didn't know the first thing it was about, and may or may not have believed it; you knew a bit and didn't believe a word; Cordelia knew about as much and believed it madly; only poor Bridey knew and believed, and I thought he made a pretty poor show when it came to explaining. And people go round saying, 'At least Catholics know what they believe.' We had a fair cross-section tonight—" (330).

Yet, even so, the narrator's identification with the "then I" seems to color all the unfavorable things uncovered by the character-persona. Carens perhaps exaggerates the results of the close narrator identification when he speaks of the treatment of the Marchmain family:

> So extravagant are Ryder's claims for them, so romanticized is their class position, so much nostalgia is lavished on the life they were able to lead before the war, so many indications are given of their exclusive right to consideration, so much of Ryder's smugness and self-satisfaction permeates the whole, that the novel seems to accept Brideshead and everything it entails and at the expense of all other beings.[24]

The trouble with the tone of the novel, then, and the reason for its notoriety among critics—particularly those who learned to appreciate Waugh from the earlier works, is not wholly with the first-person point of view but with the personality of the first-person narrator. The flaw is not with the "then I" or the "intermediate I" but in the proximity of the "now I" with the past. Despite the narrative technique, which in essence is that of the ironic mode, there is no emotional separation of personae, no

---

24. *Ibid.*, p. 109.

doubt because historical or chronological distance is obscured through ever-present "mists of sentiment."[25] As
Stopp has pointed out, there is "no present, properly
speaking, but [the novel] is suspended between past and
future, no action, but is bathed in memory and anticipation."[26] All the events are filtered through a unique
consciousness, which though seeing them in the past,
colors them with present emotion; this is detrimen-
tal, for the "now I" is a romantic, sensitive almost
to the point of femininity. Therefore, Stopp finds the
narrator "only partly comprehending, lawless, artistic,
intuitive, and romantic,"[27] and further notes that there
is "certainly a streak of maudlin sentimentality"[28] about
him. And there is abundant testimony as to his sentimentality:

> I sometimes wonder whether, had it not been for Sebastian,
> I might have trodden the same path as Collins round the cul-
> tural water-wheel. My father in his youth sat for All Souls and,
> in a year of hot competition, failed; other successes and honours
> came his way later, but that early failure impressed itself on him,
> and through him on me, so that I came up with an ill-considered
> sense that there lay the proper and natural goal of the life of
> reason. I, too, should doubtless have failed, but, having failed, I
> might perhaps have slipped into a less august academic life else-
> where. It is conceivable, but not, I believe, likely, for the hot
> spring of anarchy rose from deep furnaces where was no solid
> earth, and burst into the sunlight—a rainbow in its cooling va-
> pours—with a power the rocks could not repress (44).

What results is a romanticized, present-time commentary on past activities—memories not so much of the "intermediate I," but of the "now I." It is this persona
who continually makes use of the word "tragedy" in

---

25. *Ibid.*, p. 107.
26. Frederick J. Stopp, *Evelyn Waugh: Portrait of an Artist* (Boston:
Little, Brown and Company, 1958), p. 112.
27. *Ibid.*
28. *Ibid.*, p. 21.

reference to the story, clouding the whole novel with sentimentality (see pp. 54, 140, 164, 182, 351). Were it not for the pervading sentimentality, in some cases quite falsely based, one might easily identify with Sebastian, Julia, or even Marchmain and possibly actually even conceive of the story as a tragedy. In fact, their stories contain more serious drama than do the musings of the "now I." The deterioration of Sebastian or the spiritual struggles of Julia are indeed tragic; but, as it is, the narrator's continuing insistence upon the tragic nature of the events while ignoring the irony that might make it thus, turns the story into melodrama. The reader is cheated of all the pathos in the story by the imposition of the sublimely egotistical "now I."

The personae are not merely a tonal device, however; the technique is also the basis of the thematic development of the novel. Perhaps DeVitis provides the best analysis of the relation of tonal factors to theme:

> Waugh chose to represent his ideas through the views of Charles Ryder. All of his moral commentaries are filtered through the consciousness of the hero; and to understand Ryder is to understand Waugh's meaning. By using Ryder as a skeptical onlooker who becomes spiritually involved in the religious and social dilemma of the Catholic world of Brideshead, Waugh is able to trace his theme and make his moral commentary at the same time.[29]

Although the first part of this statement may overestimate the narrative role of Ryder, it nevertheless places him in proper relationship to theme. Therefore, it is not surprising that the theme, somewhat like the character, is both "romantic" and "religious,"[30] or as Waugh has phrased it, "romantic and eschatological."[31] Since the novel is in at least one sense the story of Ryder's conversion to the Church, and, in another, the story of a

---

29. DeVitis, p. 46.
30. See Carens, pp. 98–99.
31. Stopp, p. 108.

Catholic family, the critical consensus is that *Brideshead Revisited* is a "Catholic novel."[32] Hollis has rather dogmatically stated that it is "explicitly and consciously" a Catholic novel and that "it is about religion, but it is about nothing except religion, nor is there any question at all of any other religious truth except that of the Catholic church."[33] Spender, usually an objective and astute critic, suggests that the book is characterized by a "moralizing religion," and that in *Brideshead Revisited* Waugh "brings his novel writing [to the status of Graham Greene]."[34]

Perhaps Waugh himself has encouraged a strictly religious, even Catholic, interpretation of theme. He admitted that his objective in the novel was "to trace the divine purpose in a pagan world,"[35] specifically, "in the lives of an English Catholic family, half-paganized themselves, in the world 1923–1939."[36] Again, writing to an American correspondent who remarked that the novel "is a strange way to show that Catholicism is an answer to anything," Waugh replied, "I did my best. . . . If so I have failed indeed and my characters have got wildly out of hand once more."[37] DeVitis enlarges on Waugh's

32. This is at best a rather vague term, but it does seem to convey the consensus of critical thinking regarding the novel; see Carens, pp. 98–99 for a review of criticism centering around the problem of the Catholic writer. Perhaps Patrick Braybrooke is correct when he observes: "It has often been said that Catholics, no matter what they happen to be writing, bring in (a more favorite phrase is 'drag in') Catholicism. Fortunately this funny little querulous attack hits the right nail a tiny bump on the head. For a Catholic can no more help bringing Catholicism, either stated or implied, into his writings than a historian, writing a history of the world, can help a direct or indirect reference to Rome." *Some Catholic Novelists: Their Art and Outlook* (Freeport, New York: Books for Libraries Press, Inc., 1966), p. xi.

33. Christopher Hollis, *Evelyn Waugh* (London: Published for The British Council and the National Book League by Longmans, Green & Co., 1966), p. 17.

34. Stephen Spender. *The Creative Element* (New York: British Book Center, 1954), pp. 168, 174.

35. Quoted by Carens, p. 98.

36. Quoted by Stopp, p. 108.

37. Evelyn Waugh, "Fan-Fare," *Life* (April 8, 1946), p. 60.

first statement in light of the novel itself: Waugh's theme, becomes "the mercy of the Roman Catholic God making itself apparent in the pagan world."[38] Spender also refers to Waugh's statement of purpose and acknowledges that *Brideshead Revisited* is "to show the Catholic pattern woven through the lives of the characters." "Despite their folly, failure, and disorder," he says, "their religion is capable of saving them. . . ."[39] But in many ways the chief religious experience is that of Ryder, and the book is in that way a "conversion novel."

> The novel is, first of all and most seriously, a "conversion" novel, a story that purports to show a man in the process of becoming a new man, of being "born again," and of learning to see the world and other men with the eyes of his new identity.[40]

But no matter whether the thematic emphasis is placed on the Marchmain family and their religious experiences or on Ryder's conversion, the Catholic elements of the novel loom so large that critical reaction in general seems predicated on the critic's view of the relation of art and religion. For example, Wilson[41] and Rolo[42] find the novel too Catholic; the author's commitment to Catholicism has, in their view, completely distorted reality and has undermined his art. Such a response might be expected from non-Catholics, but even the Catholic critics are divided among themselves. Both Hollis and DiVitis praise the work highly, although for different reasons: DeVitis argues that the novel is "an apology for Waugh's faith": in this fact lies "one of the strengths of the novel."[43] Hollis, on the other hand, thinks that it "is in no way

---

38. DeVitis, p. 45.
39. Spender, p. 170.
40. John Edward Hardy, "Brideshead Revisited: God, Man, and Others," *Man in the Modern Novel* (Seattle: University of Washington Press, 1964), p. 165.
41. See chapter 1, this study.
42. *Ibid.*
43. DeVitis, p. 53.

a work of apologetics."[44] And O'Faolain, also a Catholic, finds the novel a quite unsuccessful one: "The theme . . . is universally valid; the treatment is not."[45] This is true, he says, because "a religious theme given institutional treatment is always liable to get lost in the embroidered folds of ecclesiasticism . . . ," and in *Brideshead Revisited* "detachment is sold to loyalty."[46] Thus, depending on the view, the greatest weakness or strength of the novel is in the fact that it is a "Catholic" novel.

Although it must be admitted that *Brideshead Revisited* is Waugh's first novel in which Roman Catholicism is pervasive, and that at least to a degree it has a "religious theme,"[47] it should be noted that there is a possibility that critics have overzealously pursued the ecclesiastical themes and have taken Waugh's statement much too doctrinally. It seems to be the thinking, generally, that if a devout Catholic, who by his profession of faith has not only a definite conviction but also is possessed of a message from the burning bush, writes a novel dealing as much as this novel does with Catholics, then the novel must be approached somewhat on the same theological basis as the writings of the early church fathers. Such is not the case with *Brideshead Revisited*. But only Carens, while correctly granting the artist a Catholic point of view, has had the insight to suggest that the novel is "pre-eminently aesthetic rather than didactic."[48] He explains his view of the novel this way:

> That intensely held faith which suffuses both satire and romance in Brideshead leads, in that work, neither to didacticism nor to untruthful distortion nor to propaganda for the sake of religious apology.[49]

44. Hollis, p. 17.
45. Sean O'Faolain, The Vanishing Hero: *Studies in Novelists of the Twenties* (London: Eyre & Spottieswood, 1956), p. 65.
46. *Ibid.*, p. 66.
47. Carens, p. 98.
48. *Ibid.*, p. 102.
49. *Ibid.*, pp. 101–2.

O'Faolain, going perhaps further than Carens, suggests that the Catholicism of the novel is rather incidental, or, as he says, "accidental":

> But when we have passed through these accidentals to what
> seems at first sight to be the core of the novel, its insistently per-
> vasive Catholicism, it is with a shock of dismay that we gradually
> realise that this is the most irrelevant accident of all. In fact,
> if I may be permitted to give my own personal reaction to the
> novel as a professing Catholic . . . , I fail to see why the book
> could not have been equally well written . . . by a fervent Con-
> gregationalist.[50]

Although O'Faolain overlooks the importance to the theme of the regalia and tradition associated with the Catholic church, he is correct in observing that the universal theme of the novel reaches beyond the ecclesiastical confines of even the Roman Catholic church. Therefore, while Catholicism is central to the theme, it is not by any means the theme exclusively or primarily.

Although religion in general and Catholicism particularly are vital elements in the thematic development, if one views *Brideshead Revisited* in light of the thematic progression of the earlier novels, or simply as a unified thematic entity within itself, the Catholic element is soon recognized as the positive side of a larger, more universal human dilemma, a dilemma which has been growing in intensity throughout Waugh's novels; in short, Brideshead embodies the medieval, the Victorian, even the divine concept of order, tradition, and values. Whatever residue remains on earth of human nobility and dignity is to be found here. In this way, the Church is still "a light in darkness," but not in merely a strictly religious sense. It is for this reason that the novel is not concerned with soteriology; in fact, this aspect of religion seems deliberately played down. The emphasis is

---

50. O'Faolain, p. 63.

rather on the perpetuation of culture through the "sweet-ness and light" still to be found in the domain of the Church; in this way the theme is essentially humanistic. Specifically, the theme of the novel is much the same as that of previous novels; that is, first the conflict of chaotic modern barbarism and traditional high civiliza-tion, represented by the aristocracy and the Church, and, second, the corollary theme, the plight or progress of the alien in such a world.

The novel's structure is designed to play to full ad-vantage both these aspects of theme. As indicated in the discussion of narrative, the prologue and epilogue are not merely a means to begin and end the story; only through them is the theme identified and realized and the novel thus given a kind of organic unity. The pro-logue recalls briefly, but none the less graphically and convincingly, the decadence of contemporary society so vividly portrayed in previous novels. With the scene thus established, the narrator shifts to the innocent's romantic view of life and follows this as it develops through cynicism to maturity; finally, in the epilogue, the nar-rator is able to face the reality of the prologue with a new confidence—only because of the culmination of the experiences of the main story. There is, perhaps, a kind of Hegelian triad at work here: the first stage (the "ab-stract" concept) becomes the romanticism of the main story; the second stage (the "negative"), the cruel pessi-mism of the prologue; the third stage (the "concrete" concept), the controlled, realistic optimism of the epi-logue.

As suggested, it is primarily the prologue and epilogue, featuring Captain Ryder, which are concerned directly with the encroachment of barbarism on the civilized world. Carens is correct in observing that the prologue and the epilogue are a means of expressing an "emotional attitude toward the past" and "a satirical view of the

present."[51] The contrast of past and present is placed
before the reader rather quickly:

> The smoke from the cook-houses drifted away in the mist and
> the camp lay revealed as a planless maze of short-cuts, super-
> imposed on the unfinished housing-scheme, as though disinterred
> at a much later date by a party of archaeologists.
> The Pollock diggings provide a valuable link between the
> citizen-slave communities of the twentieth century and the tribal
> anarchy which succeeded them. Here you see a people of ad-
> vanced culture, capable of an elaborate draining system and the
> construction of permanent highways, overrun by a race of the
> lowest type. The measure of the newcomers may be taken by
> the facts that their women were devoid of all personal adornment
> and that the dead were removed to burying places a great distance
> from the settlement—a sure sign of primitive taboo (7).

As Carens suggests, the setting of the prologue itself provides a "satirical-ironical projection of a sordid present
against the rich traditions of the past."[52] But, as he also
notes, there is a positive direction of the criticism; it is
Hooper who is "the principal object of satire in the prologue"[53]—not Hooper the "sallow youth with hair combed
back, without parting, from his forehead, and a flat Mid-
land accent" (7), but Hooper the "symbol of Young
England" (9). He becomes representative of national
decline:

> In the weeks that we were together Hooper became a symbol
> to me of Young England, so that whenever I read some public
> utterance proclaiming what Youth demanded in the Future and
> what the world owed to Youth, I would test these general state-
> ments by substituting "Hooper" and seeing if they still seemed
> as plausible. Thus in the dark hour before reveille I sometimes
> pondered: "Hooper Rallies," "Hooper Hostels," "International
> Hooper Co-operation" and "the Religion of Hooper." He was
> the acid test of all these alloys (9).

---

51. Carens, p. 103.
52. *Ibid.*
53. *Ibid.*, p. 104.

The fact that the prologue-epilogue and the main narrative are thematically interrelated is shown in the rather
anachronistic direct contrast of Hooper with the high-
bred and loyal relatives of Lady Marchmain within the
main narrative:

> Mr. Samgrass's deft editorship had assembled and arranged a
> curiously homogeneous little body of writing—poetry, letters,
> scraps of a journal, an unpublished essay or two—which all ex-
> haled the same high-spirited, serious, chivalrous, other-worldly
> air; and the letters from their contemporaries, written after their
> deaths, all in varying degrees of articulateness, told the same tale
> of men who were, in all the full flood of academic and athletic
> success, of popularity and the promise of great rewards ahead,
> seen somehow as set apart from their fellows, garlanded victims,
> devoted to the sacrifice. These men must die to make a world
> for Hooper; they were the aborigines, vermin by right of law,
> to be shot off at leisure so that things might be safe for the
> travelling salesman, with his polygonal pince-nez, his fat wet
> hand-shake, his grinning dentures (139).

Nor is the contrast lost in the epilogue; there is still the
awareness of advancing barbarous hordes upon the beauty
of Brideshead.

> In the epilogue the threat of destruction posed by the forces
> of the modern age (as Waugh sees it) encroaches ironically, on
> Brideshead, which is taken over by the army as a training center.
> Ryder's commanding officer surveys the "exquisite, man-made
> landscape," which Ryder has described as "sequestered," "en-
> closed," and "embraced in a single, winding valley." The officer
> then comments: "The valley has great potentialities for an as-
> sault course and mortar range."[54]

Even so, the epilogue ends on a note quite different from
the previous novels:

> Something quite remote from anything the builders intended
> has come out of their work, and out of the fierce little human

---

54. *Ibid.*, pp. 104–5.

tragedy in which I played; something none of us thought about at the time: a small red flame—a beaten-copper lamp of deplorable design, relit before the beaten-copper doors of a tabernacle; the flame which the old knights saw from their tombs, which they saw put out; that flame burns again for other soldiers, far from home, farther, in heart, than Acre or Jerusalem. It could not have been lit but for the builders and the tragedians, and there I found it this morning, burning anew among the old stones (351).

Here is a new faith and hope never before so positively stated in Waugh's fiction, not even in *Put Out More Flags* in which the hero joins society. Here, even though there is not an integration with society, there is a positive affirmation of the endurance of human values, standards, and morals, even of the dignity of man; here the author successfully defends man as being "God's creature with a defined purpose."[55] So the central theme, while based on the fundamental premise stated so effectively in the early satires—the decay of civilization—is so developed here as to show the way to faith and hope despite the all-pervasive chaos.

Yet, this affirmation can be made only because of the experiences which comprise the lengthy main story, involving Charles and the Marchmain family. In this way, the main narrative does become apologetic. Immediately, a major criticism of technique arises, not of subjectivity as noted earlier but one primarily of proportion. In this regard, Carens points out several structural flaws in the main story itself, flaws that occur, no doubt, because this part of the novel has assumed the burden of proof. Taking his cue from Henry James, he suggests that the novel has, among other faults, a "misplaced middle."[56] While this may be valid criticism, the real violation of structure seems more likely to be in the great narrative emphasis

55. "Fan-Fare," p. 58.
56. Carens, p. 105.

on the main story. The length and unity of the main story alone are enough to suggest that the prologue-epilogue sections are but appendages; hence, the reader may easily be concerned only with the events of the main story and find the thematic significance contained solely in this part. But when the novel is viewed as a whole, the main story becomes necessary in context and in length to the tentative affirmation of the epilogue.

Ryder's story becomes the second, and the most important element of theme, that is, the plight of the alien in a hostile society. In this way the "then I" becomes unmistakably the central figure in thematic development; and, as in all the previous novels, the hero is both a thematic device and the embodiment of theme. Here, however, while the basic theme is the same as that of the earlier novels, there is a new development first sensed in *Scoop,* made serious in *Put Out More Flags,* and now fully realized in *Brideshead Revisited.* To be specific, here the story ends with a pronouncement of a kind of optimism, suspended somewhere between cynicism and romanticism. DeVitis best points out the continuation of an old theme in *Brideshead Revisited* when he notes that in this novel Waugh uses the special *ingénu*-hero, slightly transformed.

> Charles is, in fact, the logical development of the innocent who so consistently figured in the earlier satirical pieces. But he has succeeded in growing out of the adolescent stage into the adult world. He loses a great deal on the way, his innocence included, but he gains something more valuable in the long run.[57]

This critic, in relating this hero to theme, suggests three stages of growth in the hero's experience within this novel, which in some ways seems to epitomize Waugh's central theme from the beginning until its culmination in the Crouchback novels:

---

57. DeVitis, p. 46.

His growth from a youthful romantic into a cynical adult and finally to a mature person capable of understanding love and the place of God in the world allows Waugh to create various moods of the period he portrays . . . .[58]

Stopp also notes this progression in the theme but chooses to divide it more closely according to the organization of the novel, particularly in reference to the two books of the main narrative: there is the period of "innocence and youth, enjoyment, charm, and dispersion to remote parts of the earth";[59] then there are "the settled years with their deeper metaphysical needs, their clearer perception of guilt, expiation and resignation."[60] Spender thinks that Ryder's development "should record the emergence of the pattern of the true religion from the unsatisfactory lives of the Marchmains and also from his own agnosticism"; yet, he finds that Ryder "lacks the character for such a role."[61] But whatever division one makes of thematic progression, and however successful the portrayal of the maturation process, it does not seem that in the "then" experiences of Ryder there emerges a real growth pattern and a corresponding solidification of theme. This comes only through the reflective meditation of the "now I."

However, the pattern that DeVitis suggests does seem a valid approach to theme although one may not agree with his view of the significance of the development of Ryder. To consider the three "stages" of Ryder's psychological, if not religious, experience is to reconstruct the thematic development of the earlier novels. Here in capsule form is the record of the alien's struggle for identity and purpose in life and the assertion of his ultimate victory over modernity. In the "Et in Arcadia Ego"

---

58. *Ibid.*
59. Stopp, p. 108.
60. *Ibid.*
61. Spender, p. 172.

section, the hero is pictured as characterized by a "funda-mental innocence" similar to the naïveté of Paul Penny-feather, Adam Fenwick-Symes, Tony Last, William Boot, and company. That Ryder's disposition is more nostalgic and romanticized cannot be denied, but his plight is nothing more than a serious, perhaps more positively real, re-creation of the plight of the alien in a hostile and awesome society. But in *Brideshead Revisited* the theme seems to suggest that the adversity arises not only from cultural and moral decadence, but from a spiritual vac-uum as well. The Arcadian period is one of almost angelic splendor, owing primarily to the isolation at Brideshead and the innocence of the hero:

> The languor of Youth—how unique and quintessential it is! How quickly, how irrecoverably, lost! . . . Perhaps in the mansions of Limbo the heroes enjoy some such compensation for their loss of the Beatific Vision; perhaps the Beatific Vision itself has some remote kinship with this lowly experience; I, at any rate, be-lieved myself very near heaven, during those languid days at Brideshead (79).

Accordingly, the nursery theme, which Carens[62] finds running throughout all Waugh's works, is there at its height, what with Sebastian and his lovable teddy bear, and with Nanny Hawkins lurking cozily in the back-ground:

> "Sebastian is in love with his own childhood. That will make him very unhappy. His Teddy-bear, his nanny . . . and he is nineteen years old" (103).

And the narrator is quick to proclaim his own innocence as the "then I":

> Lord Marchmain's mistress arrived the next day. I was nine-teen years old and completely ignorant of women. I could not with any certainty recognize a prostitute in the streets (100).

---

62. See Carens, pp. 35–39.

Both Sebastian and the hero, however, simultaneously pass out of the Arcadian stage. With Sebastian the experience is more apparent than with the hero:

> Sebastian counted among the intruders his own conscience and all claims of human affection, his days in Arcadia were numbered (127).

> A blow, expected, repeated, falling on a bruise, with no smart or shock of surprise, only a dull and sickening pain and the doubt whether another like it could be borne—that was how it felt, sitting opposite Sebastian at dinner that night, seeing his clouded eye and groping movements, hearing his thickened voice breaking in, ineptly, after long brutish silences (167).

But as Sebastian becomes more dissipated, Ryder becomes more and more cynical:

> "D'you know, Bridey, if I ever felt for a moment like becoming a Catholic, I should only have to talk to you for five minutes to be cured. You manage to reduce what seem quite sensible propositions to stark nonsense" (164).

The climax of the Arcadian period and the signal announcing the termination of innocence comes on Ryder's departure from Brideshead; he leaves with a new view of life, but, ironically, even this is rather naïve, certainly romantic.

> A door had shut, the low door in the wall I had sought and found in Oxford; open it now and I should find no enchanted garden.
> I had come to the surface, into the light of common day and the fresh sea-air, after long captivity in the sunless coral palaces and waving forests of the ocean bed.
> I had left behind me—what? Youth? Adolescence? Romance? The conjuring stuff of these things, "the Young Magician's Compendium," the neat cabinet where the ebony wand had its place beside the delusive billiard balls, the penny that folded double and the feather flowers that could be drawn into a hollow candle.
> "I have left behind illusion," I said to myself. "Henceforth

> I live in a world of three dimensions—with the aid of my five senses."

> I have since learned that there is no such world; but then, as the car turned out of sight of the house, I thought it took no finding, but lay all about me at the end of the avenue (169).

All else in this chapter is anticlimactic, for it only confirms and elaborates upon the directions established here. Sebastian is dispatched to oblivion; Charles, as a result, becomes even more bitter than before. It is merely a transitional section introducing the second stage of the experience of the "then I." But it is significant that here the tone begins to change, for the narrator begins to inject cynical observations, particularly of the Catholic church, either directly or through the "then I" or through other characters; for instance, the Jesuit quite helplessly reports critical observations made by Rex in the process of his conversion:

> " 'Look, Father, I don't think you're being straight with me. I want to join your Church and I'm going to join your Church, but you're holding too much back. . . . I've had a long talk with a Catholic—a very pious, well-educated one, and I've learned a thing or two. For instance, that you have to sleep with your feet pointing East because that's the direction of heaven, and if you die in the night you can walk there. Now I'll sleep with my feet pointing any way that suits Julia, but d'you expect a grown man to believe about walking to heaven? And what about the Pope who made one of his horses a cardinal? And what about the box you keep in the church porch, and if you put in a pound note with someone's name on it, they get sent to hell. I don't say there mayn't be a good reason for all this . . . but you ought to tell me about it and not let me find out for myself' " (193–194).

The section that deals primarily with the Arcadian experience ends with the assertion of gained reality and a cynical attitude toward positive values. After Cordelia expresses her sincere and impassioned devotion to her "vocation" as a nun, the narrator comments:

But I had no patience with this convent chatter. I had felt the brush take life in my hand that afternoon; I had had my finger in the great, succulent pie of creation. I was a man of the Renaissance that evening—of Browning's Renaissance. I, who had walked the streets of Rome in Genoa velvet and had seen the stars through Galileo's tube, spurned the friars with their dusty tomes and their sunken, jealous eyes and their crabbed hair-splitting speech (221–22).

Book Two begins with the hero (and narrator) characterized by an attitude not too far distant from that of the earlier version of Waugh's anti-innocent or cad, that is, Seal or Beaver. This may be seen as the second "stage" of thematic development in the novel and also the second stage in Waugh's progressive theme throughout all the novels. One does not have too long to discover the pervasive cynicism, even potential satire and ridicule of this section. That the original innocence and consequent inspiration is gone is a lamented fact:

But as the years passed I began to mourn the loss of something I had known in the drawing-room of Marchmain House and once or twice since, the intensity and singleness and the belief that it was not all done by hand (227).

Despite this longing for a return to innocence, the cynicism becomes increasingly bitter:

We had been given, without paying more for it, a large suite of rooms, one so large, in fact, that it was seldom booked except by directors of the line, and on most voyages, the chief purser admitted, was given to those he wished to honour. (My wife was adept in achieving such small advantages, first impressing the impressionable with her chic and my celebrity and, superiority once firmly established, changing quickly to a pose of almost flirtatious affability.) In token of her appreciation the chief purser had been asked to our party and he, in token of his appreciation, had sent before him the life-size effigy of a swan, moulded in ice and filled with caviar. This chilly piece of magnificence now dominated the room, standing on a table in the centre, thawing

gently, dripping at the beak into its silver dish. The flowers of
the morning delivery hid as much as possible of the panelling
(for this room was a miniature of the monstrous hall above) (240).

> Through and through, I thought. Through and through is a
> long way, madam. Can you indeed see into those dark places
> where my own eyes seek in vain to guide me? Can you tell me,
> dear Mrs. Stuyvesant Oglander—if I am correct in thinking that
> is how I heard my wife speak of you—why it is that at this
> moment, while I talk to you, here, about my forthcoming exhi-
> bition, I am thinking all the time only of when Julia will come?
> Why can I talk like this to you, but not to her? Why have I
> already set her apart from humankind, and myself with her? What
> is going on in those secret places of my spirit with which you
> make so free? What is cooking, Mrs. Stuyvesant Oglander? (242–
> 43).

But the cynicism and detachment of the hero are in
this section met with emotional involvement somehow
more mature and lasting than that with Sebastian and
with deep human experiences that will not allow the
spiritual qualities of man to be sneered at. He becomes
gradually more mellow and philosophical:

> Perhaps, I thought, while her words still hung in the air between
> us like a wisp of tobacco smoke—a thought to fade and vanish
> like smoke without a trace—perhaps all our loves are merely hints
> and symbols; a hill of many invisible crests; doors that open as
> in a dream to reveal only a further stretch of carpet and another
> door; perhaps you and I are types and this sadness which some-
> times falls between us springs from disappointment in our search,
> each straining through and beyond the other, snatching a glimpse
> now and then of the shadow which turns the corner always a
> pace or two ahead of us (303).

Finally, because of his association with Julia he is drawn
completely into the faith and hope promised by the
church:

> I suddenly felt the longing for a sign, if only of courtesy, if
> only for the sake of the woman I loved, who knelt in front of me,

praying, I knew, for a sign. It seemed so small a thing that was asked, the bare acknowledgment of a present, a nod in the crowd. All over the world people were on their knees before innumerable crosses, and here the drama was being played again by two men —by one man, rather, and he nearer death than life; the universal drama in which there is only one actor (338).

The concluding paragraph is perhaps the most important thematically speaking, for here the narrator puts religion, particularly Catholicism, in proper perspective:

> There was one part of the house I had not yet visited, and I went there now. The chapel showed no ill-effects of its long neglect; the art-nouveau paint was as fresh and bright as ever; the art-nouveau lamp burned once more before the altar. I said a prayer, an ancient, newly learned form of words, and left, turning toward the camp; and as I walked back, and the cookhouse bugle sounded ahead of me, I thought:—
>
> The builders did not know the uses to which their work would descend; they made a new house with the stones of the old castle; year by year, generation after generation, they enriched and extended it; year by year the great harvest of timber in the park grew to ripeness; until, in sudden frost, came the age of Hooper; the place was desolate and the work all brought to nothing; *Quomodo sedet sola civitas.* Vanity of vanities, all is vanity (350–51).

Here it is established explicitly that Catholicism is not the theme of the novel, but that it only serves as a representative, quite possibly the only representative, of eternal order, tradition, authority, standards, and—the most universal need of man—as a basis for faith, faith in himself, if nothing else. Perhaps the connection between the church and the aristocracy so paramount in this novel becomes clearer if the Church is viewed in this way. The earlier association of the two is quite definite, even to the point of insistence (see pp. 138–39). Throughout the novel there is suggested an inextricable connection between, even a common basis of, loyalty to God and to country, private morality and national honor; the inevitable union

of the two is to be later embodied by Sir Roger of Waybroke, much as it had been by the Christian knights of
the Middle Ages: Viewed in this way, the "twitch upon
the thread" becomes more than merely the attraction of
the Catholic church, more than an irresistible urge to identify with an ecclesiastical group which promises earthly security and heavenly bliss; it becomes a universal spiritual
need for "divine guidance" in its fullest implication. This
is the narrator's final note of optimism—the flame still
burns, despite the ravages of the invading barbarians;
eternal human values, however suppressed, lie smolder-
ing under the ashes, and apparently, given the time and
circumstances, could rise phoenix-like into a new splendor. If religion is triumphant as Hollis thinks,[63] it is only
because it is itself a part of something more universal
and more intrinsically human, something that transcends
religion, aristocracy, nobility, even idealism, yet contains them all. Perhaps this is the answer to the chant
sung by the half-caste choir in Guatemala, *"Quomodo
sedet sola civitas"* (237). Yet, somehow, the conclusion
of *Brideshead Revisited* seems more optative than indicative, more indicative than prophetic.

Brideshead Revisited, thus, becomes greatly important
to an understanding of Waugh's development as a novelist. It is not an aberration but a progression both in
theme and artistry. Here, however, he does reach the
extreme in both technique and theme and in both he
pushes slightly beyond the borders which are respected
universally by great art. The personae technique employed so brilliantly in the earlier more directly satirical
novels, is adapted to a first-person point of view, and,
while it proves quite suitable for narrative formulation,
and, while potentially an equally good tonal device, it
fails to produce the necessary dramatic tension in tone.
What ironic potential is present merely divides the novel

---

63. Hollis, p. 18.

against itself. The theme, although the narrative material is apparently connected with the war present or impending, is not developed through realistic experiences, but seems "staged" in a fanciful, esoteric, romantic allegory, with enough emphasis on "tragedy" to overstate the human problem and the solution. Although one may come from the novel "purged" or "inspired," he bears away neither balm nor salt for his wounds. Only in the Crouchback trilogy does Waugh successfully translate the alien, the hostile civilization, the problem and solution into real human terms; but one gets the idea that he could not have done it without the artistic and psychological experience of *Brideshead Revisited.*

6
Adaptation of Mode

Although Waugh's fiction after 1945 is characterized by the same basic artistic techniques and major themes found in the preceding novels, the fiction following *Brideshead Revisited* falls into two general categories. First, there are what may be called the "interludes," generally short works which reflect a return to the very earliest techniques and themes. Of the five such pieces, appearing between 1947 and 1957, only two may justifiably be called novels, *Helena* and *The Ordeal of Gilbert Pinfold;* two are best described as long short stories, *Scott-King's Modern Europe* and *Love Among the Ruins;* one, possibly, as a novelette, *The Loved One.* So, in genre alone, there is a departure from maturing craftsmanship in the novel form, signifying, perhaps, a falling off in the artist's power to sustain a complex narrative. Quite obvious is the suspension of development in artistry and thematic concerns. There is, in fact, what appears to be a return to earlier techniques and themes. *Scott-King's Modern Europe* (1947), *The Loved One* (1948), and *Helena* (1950), which were published in rapid succession after *Brideshead Revisited,* conspicuously depart from the thematic motifs and artistic techniques of that novel; the first two of these novels take their cue from *Decline and Fall;* the third from *Edmund Campion,* a religious biography, published in 1935. Two others, *Love Among the Ruins* (1953) and *The Ordeal of Gilbert Pinfold* (1957), also bear more affinity to the early novels than to the ones just preceding them.

In each of these works, beginning with *Scott-King*, there is a return to the satiric-ironic mode and to third-person narrative; there is also a continuation of the technique and theme introduced in *Decline and Fall*. The narrative formulation is handled through the technique of narrator-persona and character-persona, and their relationship in narrative is generally the same as in the early satiric novels, in fact, in four of the works very much like *Decline and Fall*. There is a continuation of the basic dual theme involving again the decadence of society and the plight of innocence; in *Helena*, however, there is some reflection of the optimistic faith of *Brideshead Revisited*. In each of the works the hero is an *ingénu* pitted against a corrupt, hostile, and incomprehensible world. The tonal range is from gentle comedy, *Ordeal of Gilbert Pinfold*, to the bitterest satire, *The Loved One*. The latter, a novelette, is perhaps the best example of Waugh's ability to adapt previous techniques and themes to a satirical critique of specific social areas, in this case the predatory funeral enterprise in America. Thus, the works collectively, however different they may be from each other, offer little or no development in either technique or theme.

It is significant that despite the fact that the previous techniques, themes, and tones are manifest in these works, a conscious denial of reality characterizes each of them. Each of these works is a kind of fantasy, strangely removed from the real world of the mid-twentieth century. Even *Helena*, which is thought by some to be a realistic novel, is a fanciful rendition of a semi-myth. It seems almost as though the author were trying to escape the reality of the world which has impinged upon his original fantastic world. Perhaps this is the reason Carens considers this a "period of adjustment."[1]

It is only in the war trilogy, the second category of post-*Brideshead Revisited* novels, that the author returns to the real world and to the specific thematic concerns which were introduced in *Put Out More Flags.* He returns not only with maturity of vision but also with a technical virtuosity capable of transforming wisdom into genuine art. It is the war trilogy, *Men at Arms, Officers and Gentlemen,* and *Unconditional Surrender,* that marks the culmination of Waugh's art in theme and artistry, and in the successful blending of the technical exigencies of the satiric mode with a serious moral statement in the form of a conventional novel. It is upon these novels that the final judgment of Waugh the artist must be made.

MEN AT ARMS[2]

With *Men at Arms,* Waugh confidently returns to the expanding thematic concerns and maturing artistry interrupted or postponed by the "interlude" pieces, *Scott-*

---

1. James F. Carens, *The Satiric Art of Evelyn Waugh* (Seattle: University of Washington Press, 1966) , p. 157.
2. The parts of the Crouchback trilogy were published separately and quite a distance apart: *Men at Arms,* 1952; *Officers and Gentlemen,* 1955; *Unconditional Surrender,* (or *The End of Battle*) 1961. Even so, Waugh stated at the beginning that he intended them to be read as a single progressive story dealing with the experiences of an "unchacteristic" Englishman during World War II. Accordingly, in 1961, he published "the final version of the novels" under the title, *Sword of Honour.* In the preface to this work dated 1964,, he indicates that it is a "recension" of the three books it contains. As Carens has noted, whether the narrative is read as a trilogy or in the omnibus edition, there is no denying its artistic unity (172–73) . To be fully appreciated, the narrative should be read as a unit; but to be understood as the final development of Waugh's art, the three novels are best examined separately. There is a time element separating them and there are in each novel distinctive qualities particularly of theme and tone that make a detailed analysis of each profitable. All quotations from the novels will be taken from the Chapman & Hall editions.

King's Modern Europe, The Loved One, and *Helena.*
Critics generally recognize a kinship between the war
trilogy and the earlier novels; and, although they are
not agreed as to exactly which of the three previous "prewar" or "war" novels *Men at Arms* most logically follows,
all would find its progenitor either *Brideshead Revisited,
Put Out More Flags,* or *Work Suspended.* The genealogy
is a moot point; but the significance is in the fact that
these critics find the roots of *Men at Arms* not in *Scott-
King's Modern Europe, The Loved One,* or *Helena,* but
in the earlier novels up to and including *Brideshead Revisited.* Voorhees, after briefly surveying the novels between *Brideshead Revisited* and *Men at Arms* concludes
that "the natural progression from *Brideshead* appears
in *Men at Arms* (1952) and *Officers and Gentlemen*
(1955)."[3] Bergonzi finds it "instructive" to approach
Men at Arms, the first volume of the trilogy, via *Put Out
More Flags,* because as he says, this novel also "deals
with the Phony War of 1939–40, though written much
closer to the period it describes."[4] Stopp, however, thinks
Men at Arms "continues the line of straight novels" begun with *Work Suspended.*[5] While connecting the first of
the Crouchback trilogy with this fragment, which he regards very highly, Stopp gives an even larger perspective
to *Men at Arms* by observing that the major themes and
techniques of all the previous novels, with the possible
exception of the "interlude" pieces, recur transformed
in *Men at Arms:*

> The theme is the comedy of Army life; a bitterly tragic ending
> to the life of an innocent man deeply wronged, as in *A Handful
> of Dust,* is therefore out of the question. Nor may the innocent
> return to his Limbo, as do Boot, guileless but successful, and

3. Richard J. Voorhees, "Evelyn Waugh's War Novels: A Toast to
Lost Causes," *Queen's Quarterly* 65 (Spring, 1958) : 53.
4. Bernard Bergonzi, "Evelyn Waugh's Gentlemen," *Critical Quarterly*
5 (Spring, 1963) : 31.
5. Frederick J. Stopp, Evelyn Waugh: *Portrait of an Artist* (Boston:
Little, Brown and Company, 1958) , p. 159.

Scott-King, wise and resigned; the setting of the Second World War is too real for this.[6]

But DeVitis, while finding *Men at Arms* especially comparable to *Put Out More Flags,* best delineates the affinities between this novel and both the comic and serious elements of the previous novels, and, at the same time, convincingly argues that this novel represents Waugh's highest artistic accomplishment:

> In *Men at Arms* . . . Waugh fuses the comic convention of *Decline and Fall* with the serious religious considerations of *Brideshead Revisited. Men at Arms* was the first novel of a planned trilogy dealing with the years of the Second World War. And the strides that Waugh has made can be easily discerned by comparing the novel to *Put Out More Flags,* which also dealt with the early months of the war. In *Men at Arms* there is a greater comprehension of issues and men. The earlier novel seems a child's toy by comparison. Although the satirical elements of the earlier books are present, Waugh in *Men at Arms* demonstrates a great awareness of the real world; and he makes a serious commentary on it through the medium of the comic spirit.[7]

Many things regarding the nature and development of Waugh's fiction are suggested in this generalization, but, above all, the implication that the connection between the earlier novels and *Men at Arms* is more than one of similar theme, or of setting and chronology; rather, *Men at Arms* intrinsically represents Waugh's maturation in both artistry and theme. The thematic maturation is signaled by several significant developments, especially a more conventional narrative process, realistic narrative material, and tonal modulation. Specifically, the nature of the narrative material has been changed somewhat; no longer is it taken from the fantastic world of the Bright Young Things, nor from the equally fantastic, if more

---

6. *Ibid.*
7. A. A. DeVitis, *Roman Holiday: The Catholic Novels of Evelyn Waugh* (New York: Bookman Associates, 1956) , p. 68.

cruel world of the African jungles, nor from the doomed
idyllic world of Tony Last, nor even from the Arcadian
garden of Brideshead. Here the narrative material is
taken from the real world; the reader is aware of the
"impingement of the world."[8] The narrative, comprised
as it is of events of the war period, so smoothly inter-
weaves the strands of fiction into real historical fabric
that the story seems to be almost as genuine as a CBS
documentary.

Men at Arms is essentially the story of Guy Crouchback, a story which is to be concluded in *Unconditional
Surrender*. This first novel of the trilogy impels the hero
on his journey into a world which at first seems characterized by comic confusion but finally proves to be viciously
hostile to men of values and honor. Guy, an aristocrat,
cultured and religious, devoted to God and country,
leaves the Italian villa first owned by his grandparents
to return to England to join the war effort. Guy has lived
in Italy for the eight years following his divorce from
Virginia, but now with noble purpose he returns to society because the enemy forces are for him "evil" per-
sonified, and whatever the outcome of the war he feels
that there is a place in the battle for him. The war becomes another Holy Crusade; he, Sir Roger of Waybroke,
Christian knight. After much difficulty, he receives a
temporary commission in the Royal Corps of Halberdiers, an ancient, aristocratic, ineffectual elite corps. Most
of the story concerns Guy's experiences with this band of
would-be warriors as it trains for combat, which fortunately it does not see. In many ways, the novel is a satire
of the English military; particularly graphic are the comic
portrayals of Brigadier Ben Ritchie-Hook and Apthorpe,
but there is much more serious criticism in the descrip-

---

8. Frederick R. Karl, "The World of Evelyn Waugh: The Normally
Insane," *The Contemporary English Novel*, (New York: Farrar, Straus,
and Cudahy, 1962), p. 170.

tion of the otiosity and confusion of the army. The Halberdiers finally encounter action but only in a farcical "biffing" of an unimportant coastline, a raid perpetrated against orders by the indomitable Ritchie-Hook. At the end of the novel, Guy has not found the opportunity to serve either God or country; in fact he has rather begun to be disillusioned with the unheroic, gallantless tomfoolery of the military and with the complete absence of noble aspirations among the officers and men.

The theme is still centered on the concerns that have characterized Waugh's fiction from the beginning—the decay of civilization in contemporary times, and the plight of the alien overwhelmed by modernity. But the narrative materials themselves (that is, settings, characters, plots), and the objects of the satire have become less comfortably remote, less ridiculous, more seriously real. It is a long way from the absurd politics of Azania in *Black Mischief* to the European political maze portrayed in *Put Out More Flags* and the Crouchback trilogy, but Waugh consistently moves his attack closer to reality, literally closer to home. Accordingly, the character of the alien, the hero, also undergoes a transition. This is not to say that he has completely broken out of the original *ingénu* mold nor that he has in any way proved superior to adversity, merely that he has become human—three dimensional. Paul Pennyfeather becomes little more than a comic book character when compared to Guy Crouchback, who by the end of *Unconditional Surrender* has become almost an old acquaintance who commands the narrator's, and the reader's, earnest sympathy. DeVitis explains why the reader "feels an essential kinship" with Guy:

> Paul Pennyfeather and Adam Symes had been Waugh's link with the real world in the earlier works. But where they had been flat, though fascinating, characters, Guy is real.[9]

9. DeVitis, p. 78.

The theme of *Men at Arms,* dealing with the war as it reflects the nature of contemporary civilization and influences the life of the individual, thus seems thoroughly focused on the foredoomed attempt of the hero, as Conrad would put it, to "wring some meaning out of his sinful life."

The author does not move in these directions in narrative material and theme without making corresponding adjustments in tone. The satirical element is still present in *Men at Arms,* but it has lost its harshness and has become a sincere, thoroughly ironic critique of society. DeVitis succinctly describes the nature of the satire in this novel:

> The satire of *Men at Arms* is not the malicious cut and jab of *Decline and Fall.* It is mellow, reflective; the raillery is gentle; and the situations are funny in themselves, whereas before they depended on cruelty and malice for their humor. What William Tindall termed Waugh's "monkish loathing" is replaced by a whimsical, benevolent view of the world and of man. . . . It is a far cry from the iron-fisted attacks on boys' schools and British prisons of *Decline and Fall.* The youthful extravagance is gone, replaced by a mature appraisal of the ridiculous.[10]

From *Decline and Fall* to *Brideshead Revisited* Waugh ran the gamut of the satiric-ironic spectrum, from farce to near-tragedy, then past the ironic into the melodramatic. Always the elements of the ironic mode have remained, if not in the tone at least in the substructure of the novel, usually preventing the most rollicking comedy from being altogether funny and the most intense tragedy from remaining completely serious; the comedy cannot long refresh because of its bitter implications, and the tragedy reaches no catharsis because the reader's response is short-circuited by the comic implications which the impish narrator cannot wholly suppress. Waugh does not

---

10. *Ibid.,* p. 69.

escape the double ironic perspective in *Men at Arms,* yet there is here, not an alternating comic-tragic sequence such as that in *Black Mischief,* but a thorough blending of the comic and the tragic that results in what may be best described as a kind of "ironic realism."[11] DeVitis, in this regard, speaks of "the *synthesis* of the comic and the serious";[12] in the real meaning of the word, this is an apt designation. In these aspects of the novel, narrative, theme, and tone, Waugh continues to use the basic artistic technique that, although originating in the earlier satiric-ironic approach, has characterized his fiction from *Decline and Fall* throughout his entire career. Again, the narrative, the thematic development, and the tonal control all have their center in the relationship of the narrator-persona to the character-persona.

First, in narrative Waugh has wrought to a high degree of perfection a unique kind of third-person narrative featuring an omniscient yet personable narrator who is allowed full knowledge of the character and the national and international circumstances surrounding him, who is separated from the character by time, space, and person, and yet who, by disposition and narrative process, seems very closely identified with the hero himself. The relationship of the narrator-persona and character-persona in narration is somewhat reminiscent of both *Brideshead Revisited* and *A Handful of Dust;* yet, there is not the unabashed identification of narrator with character as in *Brideshead Revisited,* nor is there the high degree of ironic tension found in *A Handful of Dust.* In both these novels, as indeed in all the others, no matter how dominating the hero, how sympathetic or subtle the narrator, there has always been the awareness of an imperturbable external presence—a "maker"—who quite outside the novel is himself directing, arranging the events, and stylizing

11. Carens, p. 157.
12. DeVitis, p. 68.

the presentation. Even in *Brideshead Revisited* there is the continuous, relentless narrator who, however different from the other narrators, steadily moves the novel.

The tried and true external method is not completely lost in *Men at Arms;* it cannot be within the ironic mode. Yet the narrator seems to function more inside the novel and, consequently, the novel is developed from within, organically. The summary method of narration coupled with a decrease in artistic detachment implied in the narrative process has a tendency to bring the narrator into the novel almost as a participant, yet not in his own person. He no longer seems to be looking over the shoulder of the hero; he is with him. In fact, at times in the narration it is difficult to distinguish between the narrator and the hero, that is, whether certain passages are to be counted dramatic reactions of Crouchback or descriptive interpretations offered by the narrator. But this does not mean that ironic perspective is given up in narrative; merely that it is less intense than in novels like *A Handful of Dust.* In the narrative of *Men at Arms,* the identification of the narrator and the character and the ironic perspective of the narrator reach a balance not heretofore achieved in Waugh's fiction. As suggested earlier, the narrator in *Men at Arms,* although more closely identified with the characters and events of the novel, still must function dramatically as the external "maker" of the novel even though his role is now more closely interwoven into the narrative itself. The narrator is responsible for the selection and ordering of the action, for the progressive movement from one event or episode to another, and for the achieving of an organic unity within the structure.

There are several factors about the structure of this novel that recall earlier novels, but here the various external techniques are handled toward a more unified effect in the dramatic presentation. First, the overall structure of the novel indicates something of the nature and importance of the narrator's role. Because this is the first of a trilogy, there is not the usual symmetry in structural organization found in the preceding novels; the prologue serves the narrator as a means of providing background information thematically but not dramatically connected to the main narrative. And, although there is the familiar circularity in plot, there cannot be circularity in structure; this is achieved to a degree with *Officers and Gentlemen* and finally completely with *Unconditional Surrender*. Within the narrative itself there is further evidence of the influence on structure of the external narrator. One of the most common narrator devices in this novel is the familiar "counterpointing" technique. Carens has noted the continuation of this device through the trilogy:

> In the works before *Brideshead*, plot is usually farcical, a distortion of reality. Scene, or episode, on the other hand, is treated ironically through "counterpoint" or montage; the technique is most obvious in the earliest novels, and it has persisted, though significantly modified in *Brideshead* and the novels following it, right down to the Crouchback trilogy, where it is again a prominent element.[13]

In *Men at Arms*, because of the narrative material and theme it is important that the narrator be able to "move about in space while remaining fixed in time and thus to spatialize his fiction, suggesting all the qualities of an atmosphere surrounding a particular group,"[14] and at the same time utilize the spatial counterpointing to advance the narrative chronologically. Waugh nowhere uses this narrative technique with greater effectiveness. The narrator seems to be intent upon establishing and maintaining an inherent unity and progression in the material by explicitly declaring in commentary or im-

---

13. Carens, p. 64.
14. *Ibid.,* p. 65.

plicitly suggesting through juxaposition of scenes not only the relationship of the various episodes, but also their thematic significance. The hero provides the final narrative and thematic unity, but there are other methods employed in the narrative which contribute to narrative progression and to the narrative unity. For instance, although there are sudden changes of scenes, whether at the chapter divisions or within the chapters, there is almost always a recognizable transition either in the narrative or within the scenes.

Probably the best example of the narrator's obviously complete control over the material and at the same time a demonstration of the author's high degree of technical skill is the handling of the lengthy flashback involving the thunderbox. The narrator moves smoothly from present time to past without any obvious contrived device; pertinent explanatory information becomes an episode within itself:

> And Guy at once knew that there must have been a new development in the tense personal drama which all that Lent was being played against the background of the Brigadier's training methods; which, indeed, drew all its poignancy from them and itself formed their culminating illustration.
>
> This adventure had begun on the first Sunday of the new regime (176).

The episode forms the major part of the chapter in which it is introduced and carries over for about half of the next chapter; then, just before the inglorious climax of the substory, the narrator returns the action to the main time stream of the novel, blends the flashback into the present narrative, and neatly concludes both the thunderbox episode and the section of the main narrative dealing with the Halberdier training school at Kut-al-Imara: as he says, the thunderbox drama provides the "culminating illustration" of the Brigadier's training methods. In sheer narrative skill—as a storyteller—Waugh never did better in the management of his material.

Another example of the narrator's function in progression and unity is found in the narrative sequence. The chapters here are characterized by what could be considered transitional "introductions" or "conclusions." There is an unhurried, noncameralike movement indicated by initial paragraphs in the various chapters:

> All that January was intensely cold. In the first week an exodus began from the dormitories of Kut-al-Imara, first of the married men who were given permission to sleep in lodgings; then, since many of the controlling staff were themselves unmarried yet comfortably quartered, the order was stretched to include all who could afford to contrive it. Guy moved into the Grand Hotel, which was conveniently placed between Kut-al-Imara and the club (138).

Even the most abrupt changes of scene and subject are less dramatic than before; the sequence is blended smoothly into a unified whole:

> Apthorpe's wildest aberration was his one-man war with the Royal Corps of Signals. This campaign was his predominant obsession during all his difficult days at Penkirk and from it he emerged with the honors of war.
>
> It began by a simple misunderstanding (228).

Moreover, there seems to be at the end of each episode or chapter a kind of summary or conclusion, many times beginning with "Thus . . .":

> Had they known it, the Halberdiers would have been even more jubilant. This was, for them, the start of the war (235).
>
> Thus the new items were added to the Most Secret index, which later was micro-filmed and multiplied and dispersed into a dozen indexes in all the Counter-Espionage Headquarters of

the Free World and became a permanent part of the Most Secret archives of the second World War (200).

If not typical, at least illustrative of the narrative continuity is the echoing of thoughts, phrases, or incidents in the chapter summary by the subsequent chapter introduction:

> The Brigadier was carried ashore to hospital. The Brigade resumed its old duty of standing by for orders (III, vi, 295).

> Three weeks later the brigade was still standing by for orders (III, vii, 296).

Sometimes the transition is found within the drama itself, not in the narrator's comments:

> Soon he heard his father lightly snoring. His last thought before falling asleep was the uneasy question: "Why couldn't I say 'Here's how' to Major Tickeridge? My father did. Gervase would have. Why couldn't I?" (Prologue, iii, 44).

> "Here's how," said Guy.
> "Cheers," said Apthorpe.
> "Look here, you two, you'd better have those drinks on me," said Major Tickeridge, "junior officers aren't supposed to drink in the anteroom before lunch" (I, i, 45).

In addition to narrative unity, the narrator attempts to maintain a sense of integrality among the various episodes; he constantly makes the reader aware of the simultaneity of the events:

> At that moment in London—for in this most secret headquarters it was thought more secret to work at unconventional hours—Guy was being talked about (198).

> This happened, though the news did not reach Penkirk for some time, on the day when the Germans crossed the Meuse (226).

Perhaps the best example of this sort of thing is found
at the beginning of chapter 2, Book Three, in which at
least four narrative strands are brought together for the
moment. Guy, at one level of narrative, receives letters
from his father telling him of Tony's capture; then the
narrator says:

> These letters arrived together on the day the Germans marched
> into Paris. Guy and his company were then quartered in a sea-
> side hotel in Cornwall (256).

In these ways the narrator seems himself drawn into the
novel; he is a very present shaping and influencing force
within the novel itself.

Other than by the necessary degree of externality required by the role of "maker" in the narrative, the narrator may be identified as a somewhat independent entity,
and one with total perspective over the novel, merely because of his necessary role as historian and source of vital
information. As a historian, he is knowledgeable of the
history of Guy's family and of England, past and present.
The novel begins with a historical review of Guy's an-
cestors; the remainder abounds with references both to
the particulars of this historic family and to the contemporary historical events surrounding its lone representative. But even in the historical accounts there is a
new closeness of the narrator to his material and to the
character.

> Gervase and Hermione were welcomed in a score of frescoed
> palaces. Pope Pius received them in private audience and gave
> his special blessing to the union of two English families which
> had suffered for their Faith and yet retained a round share of
> material greatness. The chapel at Broome had never lacked a
> priest through all the penal years and the lands of Broome
> stretched undiminished and unencumbered from the Quantocks
> to the Blackdown Hills. Forbears of both their names had died
> on the scaffold. The City, lapped now by the tide of illustrious

converts, still remembered with honour its old companions in arms (1).

Current information regarding the war is presented grimly but obliquely—"It appears, among other things, that the Germans took Boulogne yesterday" (247). Usually this information is not the object of extended explanation as in *Black Mischief* or *Scoop;* the emphasis seems to be on the character (s).

The narrator functions separately also as the source of necessary, interesting, or extraneous information other than the historical. For example, he incidentally mentions that Peregrine is "a bore of international repute" (9), and comments that the taxi driver is "quoting from an article he had lately read" (11); he keeps the reader aware of the seasons: "It was early November. Winter had set in early and cold that year" (45); and he informs the reader of peculiarities of the characters: "Boots were a subject of peculiar interest to Apthorpe" (47); "Mr. Crouchback acknowledged no monarch since James II" (34). He even notes in passing that "the proprietor was a part-time spy" (130). Or he may pause briefly to comment on one of the minor characters; of the Grand-Duchess Elena of Russia he says:

> This ancient lady lived in a bed-sitting room at Nice but she was still as loyally honoured by the Halberdiers as when, a young beauty, she had graciously accepted the rank in 1902 (88).

In the context of the narrative, only the narrator could provide such information. Yet, despite the obvious freedom and relative externality of the narrator regarding the formulation of narrative, he does not dominate the novel. Rather, his narrative function is precisely integrated with that of the central character; as a result, the narrative center is found in the inseparable fusion of the roles of narrator-persona and character-persona.

But as this synthesis is considered, it should be noted that as in the previous novels, the central character also plays a role in the narrative—a role quite distinct from that of the narrator, yet complementary. In this novel the narrator provides not only for progression of the narrative but also for narrative unity. Yet, as before, emphasis is placed in narrative on the role of the central hero, even though at times it seems to make narration rather awkward for the narrator, who has to interpose Guy into the narrative and filter information through him, and, even more awkward, has to remind the reader continually of the centrality of Guy. This is seen especially in passages that could be handled well by the narrator alone in keeping with all dramatic necessities, but in all of these Guy is interposed quite unnecessarily:

> The thaw gave place to clear, cold weather. They returned to Mudshore range but with the Brigadier in charge. This was a period before the invention of 'Battle Schools.' The firing of a live round, as Guy well knew, was attended with all the solemnity of a salute at a funeral, always and everywhere, except when Brigadier Ritchie-Hook was about. The sound of flying bullets exhilarated him to heights of levity (173).

> The newspapers, hastily scanned, were full of Finnish triumphs. Ghostly ski-troops, Guy read, swept through the sunless Arctic forests harassing the mechanized divisions of the Soviet who had advanced with massed bands and portraits of Stalin expecting a welcome (175).

The result is that the account of the adventures of the hero not only provides the grounds for entrance into several areas of society, but it also becomes a unifying factor since all the activity is in some way related to the hero.

In *Men at Arms* the story of Guy Crouchback is central to the narrative; in fact, this novel is "a study of Guy Crouchback." Yet, it is also true that the story is concerned with various other characters and with several aspects of society; these are examined through the use of the pervasive central character. Guy's narrative allows entrance first into provincial Italy and this initial view of serenity provides an ironic contrast with the same country after the ravages of war (*Unconditional Surrender*) ; second, through the central character, the narrator is able to evaluate the status of the English Catholic aristocracy represented particularly by Guy's father, whose story, intermittently told, comprises one of the major subplots of the novel; third, through the activities of the hero, a great deal is learned about the nature of modern civilization by the vivid portrayal of the general reaction, particularly that of upper-class families, to the war and national honor; and, finally, the group that most consistently commands the narrator's attention is the English military. It is into this segment of society especially that Guy provides revealing glances; in fact, the novel, on one level, may be thought of as the beginning of the story of Guy's military experiences.

Not only does Guy provide entrance into the several social areas, but it is through him that the reader is introduced to all the characters who play even the slightest role in the novel. The whole crew, Mr. Crouchback, Angela, Box-Bender, Tickeridge, Trimmer, Apthorpe, Virginia, even Chatty Corner, seem important only because of their relationship to Guy. For instance, the introduction of Ben Ritchie-Hook is made as Guy sees him (even though one gets the feeling that the narrator could have accomplished it without Guy) :

> Guy too had heard of him often. He was the great Halberdier *enfant terrible* of the first World War; the youngest company commander in the history of the Corps; the slowest to be promoted; often wounded, often decorated, recommended for the Victoria Cross, twice court-martialled for disobedience to orders in the field, twice acquitted in recognition of the brilliant success

of his independent actions; a legendary wielder of the entrenching tool; where lesser men collected helmets Ritchie-Hook once came back from a raid across no-man's-land with the dripping head of a German sentry in either hand. The years of peace had been years of unremitting conflict for him. Wherever there was blood and gun-powder from County Cork to the Matto Grosso, there was Ritchie-Hook (74).

All social areas and all subplots involving the several minor characters are held together through the central figure by several old, proved technical methods: his observations, his actual experience, his conversations, his correspondence; and—a tribute to the discrimination of the author in selection of material—they all give depth, progression, and unity to the story of the hero.

Although the narrator and the hero function separately in the formulation of narrative, there is often no clear distinction between them. Owing principally to the omniscient point of view and to the summary technique, there is consistently throughout the narrative a thorough synthesis of the roles of narrator and hero. In some passages there is a close blending of narrator comment and character response, and, although they are thoroughly interfused, both personae are still identifiable:

> Guy returned to Bellamy's as though to the Southsand Yacht Club. He washed and gazed in the glass over the basin as steadfastly as Virginia had done in hers. The moustache was fair, inclined to ginger, much lighter than the hair of his head. It was strictly symmetrical, sweeping up from a neat central parting, curled from the lip, cut sharp and slightly oblique from the corners of his mouth, ending in firm points. He put up his monocle. How, he asked himself, would he regard another man so decorated? He had seen moustaches before and such monocles on the faces of clandestine homosexuals, on touts with accents to hide, on Americans trying to look European, on business-men disguised as sportsmen. True, he had also seen them in the Halberdier mess, but on faces innocent of all guile, quite beyond suspicion. After all, he reflected, his whole uniform was a disguise, his whole new calling a masquerade (152).

But there are other passages in which the narrator, at least for the moment, seems to respond through the hero's sensibilities; these passages admit no clear separation of the personae:

> It was a bitter moment. At no previous stage in his life had Guy expected success. His 'handkerchief' at Downside took him by surprise. When a group of his College suggested he should stand as secretary of the J.C.R. he had at once assumed that his leg was being inoffensively pulled. So it had been throughout his life. The very few, very small distinctions that had come to him had all come as a surprise. But in the Halberdiers he had had a sense of well-doing. There had been repeated hints. He had not expected or desired much but he had looked forward rather confidently to promotion of some kind and he had come to want it simply as a sign that he had, in fact, done well in training and that the occasional words of approbation had not been merely 'the deference due to age.' Well, now he knew. . . . Guy felt no resentment; he was a good loser—at any rate an experienced one. He merely felt a deep sinking of spirit such as he had felt in Claridge's with Virginia, such as he had felt times beyond number through all his life. Sir Roger, maybe, had felt thus when he drew his dedicated sword in a local brawl, not foreseeing that one day he would acquire the odd title of 'il Santo Inglese' (210–11).

What must be concluded is that despite their separate roles and independent functions, there is at several points in the novel and potentially at any time the complete synthesis of narrator and character in narrative formulation. This synthesis provides not only a more organic, self-contained narrative, but also dictates the whole tone of the novel.

From the discussion of the relationship of the narrator and character personae in narrative, it is apparent that the tone of the novel also represents a synthesizing and refining of previous tonal qualities. As a result, the precise tone of this novel may be difficult to determine and even more difficult to describe, for on the one hand there is a degree of real identification and sympathy of the narrator with the character; yet, on the other hand, there is ironic detachment and perspective. It is for this reason that O'Donnovan can speak of *Men at Arms* as the beginning of a "continuous mounting tragedy," but also can find in this first installment "the best lavatory joke in English history."[15] It is "almost as funny as *Decline and Fall*,"[16] he says. Bergonzi finds it characterized by "grim comedy"[17] and at the same time "one of the most thoroughgoing satires of military life on record."[18] Carens, noting that after *Brideshead Revisited* Waugh attempts "to adjust his satirical vision to a more conventional and realistic novel form,"[19] suggests that "in the Crouchback novels Evelyn Waugh successfully adjusts his conservative satirical vision to the conventions of the novel."[20] He also finds a synthesis of the previous primary tonal qualities when he observes that the satire of the Crouchback novels is a blend of "burlesque" and "low-keyed ironic realism."[21] DeVitis mentions specifically the "synthesis of the comic and serious," which brings this novel, as he says, "above the level of amusing farce to that of tragicomedy."[22] He still finds the ironic perspective of the earlier works, but it has become "more understanding and tolerant."[23] He suggests that "it is as though Waugh has come down from the summit and identified himself as one of men."[24] This is exactly what he has done.

Waugh accomplishes this successful synthesis of the comic and tragic, the satiric and romantic, through a re-

15. Patrick O'Donnovan, "Evelyn Waugh's Opus of Disgust," *The New Republic* (February 12, 1962), p. 21.
16. *Ibid.*
17. Bergonzi, p. 32.
18. *Ibid.*
19. Carens, p. 157.
20. *Ibid.*, p. 158.
21. *Ibid.*, p. 157.
22. DeVitis, p. 68.
23. *Ibid.*
24. *Ibid.*, p. 69.

fined control of the relationship of the narrator-persona and the character-persona. The peculiar feature of this novel is that here the narrator is detached enough to retain ironic perspective conducive to even caustic satire, yet to be both artistically and emotionally involved with the hero. Rather than alternating comedy and tragedy, or even creating tragedy with a comic basis or comedy with tragic overtones, Waugh here has gained more the effect of a fusion in which neither tonal element ever quite overshadows the other; there is a fusion in which both ends of the ironic spectrum are recognizable but are perfectly intermeshed into what Carens calls a kind of "ironic realism," a tone intensified in the subsequent war novels.

The narrator first reveals his detached posture both by the content of his frequent ironic comments and sometimes by the style itself. First, by narrator comments themselves ironic and indicative of detachment:

> They dug drains and carried tent-boards (the most awkward burden even devised by man for man) (203).

> There were moments, as in the gym in barracks, when Apthorpe rose above the ridiculous. This was one of them (222).

Or, the narrator's style may reflect his ironic detachment:

> He nothing common did or mean on the morning of their departure (194, 195).

> The Training Programme followed no text-book. Tactics as interpreted by Brigadier Ritchie-Hook consisted of the art of biffing. Defence was studied cursorily and only as the period of reorganization between two bloody assaults. The Withdrawal was never mentioned. The Attack and the Element of Surprise were all. Long raw misty days were passed in the surrounding county with maps and binoculars. Sometimes they stood on the beach and biffed imaginary defenders into the hills; sometimes they biffed imaginary invaders from the hills into the sea. They invested

downland hamlets and savagely biffed imaginary hostile inhabitants. Sometimes they merely collided with imaginary rivals for the use of the main road and biffed them out of the way (172).

Both these methods are utilized by the narrator throughout the novel to heighten the comedy of the escapades of Apthorpe, Trimmer, and Ben Ritchie-Hook especially.

But the narrator maintains the same kind of artistic distance with respect to the central character; the very name "Crouchback" is significant in this regard. For instance, he describes Guy quite objectively:

> Everything was now in order at the Castello. His formal farewells were made. The day before he had visited the Arciprete, the Podesta, the Reverend Mother at the Convent, Mrs. Garry at the Villa Datura, the Wilmots at the Castelletto Musgrave, Grafin von Gluck at the Casa Gluck. Now there was a last piece of private business to transact. Thirty-five years old, slight and trim, plainly foreign but not so plainly English, young, now, in heart and step, he came to bid good-bye to a life-long friend who lay, as was proper for a man dead eight hundred years, in the parish church (5).

And he is able to describe or comment on Guy's experiences with the same air of objectivity; there is neither the complete detachment of the earlier novels nor the complete attachment of *Brideshead Revisited*:

> Guy travelled through the familiar drab landscape. The frost was over and the countryside sodden and dripping. He drove through the darkling streets of Southsand where blinds were going down in the lightless windows. This was no homecoming. He was a stray cat, slinking back mauled from the rooftops, to a dark corner among the dustbins where he could lick his wounds (166).

The narrator may even rather gently satirize Guy much like the other characters:

> It was a moment of heightened emotion; an historic moment,

had Guy recognized it, when in their complicated relationship Apthorpe came nearest to love and trust. It passed, as such moments do between Englishmen (188).

Thus Guy stood high in Apthorpe's favor and became with him joint custodian of the thunder-box (188).

Or, the narrator may so detach himself as to allow even more severe, though comic, satire of Guy:

The words were not well chosen; lame or sound, Guy was not built to inspire great physical fear, but sudden wrath is always alarming, recalling as it does the awful unpredictable dooms of childhood; moreover Guy was armed with a strong stick which he now involuntarily raised a little. A court martial might or might not have construed this gesture as a serious threat against the life of brother officer. Trimmer did.

'Here, I say, steady on. No offence meant.'

Anger carries its own propulsive mechanism and soars far from the point of ignition. It carried Guy now into a red incandescent stratum where he was a stranger. . . .

Was it for this that the bugles sounded across the barrack square and the strings sang over the hushed dinner table of the Copper Heels? Was this the triumph for which Roger of Waybroke took the cross; that he should exult in putting down Trimmer?

In shame and sorrow Guy stood last in the queue for boiling water, leaning on his fouled weapon (126–27).

Although the narrator is detached enough from the central character to satirize him, he is at the same time closely identified with him. And the identification is not merely implied; it is achieved within the narrative process itself. In the early novels the narrator was, for the most part, scarcely apparent between the reader and the

character, or if he was present it was only as an external
director of the events or thoughts involving the character. But in *Men at Arms* there seems to be little separation of the narrator and character in point of view, even
in extreme instances of narrative emphasis, hence little
separation of sympathies. This is why many critics, who
consider Waugh the man to be the narrator, conclude
that the novel is autobiographical; but the question here
is not the author identity but narrator identification with
the central character, and the subsequent tone. Voorhees, while recognizing that "the identity between author
and hero is not absolute" and is "more a matter of point
of view than of personality,"[25] suggests, nevertheless that
the narrator's "identity with his hero has become closer."[26]
Stopp goes even further and suggests that the author and
the hero are the same:

> For all the author's disclaimer that he has nothing in common
> with his observer-hero, Guy Crouchback, beyond their common
> faith and age, the sequence of events follows roughly the author's
> own experiences till after the fall of Crete.[27]

Therefore, the center of the narrator's concern is Guy
and not Apthorpe as the chapter titles may indicate; Guy
is not only the central narrative figure but also the chief
thematic force, and the narrator's sympathetic identification with him informs the whole tone of the novel. There
are several ways in which narrator identification with
the hero is demonstrated, most of which are refinements
of the previous technique. First, there are passages in
which the narrator seems to report directly the thoughts
of Guy; even in these instances there is retained the presence of the narrator, for the method is primarily summary:

25. Voorhees, p. 57.
26. Stopp, p. 39.
27. *Ibid.*

Well, he reflected, he had not joined the army for his own comfort. He had expected a grim initiation. Life in the barracks had been a survival from long years of peace, something rare and protected, quite unconnected with his purpose. That was over and done with; this was war (109).

Some lengthy passages are introduced by narrator transitions and while ostensibly the thoughts of the hero are directly presented, there is still the summary form, indicating the closeness of the narrator:

He could imagine a row of little boys struggling to sit on them, tight-trousered boys with adenoids and chilblains; or perhaps it was a privilege to sit there enjoyed only by prefects and the First Eleven. In its desolation he could see the whole school as it had been made familiar to him in many recent realistic novels; an enterprise neither progressive nor prosperous. The assistant masters changed often, he supposed, arriving with bluff, departing with bluster; half the boys were taken at surreptitiously reduced fees; none of them ever won a scholarship or passed into a reputable school or returned for an Old Boys' Day or ever thought of his years there with anything but loathing and shame. The History lessons were patriotic in design, turned to ridicule by the young masters. There was no school song at Kut-al-Imara House. All this Guy thought he snuffed in the air of the forsaken building (109).

Since most of the reporting of Guy's mental activity is done through the summary method the narrator is able to color and shape the material and hence to direct the reader's response to Guy; at the same time, he can insert at the proper moment bits of information related to the circumstance at hand. There are some instances in which the narrator seems to dominate completely:

But to Guy sitting there with them in the anteroom among all the trophies of the Corps, in the order and comfort of two centuries' uninterrupted inhabitation, it seemed impossible that anything conducted by the Halberdiers could fall short of excellence. And to him now, as the train rolled through the cold and misty darkness, there remained the same serene confidence. His knee was stiff and painful. He shifted his leg among the legs that crossed and crowded in the twilight. The little group of subalterns sat listless. High overhead their piled kitbags, equipment and suitcases loomed darkly and were lost in the shadows. Faces were hidden. Only their laps were lit by shafts too dim for easy reading. From time to time one of them struck a match. From time to time they spoke of their leave. Mostly they were silent (101).

There are other instances in which nothing in the narrative process allows any sure distinction between the sentiments of the narrator and those of the character:

He was thinking of this strange faculty of the army of putting itself into order. Shake up a colony of ants and for some minutes all seems chaos. The creatures scramble aimlessly, frantically about; then instinct reasserts itself. They find their proper places and proper functions. As ants, so soldiers (205–6) .

Such close but unobtrusive identification of narrator with character both artistically and to a degree emotionally, although still within the ironic mode, means that the satiric potential is not reached, not even attempted. In fact, the ironic perspective itself is lessened, although it is not lost. The result is one of carefully controlled balance between satire and romance, ironic perspective and sympathetic identification—a harmony which could have been achieved only by a master of both, the author of both *Decline and Fall* and *Brideshead Revisited*. Carens has assessed the tonal achievement of the novel in this way:

The satire is handled here with marvelous delicacy, for Waugh manages to suggest both the attractiveness and the illusoriness of everything that Guy has committed himself to, at the same time that he ridicules with restraint and poise Crouchback's failure to recognize his illusions.[28]

The vision that could not sustain pure comedy nor ac-

28. Carens, p. 43.

cept simple tragedy finds its greatest artistic expression in this hard-minded "ironic realism." Waugh has learned literally to "tone down" his fiction to a more realistic level; he has found the delicate equilibrium between the bitter satire and cruel farce of the early works and the romanticism of *Brideshead Revisited.* And, because tone is the chief influencing factor in the development of Waugh's theme, it is necessarily implied that in theme also he has found the mean between "monkish" rejection of the modern age and prophetic assurance of the endurance of spiritual values and corresponding human traditions.

The theme of *Men at Arms* finds its origin in the previous novels. Most of the previous thematic elements are present, but here they are more purposefully directed toward a realistic portrayal of contemporary civilization and the consequent plight of the individual who by nature and cultural precedent remains an alien. Both elements of this theme are present, but here the emphasis is on the plight of the hero. Waugh says as much in the preface to *Sword of Honour:*

> This product is intended (as it was originally) to be read as a single story. I sought to give a description of the Second World War as it was *seen* and *experienced* by a single, uncharacteristic Englishman, and to show its *effect on him* [italics mine].[29]

But the author does not seem to be interested in Guy merely as an individual, but more as a representative of an old order that is being gradually disintegrated by both weaknesses within and barbarous opposition. His experiences signal the decline and fall of the Catholic aristocracy as well as the end of societal order, morals, and spiritual values. It is because of the implied commentary on contemporary society that Didion finds this

---

29. "Preface," *Sword of Honour* (Boston: Little Brown and Company, 1961), p. 9.

novel a "study of the breakdown of civilization,"[30] and Amis would agree that its primary concern is with "disintegration, social and moral."[31] The picture of a collapsing civilization in *Men at Arms* is similar to that of the early novels, a mosaic made up of views of various elements of the society. DeVitis notes that "most of the satire is directed at the army";[32] while this may be true, it is by no means concerned only with the ineffectuality of the British military forces. There is also a continual ironic view of the aristocracy, primarily in the portrait of Mr. Crouchback, later in Ivor Claire, finally (in *Unconditional Surrender*), in Guy himself. Mr. Crouchback, indeed his whole family, is the epitome of the decline of the aristocracy. The initial portrait of Mr. Crouchback is a picture of a gradual but certain, possibly somewhat stubborn, deterioration:

> Despite the forty years that divided them there was a marked likeness between Mr. Crouchback and Guy. Mr. Crouchback was rather the taller and he wore an expression of steadfast benevolence quite lacking in Guy. "*Racé* rather than *distingué*" was how Miss Vavasour, a fellow resident at the Marine Hotel, defined Mr. Crouchback's evident charm. There was nothing of the old dandy about him, nothing crusted, nothing crotchety. He was not at all what is called 'a character.' He was an innocent, affable old man who had somehow preserved his good humour—much more than that, a mysterious and tranquil joy,—throughout of life which to all outward observation had been overloaded with misfortune. He had like many another been born in full sunlight and lived to see night fall (33–34).

The deterioration is complete only in *Unconditional Surrender*, but even here Mr. Crouchback is surrounded

30. Joan Didion, "Gentlemen in Battle," *National Review* 12 (March 27, 1962) : 316.
31. Kingsley Amis, "Crouchback's Regress," *The Spectator* (October 27, 1961), p. 581.
32. DeVitis, p. 69.

by ominous circumstances. Reduced to near poverty by the conditions of war and fortune; gently tolerated by friends; exploited by landlords who used to be his servants; sporadically teaching a forgotten language to silly, young scholars, he seems merely waiting for death. Ivo, a son, years before died insane; Gervase, another son, while wearing a religious badge which was supposed to provide divine protection, was killed during his first day in battle; Angela, his daughter, is married into the political, commercial world of Box-Bender, whose career fluctuates precariously; Guy, the youngest son, and the only hope of continuing the Crouchback line and restoring it to its original splendor, is divorced and his wife now little more than a prostitute.

Very closely related to the deterioration of society and fall of the aristocracy is the account of Guy's unsuccessful marriage and the activities of his wife. She, very much like Brenda Last, cannot understand the church's concept of the sanctity of marriage, nor can she fully realize the impact that her leaving him has had on Guy; for Guy the divorce is a "deep wound" that sets him apart "from his fellows" (4). For Mr. Crouchback, it means the end of the line. In fact, the relationship of Guy and Virginia contributes much to the plot of *Men at Arms* and even to the plots of the subsequent novels in which Virginia and the marriage problem figure more importantly in the central theme. In *Men at Arms,* while she possibly accounts for some of Guy's melancholy, she is primarily symbolic, not dramatic, contributing to the overall picture of disintegration surrounding Guy. Through Mr. Crouchback and Virginia another thematic element is introduced. There is among the main thematic elements a continuing interest in the state of religion, particularly of the Catholic Church. So much so, in fact, that DeVitis supposes the theme of *Men at Arms* very nearly that of *Brideshead Revisited,* "divine purpose making itself ap-

parent in the phenomenal world."[33] The only difference
between this novel and *Brideshead Revisited,* he says, is
that here "the element of apology is gone."[34] Although
Waugh contends that *Sword of Honour* "was not specifically a religious book," he admits that it is "an obituary
of the Roman Catholic Church in England as it had existed for many centuries."[35]

These thematic concerns are not dealt with in the
rapid-fire camera method of *Decline and Fall* or *Vile
Bodies,* but they are thoroughly synthesized into the experience of the character-persona; they overlap, inter-
mingle, and interact inseparably in the activities of this
hero. Guy Crouchback is the narrative device through
which these areas are explored, but more important he
is the figure who embodies the total thematic significance
of the novel. Once more Waugh chooses as the chief
means in the development of theme the character-persona
who, in this case particularly, has been stylized "something of a literary surrogate for Waugh."[36] Though somewhat changed, Guy Crouchback is strictly in the tradition
of Paul Pennyfeather, Adam Fenwick-Symes, Tony Last,
or even Charles Ryder. DeVitis notes that

> Guy is made of the same idealistic stuff as his predecessors;
> he is romantic. Like Charles Ryder and like Tony Last he lives
> in the world of the nursery and the schoolroom.[37]

Karl describes Guy as "a Tony Last converted to Catholicism"[38] and as "a Basil Seal who has effaced himself
and gained social responsibility and religious fervor."[39]
Thus, the innocent who in *Put Out More Flags* sup-

---

33. *Ibid.,* p. 70.
34. *Ibid.*
35. "Preface," *Sword of Honour.*
36. Karl, p. 168.
37. DeVitis, p. 72.
38. Karl, p. 179.
39. *Ibid.,* p. 181.

planted completely the cad, here is extended into realistic proportions. DeVitis notes the continued use of the innocent and his gradual movement toward reality:

> In Guy Crouchback Waugh introduces again the character of the innocent, but the uncomprehending naïveté of a Paul Pennyfeather is replaced by a sense of inadequacy of modern man in the confusion of the modern world.[40]

Carens also suggests that

> Crouchback, who has obvious links to the earlier and younger men in Waugh's novels, is not the one-dimensional earlier type but a fully developed character.[41]

Possibly this sense of "roundness" results from Guy's more positive idealism; although he is buffeted and his relatively mild ambitions are suppressed by social machinery, he is hardly the totally passive pawn, like Paul or Tony. Somewhere in the evolution of the innocent, the jellyfish has developed a backbone: Paul had had no real dream, little energy, reacted only to stimuli; Tony, who introduced the quest motif, proved too ineffectual even to pursue it; Basil had the necessary pluck and ambition but less than noble goals; only Guy has both an ideal and the energy to seek its fulfillment. DeVitis sees in Guy both dedication to his country and deep religious convictions.[42] O'Donnovan finds him "dedicated and courageous."[43] Carens says of him:

> Inarticulate, frequently foolish, an easy dupe of illusion, limited by his social bias . . . Guy Crouchback is still a man of honor and courage.[44]

---

40. DeVitis, p. 70.
41. Carens, p. 41.
42. DeVitis, pp. 70–71.
43. O'Donnovan, p. 21.
44. Carens, p. 158–59.

But Bergonzi offers the most heroic concept of Guy:

> In the person of Guy Crouchback Waugh offers us his fullest
> and most sympathetic delineation of the Gentleman, the embodi-
> ment of the Gothic dream, a gallant officer who would be, if he
> could, a twentieth-century reincarnation of Roger of Waybroke.[45]

It is this fact that separates Guy from the earlier heroes
and from the world of common mortals; Guy is not "potentially an every-man";[46] he is, as Waugh says, "unchar-
acteristic,"[47] first because of his Catholic aristocratic heritage, second because of his heroic ideal. As a result
he is anything but "tedious," and is obviously not "too
will-less to sustain a tragic apparatus."[48] In fact, DeVitis
finds heroic qualities about Guy that necessarily relate to
the deepening tone of the novel: "more than pathetic
. . . he verges on the tragic."[49] And Didion perceives a
note of heroic tragedy when she describes *Men at Arms*
as "about one man's aridity, and his foredoomed attempt
to make a social cause a moral cause in a society bereft
of moral meaning."[50] But if the trilogy is of a tragic
bent, there is only premonition in *Men at Arms* as to the
outcome of Guy's struggles. In this novel, the quest is
undertaken with serious resolve and optimism, and, although thwarted in the course of the novel, Guy is un-
daunted at its conclusion.

Two things characterize Guy: isolation and search, one
arising out of the other, and the latter essentially the
theme of the novel. Guy, like the previous innocents,
partly by choice and partly of necessity, lives in isolation.
No matter what the circumstances, Guy throughout the
novel is separate: "set apart from his fellows" (4); "his

---

45. *Bergonzi*, p. 34.
46. Karl, p. 180.
47. "Preface," *Sword of Honour*.
48. Karl, p. 179.
49. DeVitis, p. 76.
50. Didion, p. 316.

heart was lonely" (22) ; "Guy belonged to neither world" (28) ; "he . . . hobbled back alone behind them" (113) "different from the rest of the crowd" (57) are but a few of the many suggestions of his isolation. Guy seeks both personal satisfaction in honorable service to his country and integration into his society on a level that that society cannot comprehend. Guy is "trying to find a place in a scheme that excludes him," but not strictly for selfish motives:

> The enemy was at last in plain view, huge and hateful, all disguise cast off. It was the Modern Age in arms. Whatever the outcome there was a place for him in that battle (5) .

To that purpose he dedicates himself on the tomb of Sir Roger of Waybroke: "Sir Roger . . . , pray for me and for our endangered kingdom" (7). Sir Roger becomes the symbol of the aristocratic Catholicism and the attendant devotion to God and country, either or both of which are implied in "kingdom." To Guy, the war provides opportunity to fulfill both the aristocratic code of duty and the church's demand for eternal vigilance against evil; thus, he undertakes his personal mission much like a Christian knight errant dedicating himself to service in a "Holy Crusade."[51]

Guy soon learns that his idealism and dedication to truth, justice, and all other virtues, are not shared by his society. He is introduced into a world which knows no ideals or virtues; *Men at Arms* merely records the initial cognition. He first learns that "others do not approach the war with the same high purpose, devotion to moral cause, and disdain for the modern age in arms" through discussions at Bellamy's:

> 'Then why go to war at all? If all we want is prosperity, the hardest bargain Hitler made would be preferable to vic-

---

51. Karl, p. 168.

tory. If we are concerned with justice the Russians are as guilty as the Germans.'

'Justice?' said the old soldiers. 'Justice?' (21).

His subsequent military experience does little to convince him of the high calling of those involved or even of professionalism among the soldiers. The various "flaps," "alternating chaos and order" (248) the petty jealousies, the careless, lazy, eccentric characters he encounters can only convince him that his unit is a small part of a nation without virtue or excellence. There is little of the swagger and daring of Captain Truslove anywhere to be seen. Yet, eternal hope and assignment to the Royal Corps of Halberdiers keep alive Guy's own personal faith and sense of heroic destiny:

> He held his audience for a moment with his single eye. Then he said: 'Gentlemen, these are the officers who will command you in battle.'

> At those words Guy's shame left him and pride flowed back. He ceased for the time being to be the lonely and ineffective man —the man he so often thought he saw in himself, past his first youth, cuckold, wastrel, prig—who had washed and shaved and dressed at Claridge's, lunched at Bellamy's and caught the afternoon train; he was one with his regiment, with all their historic feats of arms behind him, with great opportunities to come. He felt from head to foot a physical tingling and bristling as though charged with galvanic current (167).

But the Halberdiers are not destined for glory; at best, only a farcical midnight raid on an unimportant coastline. Although he recognizes that the war and those involved are somehow strangely foreign to his own convictions of right and wrong, justice and injustice, he continues alone to pursue his ideal which, unknown to him now, will ultimately prove a disillusionment.

> He was a good loser, but he did not believe his country would

lose this war; each apparent defeat seemed strangely to sustain it. There was in Romance great virtue in unequal odds. There were in morals two requisites for a lawful war, a just cause and the chance of victory. The cause was now, past all question, just. The enemy was exorbitant. His actions in Austria and Bohemia had been defensible. There was even a shadow of plausibility in his quarrel with Poland. But now, however victorious, he was an outlaw. And the more victorious he was the more he drew to himself the enmity of the world and the punishment of God (220).

There is in *Men at Arms* no consummation of the quest, and only little, if any, hope offered of sustaining for long the grand illusion. There cannot be, for, although *Men at Arms* is a complete unit, there is no air of finality about the conclusion. Even in the last sentence there seems to be a note of anticipation; the quest continues:

He had momentarily been of them; now he was an alien; someone in their long and varied past, but forgotten (314).

OFFICERS AND GENTLEMEN

It is difficult to understand why critics in the mid-fifties generally did not respond to *Officers and Gentlemen* with the same enthusiasm with which they had greeted its predecessor. DeVitis, writing in 1955, concludes that "the sequel to *Men at Arms* is not a success" because it "lacks the warmth" of the previous novel and because it "fails to maintain an interest in the characters."[52] In fact, he suggests that *Officers and Gentlemen* is something of an antithesis of *Men at Arms*. Stopp, while discussing primarily only the theme of *Officers and Gentlemen*, seems somehow to avoid any real assessment of the novel, although he finds it the most "deflating"[53] of Waugh's novels; it is clear, however, that he, always a defender of Waugh, expects better things of the third installment

---

52. DeVitis, p. 80.
53. Stopp, pp. 169–70.

in the trilogy. Yet, *Officers and Gentlemen* is a worthy
sequel to *Men at Arms.* Not only is there a logical progression from the tentative conclusion of *Men at Arms*
into a complexity of historically and thematically related
events, but the high degree of artistry achieved in the
previous novel is sustained and refined. The theme, still
essentially a serious examination of modern values, increases in intensity as the adventures of Guy offer intimate
views of several areas of contemporary society, and as
they eventually lead to his disillusionment.

Perhaps it is because *Officers and Gentlemen* can now
be viewed not so much as a sequel and therefore the final
statement of a serious theme, but as only the second of a
trilogy, or even as the central portion of one novel, *Sword
of Honour,* that critics of this decade have begun to look
more favorably on the work. Amis finds particularly the
artistry superior to that of *Men at Arms;*[54] and Carens
sees *Officers and Gentlemen* as a continuation of the
successful adjustment of a "conservative satirical vision
to the conventions of the novel."[55] Themes begun in *Men
at Arms,* he says, emerge in *Officers and Gentlemen* "in
full force."[56] That the ironic technique of the earlier
novels here reaches a kind of culmination is also suggested, Carens thinks, by the expert handling of the
counterpointing technique, particularly in the episode involving the disaster in Crete.[57]

Whatever the final critical view of this novel as it
stands in relation to the other novels, as a unit of fiction
itself *Officers and Gentlemen* is a highly successful novel.
In the fine manner of *Men at Arms,* the narrative, show-
ing new refinements in even very early methods, is expertly managed through the harmoniously interfused
roles of the narrator-persona and the character-persona;

---

54. Amis, p. 581.
55. Carens, p. 158.
56. *Ibid.,* p. 160.
57. *Ibid.,* pp. 65–66.

the theme remains essentially the same as in *Men at Arms,* but here, by a shift reminiscent of *Vile Bodies,* the primary emphasis seems to be not on the personal quest of Guy, but on the barbarous society which mocks his ambition and turns his ideals into illusions. Consequently, the narrator's ironic accounts of the adverse circumstances and personages in the civilized world become more embittered, while the tone surrounding Guy's growing disillusionment deepens gradually toward tragedy.

Officers and Gentlemen finds Guy still pursuing his ideal much in the same way that he thinks Roger of Waybroke would have done. But this novel ends in bitter disillusionment. Early in the story, Guy's quest is parodied in his compelling mission to deliver Apthorpe's gear to Chatty Corner, man of the wilds. On the island of Mugg, Guy subsequently undergoes commando training, which is to prepare him for military action that finally materializes as the fiasco in Crete. While in training, he meets Trimmer (ex-hairdresser) who through a secret raid on a friendly coastline is made a national hero by the press; consequently, Trimmer begins a liaison with Virginia. While these and other farces are being enacted on the home front, Guy's unit moves into the combat area; the military operations likewise prove a farce: the defeat in Crete, the withdrawal, and the rearguard action are shameful and inglorious. Epitomizing the spirit of the defeat is Major Hound—exact opposite of Roger of Waybroke—who is the most despicable character Waugh ever conceived; he forsakes national interests and later loses his own personal honor. Yet, Guy, aware that "all gentlemen are now very old," still clutches his ideal of the Christian knight. In fact, his ideal is embodied in an associate, Ivor Claire, "flower of the nation," the man whom Hitler failed to take into account. But when Claire also proves coward and traitor, the illusion is shattered. Guy escapes from Crete; but the illusion does

not. "After less than two years' pilgrimage in a Holy
Land of Illusion," Guy returns to the old world, "where
priests are spies and gallant friends prove traitors and
the country is led blundering into dishonour."

As a novel, as a sequel, as the center section of a longer
work, *Officers and Gentlemen* demonstrates Waugh's
artistic maturity and, while it may not seem so on the
surface, this novel reflects, possibly more than *Men at
Arms,* a tempered, if not resigned, view of modern civilization. Waugh in *Officers and Gentlemen* is moving
inevitably toward the congenial blend of the satiric-
ironic mode with a serious moral statement, within the
bounds of the conventional novel.

The narrative technique of *Officers and Gentlemen*
is essentially the same as that of *Men at Arms,* yet there
are differences which make not only the narrative but
also the tone of *Officers and Gentlemen* distinctive. The
narrator continues to function in close identification
with the central hero. There is much narrator summary
of the activities and thoughts of the hero; the distinction
between narrator and character frequently is obscured.
But the narrator seems to be a bit more independent as
a narrative device. The narrator's function becomes
reminiscent of the method of the narrator of *Decline and
Fall,* who almost totally effaces himself from the internal
narration but who externally directs the events and continues to make ironic commentary. In *Officers and Gentlemen* the narrator manipulates, rather externally, the
narrative material, but at the same time he provides by
his identification with the hero internal progression and
unity within the narrative itself. In this manner, the
omniscient narrator is able not only to relate and comment on simultaneous activity in a number of locations,
but continually to draw all this activity into the experience of Guy. Thus, there is a detached overview of national and international events and their consequences,

and at the same time there is something of a psychological penetration into Guy's frustrations. This is not to say that in this dual role the narrator reaches either the extreme distance and externality of *Vile Bodies* or the extreme identification with the hero of *Brideshead Revisited*. Both are modulated versions of the previous stances and here they are so complementarily fused that the reader is scarcely aware of the narrator's double perspective.

Because the externality of the narrator is somewhat more pronounced in *Officers and Gentlemen* than in *Men at Arms,* and because it results in the major tonal and narrative differences between the novels, perhaps the narrator's function should be the first consideration in determining this novel's relation to *Men at Arms,* and its own intrinsic merit.

The external control of the narrator and consequently his ironic distance from the material is manifest in several ways in *Officers and Gentlemen*. First, this novel is much more episodic than *Men at Arms,* and the narrator makes no attempt to force a smooth connection between the various narrative units. Thus, the story proceeds without transition from Trimmer's leading his detachment "into the unknown" to Ivor Claire's sighting of the *Cleopatra,* Julia Stitch's ship (123–24). Or the transition may be quite brief: "So the days passed until in the third week of May war came to Major Hound" (209). The overall structure is, however, rounded off with an epilogue which somewhat concludes the activity begun in *Men at Arms*. But the narrator's influence is nowhere better seen than in his juxtaposing the various scenes and events for ironic effect, as Carens points out, both spatially and chronologically.[58] In this way the narrator also insures the logical progression of the novel. Within the novel itself, the narrator's control is apparent in the

---

58. *Ibid.,* pp. 65–66; 162.

reappearance of the old cinematic shifting of scenes without narrative transition:

> Given time, given enough confidential material, he [Marchpole] would succeed in knitting the entire quarrelsome world into a single net of conspiracy in which there were no antagonists, merely millions of men working, unknown to one another, for the same end; there would be no more war.
>
> Full, Dickensian fog enveloped the city. Day and night the streets were full of slow-moving lighted trams and lorries and hustling coughing people (99).

> 'He must be here somewhere. Someone must know. You and Charles find him while I collect a submarine.'
>
> While the first bells of Easter rang throughout Christendom, the muezzin called his faithful to prayer from the shapeless white minaret beyond the barbed wire (155).

There is in many of these shifts an attempt to capture the simultaneity of the events:[59]

> At that moment in London Colonel Grace-Groundling-Marchpole, lately promoted head of his most secret department, was filing the latest counter-intelligence (98).

> Another day; another night.
>
> 'Night and day,' crooned Trimmer, 'you are the one. Only you beneath the moon and under the sun, in the roaring traffic's boom—' (283).

The narrator reports directly a great deal of the conversation, something quite uncommon in *Men at Arms,* where the narrative summary is the usual method:

> Guy removed his mask and let it hang, in correct form, across his chest to dry.
>
> 'Haven't you read the Standing Orders?'
>
> 'No, sir.'
>
> 'Why the hell not?'
>
> 'Reporting back to-day, sir, from overseas.'

---

59. DeVitis, p. 81.

'Well, remember in future that every Wednesday from 1000 to 1100 hours all ranks take anti-gas precautions. That's a Command Standing Order.'

'Very good, sir.'

'Now who are you and what do you want?'

'Lieutenant Crouchback, sir. Second Battalion Royal Halberdiers Brigade.'

'Nonsense. The Second Battalion is abroad.'

'I landed yesterday, sir' (12–13).

As further evidence of the narrator's relative independence from the character-persona, many scenes, some quite lengthy, are reported and commented upon without the presence of Guy. In fact, quite frequently it seems that the hero "momentarily slips through one of the cracks in the [narrative] floor" (see pp. 19–43; 90–101; 176–99; 257–72).

The narrator's style itself many times reflects his distance from the material and his comfortable control over it; the ironic potential of this manner is not subdued:

Selections from Livy in Mr. Crouchback's form-room. Black-out curtains drawn. Gas fire hissing. The customary smell of chalk and ink. The Fifth Form drowsy from the football field, hungry for high tea. Twenty minutes to go and the construe approaching unprepared passages (19).

He laughed, Tommy laughed, they laughed all four (208).

In this green pasture Trimmer and his section for a time lay down (176).

And, as before, the narrator's superior knowledge detaches him from the narrative; but in *Officers and Gentlemen* the narrator is more obviously the external "storyteller" chiefly because he constantly views the events in terms of the realized future. But the narrator's externality is also distinguished because of the various kinds of general information which he provides. First, he has an omniscient knowledge of the characters. For instance, of Kerstie he says:

> Kerstie was a good wife to Ian, personable, faithful, even-tempered and economical. All the pretty objects in their house had been bargains. Her clothes were cleverly contrived. She was sometimes suspected of fabricating the luncheon vin rose by mixing the red and white wines left over from dinner; no more damaging charge was ever brought against her. There were nuances in her way with men which suggested she had once worked with them and competed on equal terms. Point by point she was the antithesis of her friend Virginia Troy (176).

Second, he has a complete historical, geographical, and climatic information about most of the various locales; the description of the Isle of Mugg is perhaps the most entertaining:

> The Isle of Mugg has no fame in song or story. Perhaps because whenever they sought a rhyme for the place, they struck absurdity, it was neglected by those romantic early-Victorian English ladies who so prodigally enriched the balladry, folk-lore and costume of the Scottish Highlands. It has a laird, a fishing fleet, an hotel (erected just before the first World War in the unfulfilled hope of attracting tourists) and nothing more. It lies among other monosyllabic protuberances. There is seldom clear weather in those waters, but on certain rare occasions Mugg has been descried from the island of Rum in the form of two cones. The crofters of Muck know it as a single misty lump on their horizon. It has never been seen from Eigg (55).

Third, the narrator is aware of the real events in contemporary history and understands their implications:

> This was February, 1941. English tanks were cruising far west of Benghazi; bankers, labelled 'AMGOT', were dining nightly at the Mohamed Ali Club in Cairo, and Rommel, all unknown, was even then setting up his first headquarters in Africa (142).

Moreover, he is able to blend perfectly the historical with the fictional:

Major-General Whale held the appointment of Director of Land Forces in Hazardous Offensive Operations. He was known in countless minutes as the DLFHOO and to a few old friends as 'Sprat'. On Holy Saturday 1941 he was summoned to attend the ACIG's weekly meeting at the War Office. He went with foreboding. He was not fully informed of the recent disasters in the Middle East but he knew things were going badly. Benghazi had fallen the week before. It did not seem clear where the retreating army intended to make its stand. On Maundy Thursday the Australians in Greece had been attacked on their open flank. It was not clear where they would stand. Belgrade had been bombed on Palm Sunday (151).

All these narrative devices have the effect of identifying the narrator as an external "maker" of the novel and allow a broad historical perspective of events as well as a high degree of ironic potential. And yet, this does not exclude the narrator's almost complete identification with characters, even characters other than the hero, in the narrative process. Here, as in *Men at Arms,* it is often impossible to distinguish between what appears to be an "internal" summary by the narrator and the direct thought of the character, especially in the case of those characters whom the narrator treats sympathetically. In such passages, which indeed dominate the narrative involving Guy, the narrator is able to fuse his narrative role with that of the hero; but the narrator also at times utilizes other characters in much the same way. For example, Mr. Crouchback:

> Now he cut the string with his nail scissors and spread the contents in order on his table.
> First came six tins of 'Pullitzer's Soup.' They were variously, lusciously named but soup was one of the few articles of diet in which the Marine Hotel abounded. Moreover, he had an ancient conviction that all tinned foods were made of something nasty. 'Silly girls. Well, I daresay we shall be glad of it one day.' Next there was a transparent packet of prunes. Next a very heavy little tin labelled 'Brisko. A Must in every home.' There was no indication of its function. Soap? Concentrated fuel?

Rat poison? Boot polish? He would have to consult Mrs. Tickeridge. Next a very light larger tin named 'Yumcrunch.' This
must be edible for it bore the portrait of an obese and badly
brought-up little girl waving a spoon and fairly bawling for the
stuff. Last and oddest of all a bottle filled with what seemed to
be damp artificial pearls, labelled 'Cocktail Onions.' Could it be
that this remote and resourceful people who had so generously
(and, he thought, so unnecessarily) sheltered his grand-children;
this people whose chief concern seemed to be the frustration
of the processes of nature—could they have contrived an alcoholic
onion? (24).

But there is a noticeable difference between the almost
complete identification in such passages and those which
externally summarize the thoughts and actions of characters treated less sympathetically. While the narrator's
antipathetic view is seen in regard to Trimmer and other
even more minor characters, perhaps, Fido Hound offers
the best example of the distinct detachment of narrator:

> Fido watched. He craved. Not Guy nor the ragged, unshaven
> Sergeant, not Fido himself who was dizzy with hunger and lack
> of sleep, nor anyone on that fragrant hillside could know that
> this was the moment of probation. Fido stood at the parting of
> the ways. Behind him lay a life of blameless professional progress;
> before him the proverbial alternatives: the steep path of duty
> and the heady precipice of sensual appetite. It was the first great
> temptation of Fido's life. He fell (235).

Although the narrator is the major factor in external
organization and in progression of the narrative, the character-persona is the central device in progression and unity
of plot. Although the narrator operates frequently without the character, the entire novel is focused on Guy
and all the events either become a part of or are held
together by his experience. All somehow contribute to
his story and all are given thematic significance by his
story.

Guy provides entrance into the several areas of society

and into the lives of the many illustrative characters. Both the method and the areas explored are similar to *Men at Arms:* specifically examined are the aristocracy, the church, the British military, the civilian response to the war, the typical military snafus, even the press. Only here Guy's experience leads to the actual horrors of war and its accompanying chaos, militarily and morally:

> The sick-bay was crowded now. Two army doctors and the ship's surgeon were dealing with urgent cases. While Guy stood there beside Tommy's bunk a huge, bloody, grimy, ghastly Australian sergeant appeared in the door. He grinned like a figure of death and said: 'Thank God we've got a navy,' then sank slowly to the deck and on the instant passed into the coma of death (222–23).

It is through the hero that the narrator not only explores these areas of society, but by his close identification with the hero also is able to imply his own serious attitudes about the various circumstances. A narrative technique which simultaneously reflects both narrator externality and narrator identification with the hero signifies the possibility of tonal effects at both ends of the satiric-ironic scale. In *Men at Arms,* Waugh achieves a delicate balance in tone between the extremes of the early bitter satire and the later romanticism; the result is a mellowed satire and a more realistic view of contemporary society. A similar kind of tonal effect is achieved in *Officers and Gentlemen,* except that the poles of the irony are more extreme, at times separable, and more easily identified. Whereas most critics find the tone of *Men at Arms* modulated, *Officers and Gentlemen* is considered more "violent,"[60] more "bitter,"[61] and "more serious"[62] than the earlier work. DeVitis says:

---

60. Carens, p. 160.
61. *Ibid.*
62. Voorhees, p. 62.

It is not the gentle remonstrance that characterized the earlier book. Rather it is a contemptuous and biting appraisal of incompetence and bad management.[63]

Yet, on the other hand, the same critics note "a profusion of comic plots," "farcical footnotes,"[64] and a return to the satiric-comic in burlesque.[65] This does not mean, however, that there is not the same kind of simultaneous intermingling of the comic and tragic, the satiric and the sympathetic, that is found in *Men at Arms*. The fusion in *Officers and Gentlemen* is merely stretched in both directions, with the unifying bond of irony never broken.

In *Officers and Gentlemen* Waugh approaches a tone which reflects what may best be described as "hardness of mind."[66] The narrator's handling of the bombing of Crete is an example:

> From the boat they saw havoc. One of the aeroplanes dipped over their heads, fired its machine-gun, missed and turned away. Nothing further was done to molest them. Guy saw more bombs burst on the now-deserted waterfront. His last thoughts were of X Commando, of Bertie and Eddie, most of all Ivor Claire, waiting at their posts to be made prisoner. At the moment there was nothing in the boat for any of them to do. They had merely to sit still in the sunshine and fresh breeze.
>
> So they sailed out of the picture (302).

Dominant throughout the novel, this attitude is characterized by ironic detachment, disgust, and bitter remonstrance regarding contemporary civilization, and by an ironic though sympathetic identification with the representative of the aristocratic code of national morality and individual responsibility. It is an attitude difficult to comprehend, even more difficult to share by those given to single-minded emotional responses. But the

---

63. DeVitis, p. 80.
64. Voorhees, p. 62.
65. Carens, p. 161.
66. Didion, p. 315.

narrator (and one supposes by now, Waugh) can resolve tragedy through admission of tragedy's intrinsic comedy, and can bring comedy to fruition only through awareness of its underlying tragic implications. As the tone deepens in *Officers and Gentlemen,* Waugh succeeds in expanding his ironic tone beyond either simple tragedy or comedy into ironic realism. Didion attempts to explain in practical terms what "hardness of mind" means in *Officers and Gentlemen,* indeed in the whole trilogy:

> One of the virtues of the hard mind is that it can deal simultaneously with an individual, his God, and his society, neither slighting nor magnifying the subtle delicate pressures each exerts upon the others.[67]

What this means in *Officers and Gentlemen* is that the tension created by the conflict of the narrator's overview with his implied sympathy for the hero, as in *Decline and Fall* or *A Handful of Dust,* is greatly lessened and therefore generates a more straightforward, realistic evaluation of society. This is true for two reasons. First, the setting of this novel, like *Men at Arms,* is historically real; it is the actual "modern age in arms"; Guy also, although a descendent of Paul Pennyfeather, is real—there is no longer any question of the hero's human dimensions. Second, Guy himself in the process of the two novels, especially in *Officers and Gentlemen,* gradually comes to an awareness that quite destroys all his early fond illusions about justice and honor, about all other noble medieval notions. These, plus the fact that the narrator continues to identify with the character even while most unmercifully satirizing his society, cause the novel to become not another satiric renunciation of modernity, but one which, while pessimistic and negative regarding civilization, is positive in its assertion of the superiority of the hero's values, although these values are doomed to annihilation.

---

67. *Ibid.,* p. 316.

The fact that the narrator can accept with resignation the foredoomed failure of Guy's pursuit of ideals, yet all the while confidently defend the superiority of these ideals, demonstrates a deepening of the ironic realism which characterized *Men at Arms*.

This particular tone is developed through the relationship of the narrator-persona with the character-persona, a relationship that stands in stark contrast to his detached stance in regard to the other significant characters and events in the same novel. The detachment of the narrator from the material first provides the basis of ironic commentary ranging from mild comic remarks to verbal barbs. For instance, in some cases the narrator appears to view the events in the friendly good humor which characterized most of *Men at Arms:*

> But the rebuke never took full shape; the strip, as he would have preferred it, was not torn off, for that moment there appeared from the outer hall the figure of Job, strangely illuminated. In some strictly private mood of his high drama Job has possessed himself of one of the six-branched silver candelabra from the dining room; this he bore aloft, rigid but out of the straight so that six little dribbles of wax bespattered his livery. All in the backhall fell silent and watched fascinated as this fantastic figure advanced upon the Air Marshal. A pace distant he bowed; wax splashed on the carpet before him (8–9).

Sometimes the narrator seems a bit less friendly, perhaps more serious:

> Generations of military history, the smoke of a hundred battlefields, darkened the issue (113).

> Half a dozen male figures stood at the rail. Tommy Blackhouse was there beside a sailor deeply laced with gold; General Whale was there; Brigadier Ritchie-Hook was there. Even, preposterously, Ian Kilbannock was there (125).

But the narrator is not always mild in his criticism; repulsed by what he is recording, he may engage in the most scornful ridicule, particularly of certain military activities. Describing Creforce HQ, he says:

> The headmen of the defeated tribe huddled on their haunches like chimps in a zoo. The paramount chief seemed to recognize Fido.
> This was not a people among whom toothless elders were held in honour. Strong yellow fangs gnawed the human sacrifice (264–65).

However, the extremes in tonal range in this novel, as noted earlier, are produced not merely by the narrator's overall view of activities, but primarily by his close relationship to the hero in contrast to his withdrawal from less noble characters. The most bitter elements of tone arise from the narrator's detachment from and rejection of the characters who do not embody the chivalric code as does Guy. Before in Waugh's novels the narrator relationship to significant minor characters has generally enhanced or complemented his relationship with the central character: for instance, by implication, the narrator views Brenda Last with a note of pathos; Apthorpe with good humor; Courteney with mild disgust; Hooper with benevolent superiority; even Lady Beste-Chetwynde with a kind of respect. But the minor characters have never figured as much in the tonal control of the novel as they do in *Officers and Gentlemen*. But the narrator's identification with the minor characters is distinguished from that with the hero; the narrator seems to assume what may be thought of as a "mock identity" with them, which allows him to satirize them even more thoroughly. And there is tonal and thematic purpose in this, for, in this way, he can offer a striking contrast between them and Guy, and at the same time imply his attitude toward both. Although the narrator assumes this mock identity with

several of the characters, including Virginia (97–98),
Marchpole (98–99), and even the nameless guests at Lady
Stitch's party (171), the most sustained satiric relationship is with Trimmer and Hound. And it is only logical
that the narrator's attitude toward these characters be
quite harsh. As noted in *Men at Arms*, the hero's plight
centers around his single-minded attempt to realize within his own life two interrelated ideals. One involves his
deeply rooted religious conviction, particularly regarding
his service to the Church but also his concern with a
successful marriage and the continuation of the Crouchback line; the other, his keen sense of duty to his country
not only as an aristocrat but as a citizen. Trimmer, thus,
becomes the antithesis of the first; Hound, of the second.

The satiric-ironic detachment and the consequent mockery characterizes all of the narrator's relationship with
Trimmer, although there does seem to be a glimmer of
humor in his view of this character:

> Trimmer was both shocked and slightly exhilarated by this
> news. The barrier between hairdresser and firstclass passenger
> was down. It was important to start the new relationship on the
> proper level—a low one. He did not fancy the idea of often acting
> as host at the Chateau de Madred (95).

> A telephone message bade him report next day at HOO HQ at a
> certain time, to a certain room. It boded only ill. He had come
> to the bar for stimulus, for a spot of pleasantry with 'les girls'
> and here, at his grand climacteric, in this most improbable of
> places, stood a portent, something beyond daily calculation. For
> in his empty days he had given much thought to his escapade
> with Virginia in Glasgow. So far as such a conception was feasible
> to Trimmer, she was a hallowed memory. He wished now
> Virginia were alone. He wished he were wearing his kilt. This
> was not the lovers' meeting he had sometimes adumbrated at his
> journey's end (178).

In the case of Fido Hound there is no humor, only a
very bitter, perhaps pathetic ridicule as the inglorious

major gradually but with calculable certainty falls irretrievably, absolutely from grace. Hound is without doubt Waugh's most despicable character. Even though the narrator is identified with him to the point of being able to describe directly and in minute detail the unrelenting torturous attack on his senses, there is obviously a pervasive contempt for this character; here the narrator's identity with the character works to intensify the satire, for it is counterbalanced by a rigid detachment akin to loathing:

> Nothing disturbed him. . . . There were no bombs or bullets here. All that was left of Hookforce rolled down the road overhead, but Fido did not hear. No sound penetrated to his kennel and in the silence two deep needs gnawed at him—food and orders. He must have both or perish. The day wore on. Towards evening an intolerable restlessness possessed him; hoping to stay his hunger, he lit his last cigarette and smoked it, slowly, greedily sucking until the glowing stub began to burn the tips of his fingers. Then he took one last deep breath and, as he did so, the smoke touched some delicate nerve of his diaphragm and he began to hiccup. The spasms tortured him in his cramped position; he tried lying full length; finally he crawled into the open. . . . It was the moment of evening when the milky wisp of moon became sharp and luminous. Fido saw none of this, each regular hiccup took him by surprise and was at once forgotten; between hiccups his mind was dull and empty, his eyes dazzled and fogged; there was a continuous faint shrilling in his ears as though from distant grasshoppers (257–58) .

Moreover, the narrator when referring to "Hound" does so constantly in canine analogies ("crouched," "kennel," "doggy," "sniffed") ; or, he may do so in pastoral, mock-heroic terms:

> Scattering Greek currency among the leaves, he subsided quite gently from branch to branch and when he reached ground continued to roll over and over, down and down, caressed and momentarily stayed by bushes until at length he came to rest as though borne there by a benevolent Zephyr of classical myth,

> in a soft, dark, sweet-smelling, empty place where the only sound
> was the music of falling water. And there for a time his descent
> ended. Out of sight, out of hearing, the crowded boats put out
> from the beach; the men-o'-war sailed away and Fido slept (266).

Sometimes even the style itself mocks Hound: "Fido snoozed," "Fido wept," "Fido stood," "Fido slept," "Fido subsided"; the narrator's choice of descriptive words also somewhat repulses the reader: "he gulped and panted and blubbed."

As the bitterly satiric elements of tone are thus sustained by the relationship of the narrator with Trimmer and Hound, the opposite end of the spectrum, the tragic, is approached through his relationship with Guy. In the narrator's identification with Guy there is explicit sympathy, particularly as Guy becomes more and more disillusioned. Even though there is frequently irony or at least the hint of ironic perspective, the narrator is implicitly sympathetic even in these passages:

> In Guy's dreams there were no exotic visitants among the shades
> of Creforce, no absurdity, no escape. Everything was as it had
> been the preceding day, the preceding night, night and day since
> he had landed at Suda, and when he awoke at dawn it was to
> the same half-world; sleeping and waking were like two airfields,
> identical in aspect though continents apart. He had no clear
> apprehension that this was a fatal morning, that he was that day
> to resign an immeasurable piece of his manhood. He saw himself
> dimly at a great distance. Weariness was all (296).

In all other passages dealing with Guy there is definite sympathetic identification. Particularly is this identification intense in the passages dealing with Guy's delirious reflections after the evacuation:

> Guy lay with his hands on the cotton sheet rehearsing his
> experiences.
> Could there be experience without memory? Could there be
> memory where fact and fancy were indistinguishable, where time

was fragmentary and elastic, made up of minutes that seemed like days, of days like minutes? He could talk if he wished to. He must guard that secret from them. Once he spoke he would re-enter their world, he would be back in the picture (305–6).

Because the narrator commonly appears in straightforward identification with Guy, there can be no doubt of his sympathy for Crouchback. Guy becomes a pathetic, even tragic, figure.

It is through this "broadness" of tone that the author is able to give serious dimensions of reality to the continuing theme originating in the alien's plight in a chaotic world; and, while this novel because of its dealing with the real world becomes more seriously pessimistic than its predecessor regarding the survival of values, it becomes at the same time, through the contrast offered by the narrator's obvious approval of the hero's ideals, a more positive affirmation of the superiority of the aristocratic code of responsibility and the public and private morality upheld by the doctrines of the Church.

Guy appears in *Officers and Gentlemen* as the same knight errant he was in *Men at Arms.* In fact, the narrator considers the second novel "the second stage of [Guy's] pilgrimage, which had begun at the tomb of Sir Roger" (17). Guy in *Officers and Gentlemen* continues to play the role of the crusading, Christian knight, epitomizing the chivalric ideal pitted against modern moral anarchy and sloth. Much like his earlier prototypes and especially like the Guy of *Men at Arms,* he is both devoted to his religion and dutifully loyal to his country, particularly in times of peril. But it may be that in the first few pages of *Officers and Gentlemen* Waugh ironically depicts the ineffectual though determined nature of the English Catholic aristocracy and already forecasts Guy's ultimate disillusionment with both religion and patriotism. Throughout the novel the quest is paramount, but there may be an ironic premonition in the first major episode in which the quest is ironically transformed into the search for Chatty Corner, the heir of Apthorpe's gear:

> An act of pietas was required of [Guy]; a spirit was to be placated. Apthorpe's gear must be retrieved and delivered before Guy was free to follow his fortunes in the King's service. His road lay backward for the next few days, to Southsand and Cornwall. 'Chatty' Corner, man of the trees, must be found, somewhere in the trackless forests of wartime England (18).

This lowly, even ridiculous, quest may be taken as a parody of Guy's original crusade, replete with high purpose and heraldry. What had begun as a holy crusade becomes, as a result of his entanglement in the chaos of the age, an attempt to deliver a preposterous bundle of gear to a monstrous caricature of civilization. Guy's attempts to deliver the inheritance is even referred to as a "quest": "The early stages of his quest had been easy" (44). It is not fanciful to think that Apthorpe's heterogeneous collection somehow parallels Guy's traditions and sense of honor, the awkward and cumbersome trappings of aristocracy; indeed, both seem quite out of place wherever they are found. Guy is thus appropriately rendered "immobile" and "alone" by Apthorpe's gear (45).

> Here it seemed he was doomed to remain forever, standing guard over a heap of tropical gadgets, like the Russian sentry he had once been told of, the Guardsman who was posted daily year in, year out, until the revolution, in the grounds of Tsarkoe Seloe on the spot where Catherine the Great had once wished to preserve a wild flower (46).

Chatty Corner, if the analogy is to be complete, must symbolize the depravity and beastliness of the contemporary age; although his "lair" reflects both medieval and Victorian architecture, there is nothing about the dwelling or the man that in any way suggests the survival of the values from either of these ages (see pp. 66–68). With the delivery of the materials and the signing of the receipt, the transaction is complete, the "quest" fulfilled:

> Suddenly the wind dropped. It was a holy moment. Guy rose in silence and ritually received the book (71).

However valid this interpretation of the Chatty Corner episode may be, there is in *Officers and Gentlemen* a complete fusion of the two primary thematic elements characteristic of the earlier novels: the typical Waugh theme thus far has included both the "theme of national irresponsibility and dislocation of value"[68] and also the complementary theme of the alien's pilgrimage and its significance as it relates to twentieth-century man in general. In *Officers and Gentlemen,* more than in any previous novel, these two elements merge almost into one integral portion of contemporary society, no doubt because the hero himself is almost completely integrated into that society. The hero cannot, like Paul Pennyfeather, detach himself from the world around him; nor is he allowed to be destroyed by his complete refusal to recognize reality; nor is he able to sentimentalize the prospects into optimism—his plight is indeed that of contemporary civilization, particularly that of England.

Guy, by birth an aristocrat, by nature honorable and patriotic, like his predecessors, is alienated from the masses who have already succumbed to the ravages of the modern age: the Cuthberts, for instance. Yet his experiences in *Officers and Gentlemen* begin to crack his knightly armor. As might be expected, Guy is portrayed consistently as an isolated figure, not physically, but spiritually; he is never quite "one of the family at all, merely a passing guest" (106–7):

> Guy stood between his friends, isolated. A few hours earlier he had exulted in his loneliness. Now the case was altered. He was

---

68. Carens, p. 160.

a 'guest from the higher formation,' a 'Hookforce body,' without place or function, a spectator. And all the deep sense of desolation which he had sought to cure, which from time to time momentarily seemed to be cured, overwhelmed him as of old. His heart sank. It seemed to him as though literally an organ of his body were displaced, subsiding, falling heavily like a feather in a vacuum jar; Philoctetes set apart from his fellows by an old festering wound; Philoctetes without his bow. Sir Roger without his sword (280–81).

Yet in *Officers and Gentlemen,* more even than in the preceding novel, reality begins to impinge upon his experience and hence upon his illusion. Here is the first element of theme: the decline of civilization; Waugh pushes to the front the theme of dislocation of values and moral anarchy. First, there is the deterioration of religion epitomized by Virginia; then society's loss of any sense of values or justice, its disorder and instability, represented by Trimmer; the decay of social order, seen expressly in the Cuthberts' treatment of Mr. Crouchback; finally, the loss of manly honor, epitomized by Major Hound. Guy soon learns, as Ludovic notes in his diary, that "all gentlemen are now very old" (249).

But one gets the idea that Guy could have endured these harsh realities, that the ideal is stronger than these, and that the illusion provides the invisible shield which protects Guy from the abrasion of his corrupt society. Guy can accept Virginia's unprincipled activity and bear the resulting cross; he can endure the realization that some priests are spies; he accepts Hound as he does the rest of the army, and can easily "dissociate himself from the army in matters of real concern" (161). These things weaken Guy's zealous trust in a higher order, but they are not lethal because his illusion is nurtured and sustained within himself and because his ideal of the officer and gentlemen is transformed into reality before his eyes in the person of Ivor Claire:

Guy thought instead with deep affection of X Commando. 'The
Flower of the Nation,' Ian Kilbannock had ironically called them.
He was not far wrong. There was heroic simplicity in Eddie
and Bertie. Ivor Claire was another pair of boots entirely, salty,
withdrawn, incorrigible. Guy remembered Claire as he first saw
him in the Roman spring in the afternoon sunlight amid the
embosoming cypresses of the Borghese Gardens, putting his horse
faultlessly over the jumps, concentrated as a man in prayer. Ivor
Claire, Guy thought, was the fine flower of them all. He was
quintessential England, the man Hitler had not taken into account, Guy thought (146–47).

Guy finds in Claire strength to sustain his illusion; Claire
provides the concrete realization of the spiritual values
Guy is committed to. Therefore, it is not unusual that
Guy should identify himself with this symbol:

> As for Guy, he had recognized from the first a certain remote
> kinship with this most dissimilar man, a common aloofness, dif-
> ferently manifested—a common melancholy sense of humour; each
> in his way saw life *sub specie aeternitatis;* thus with numberless
> reservations they became friends, as had Guy and Apthorpe (110).

It is only when this "flower of the nation" crumbles
before the onslaught of the modern age that Guy's ideal
is shattered. With Claire the deterioration begins slowly,
philosophically, but internally:

> 'I was thinking about honour. It's a thing that changes, doesn't
> it? I mean, a hundred and fifty years ago we would have had to
> fight if challenged. Now we'd laugh. There must have been a
> time a hundred years or so ago when it was rather an awkward
> question' (295).

> 'And in the next war, when we are completely democratic, I
> expect it will be quite honourable for officers to leave their men
> behind' (295).

When these musings are translated into cowardly deser-
tion in Crete, there can be no hope for Guy's maintaining the illusion:

> Guy lacked these simple rules of conduct. He had no old love
> for Ivor, no liking at all, for the man who had been his friend
> had proved to be an illusion (320).

Claire's betrayal has far-reaching effects on Guy; here
is the final bitter disillusionment. It is at this point, Bergonzi notes, that "Guy's self-knowledge is complete, and
the dominating myth of much of Waugh's work is deflated. Reality is too terrible and too various to be accounted for by any simple myth, any easy pattern of
heroics, no matter how splendid."[69] "The crusade turns
into an illusion."[70]

> He was back after less than two years' pilgrimage in a Holy
> Land of illusion in the old ambiguous world, where priests were
> spies and gallant friends proved traitors and his country was led
> blundering into dishonour (322).

This seems to signal the end of the original chivalric
quest which was begun in *A Handful of Dust*. Although
intermediate novels offered some little hope of success,
it ends as it must inevitably in disillusionment and failure;
Roger of Waybroke is hopelessly anachronistic. Overwhelmed, Guy becomes a reluctant accomplice of the
forces of evil by destroying evidence that would incrim-
inate Claire:

> That afternoon he took his pocket-book to the incinerator
> which stood in the yard outside the window, and thrust it in.
> It was a symbolic act; he stood like the man at Sphakia who
> dismembered his Bren and threw its parts one by one out into the
> harbour, splash, splash, splash, into the scum (322).

At this moment Guy loses his identity as the embodiment of aristocratic codes of duty and honor; the Waybroke fantasy is shattered. He seems to have become a

69. Bergonzi, p. 35.
70. O'Donnovan, p. 21.

part of a vicious, impersonal mechanism which is appeased only by the sacrifice of values for expediencies; he has become, like the machine-gunner, one who reacts only to imposed, if perverted, authority. Personal responsibility is given up; personal honor seems unimportant. Carens is correct in noting that:

> *Officers and Gentlemen* is not solely an aristocracy-worshipper's description of the collapse of values in the lower and middle classes during warfare, for Evelyn Waugh reveals, as burlesque turns to bitter irony, that even his aristocrats have failed him.[71]

Yet this does not in any way sully the "aristocratic principle of devotion and honor to God, which the symbolic figure of Sir Roger embodies";[72] this "remains untarnished."[73] Merely the collapse of those whom Waugh believes should embody Sir Roger's ideals is depicted. This is seen not only in Claire but also in Julia Stitch, a carryover from the world of Lady Metroland, who, as the pagan antithesis of Sir Roger, disregards both national and religious solemnities by tossing into the waste can the dog tags of the soldier whom Guy found dead in Crete. The immediate reference to Cleopatra drives home the paganism of the act: "Her eyes were one immense sea, full of flying galleys" (327).

As *Men at Arms* begins "with its hero inspired by an illusion," *Officers and Gentlemen* "ends with its deflation."[74] But the ideal is not completely forgotten; personal honor, although treacherously compromised, is not altogether lost. At least Waugh would have it that way at the beginning of the third installment in the trilogy. In the introduction of *Unconditional Surrender*, which provides a summary of the first two volumes, he says of Guy: "Personal honor alone remains" (4). Yet this re-

---

71. Carens, p. 163.
72. *Ibid.*, p. 164.
73. *Ibid.*, p. 165.
74. Stopp, p. 169.

mark comes six years after *Officers and Gentlemen* and, coming at the first of *Unconditional Surrender,* is likely more of an anticipation of the hero's response to the activities of that novel than a reflection of *Officers and Gentlemen.* One thing is certain, however: *Officers and Gentlemen* is the most pessimistic of all Waugh's novels, and, if taken as it must have been intended, strictly in a serious vein, it represents the kind of world view held later by Spruce in *Unconditional Surrender,* who, although editor of the magazine called *Survival,* believes "that the human race [is] destined to dissolve in chaos" (41).

There is little in the novel to indicate that Waugh holds out significant hope for aristocratic principles, for morality, or, consequently, for civilization at large. Yet, already Guy's disillusionment begins to engender not caustic rejection but resigned acceptance of the modern age and its helter-skelter moral codes; perhaps this indicates the achieving of a kind of compassionate wisdom, if not of human understanding. It is at least worth noting that the Halberdiers, that unfashionable, tedious, tradition-laden, ineffectual, but elite corps does endure; the last paragraph or so may be more thematic than dramatic:

> That afternoon Guy paraded on the square with a mixed squad of recruits and officers in training under Halberdier Colour-Sergeant Oldenshaw.
> '. . . I'll just run through the detail. The odd numbers of the front rank will seize the rifles of the even numbers of the rear rank with the left hand crossing the muzzles—all right? magazines turned outward—all right?—at the same time raising the piling swivels with the forefinger and thumb of both hands—all right?'
> All right, Halberdier Colour Sergeant Oldenshaw. All right.

7

The Finality of Mode

Unconditional Surrender (or, the American edition, *The End of Battle*), unlike the two previous installments of the Crouchback trilogy, cannot easily be read as a separate, self-contained work, for it is indeed a novel of denouement, particularly of the Crouchback saga and, in a sense, of all Waugh's fiction.

Unconditional Surrender brings Guy's quest to a conclusion, in the final analysis not so pessimistic as the title of the novel indicates. Throughout the novel there is as before evidence of military ineffectuality, decay of the aristocracy (Guy's father's death marks the passing of an order), and the inability of the Church to offer any real positive force for good in a confused and evil world. Guy returns to his unit convinced that the war is no longer a matter of justice or of right versus wrong; yet he believes that "personal honour alone remains." He sets about satisfying this honor: First he gallantly remarries Virginia, who is pregnant by Trimmer, but somehow this knightly deed does not fit his notion of genuine honor. Next, he self-consciously aids the Jewish refugees in Yugoslavia, assuming for the occasion the figure of Moses, Roger of Waybroke transformed, but even in this noble deed the illusion separates him from real humanity. Finally, after Virginia's death, Guy returns to England

and marries a rough-speaking, uncultured farm girl, thus effecting a rather strange union of the aristocracy and the common people; the ideal is finally brought into the realm of reality. The ideal, which began its development in the very earliest works, has not destroyed him but has integrated him into the world of real men.

Here, either in the novel proper or in the epilogue, characters and conflicts which were introduced previously in either *Men at Arms* or *Officers and Gentlemen* are neatly and finally dealt with; the novel reminds one of *Put Out More Flags*, with its summary dismissal of familiar characters of the previous novels, and the epilogue's catalogue of personal destinies is reminiscent of the final few pages of *Scoop*. There is no question that there is a note of finality in the author's dealings with the characters; for instance, of Virginia, the last of the Bright Young Things, the narrator has one of the minor characters comment:

'Virginia Troy was the last of twenty years' succession of heroines,' he said. 'The ghosts of romance who walked between the two wars.'

'Virginia was the last of them—the exquisite, the doomed and the damning, with the expiring voices—a whole generation younger. We shall never see anyone like her again in literature or in life and I'm very glad to have known her' (258–59).

There is implied here more than the mere "rounding off"[1] of the previous novels and the concluding of the activities of the various characters. It is as though in this novel, after much soul-searching and many tentative or oblique solutions, Waugh comes to grips at last with the implications of historical realities and with a real society which is evidently bent on destroying itself; now he is

1. James F. Carens, *The Satiric Art of Evelyn Waugh* (Seattle: University of Washington Press, 1966), p. 169.

able to offer a final realistic appraisal of the alien's chance of survival. Waugh has dealt with the real world before, beginning with *Put Out More Flags,* and the hero, in the course of the novels, has taken on human proportions, but it is not until *Unconditional Surrender* that the romanticism of *Brideshead Revisited* or the comic fantasy of even *Men at Arms* completely disappears. Any symbol of unreality that remains is quickly and unmercifully dispelled by the reality of war—Mr. Crouchback and Ritchie-Hook, for example. *Unconditional Surrender* is Waugh's *de profundis:* here is a final view of the predicament of contemporary man and, perhaps surprisingly, a rather positive assertion of the "survival of values" (56). And the artistry is up to the demands of the theme, which must be methodically and persistently worked out and emphatically concluded. It is as though Waugh summons up the best of the previous techniques, refines and adapts them to the material and theme at hand, and so manipulates these factors as to produce a truly well-wrought conventional novel.

In *Unconditional Surrender,* obviously a more conventional novel than even the two immediate predecessors, the typical satiric-ironic techniques used previously in formulation of narrative, theme, and tone, while still present, are kept well below the surface. Even though the cutting edge of the irony is gone, one gets the notion that this novel could not have been written by anyone other than the author of both *A Handful of Dust* and *Brideshead Revisited,* for elements of these two novels recur refined and modulated in this novel. And, while these previous novels at first may seem nothing at all like *Unconditional Surrender,* close observation coupled with a recognition of the continuing and developing techniques and themes of all the preceding fiction not only reveals an affinity of this novel with the others, but also demonstrates the extent to which Waugh has refined and modified his original basic technique and the degree to which he has tempered the original satirical attacks and subdued the later burst of romantic optimism.

However subtle the technique of this novel, the narrative devices, the thematic development, and the tonal control all find their origin again in the author's controlled relationship of the narrator-persona and the character-persona, why by now are frequently not only one in narrative point of view but evidently one in sentiment as well; yet, in dramatic function they remain distinct entities. Thus, there is variation within the narrative process, realistic perspective in theme, and enough tension in tonal factors to prevent sentimentality but enough identification to suffuse the novel with a completely serious tone. There is a blending of the novel's narrative, tonal, and thematic qualities not seen to this degree in Waugh's fiction since *A Handful of Dust,* and there not within the framework of a conventional novel nor in the expression of positive moral views.

First the narrative. Essentially, the narrative formulation of *Unconditional Surrender* is a modified extension of that found in *Officers and Gentlemen;* that is, there is an active, identifiable narrator who omnisciently commands a dramatic overview of the events, historical or fictional, and who, at the same time, is able to see from various points of view within the story—particularly that of the central character. Again, the narrator relates the episodes in effective dramatic sequence, maintaining throughout his own identity and an appreciable degree of detachment. But there are some distinctions to be made between the narrative formulation of *Officers and Gentlemen* and that of *Unconditional Surrender,* distinctions that indicate the degree of refinement to which Waugh brings his art in this novel. The dual vision of *Officers and Gentlemen,* which allowed simultaneously explicit rejection of unsavory characters and sympathetic identification with the hero, is manifest in *Unconditional Surrender,* but the extreme polarity (particularly as affects tone) is diminished. In fact, there seems to be a return to the synthesis of the narrator and character roles as in *Men at Arms.* In other words, the expanded narrative roles of narrator and character, particularly of the narrator, and hence the wider tonal range, as found in *Officers and Gentlemen,* are here contracted into a union in narrative which centers primarily on the narrator's internal function and his identification with the hero. In narrative process the narrator is more reliant upon the characters, particularly the minor characters, such as Virginia and Ludovic; and his narrative and tonal identification with the hero becomes not only a matter of point of view, but an "absolute"[2] identification.

This is not to say that the narrator and Guy do not have separate dramatic roles, but that these roles are drawn into greater unity and ultimately into a precisely modulated ironic realistic tone. Here as before the narrator functions separately outside the structure of the novel. He is easily identified as the external "maker" of the novel, who with an omniscient perspective also enjoys ironic potential; yet, there seems to be in *Unconditional Surrender* a rather successful attempt to interfuse the external dramatic necessities into the internal developments in plot. The narrator unifies the novel by the arrangement of the episodes surrounding the hero; the order of his narrative sequence provides both progression of plot and thematic emphasis. Yet it is left primarily to the central character to provide the internal unifying factor in both plot and theme.

Perhaps the nature of the narrator's function may be quickly summarized by noting the general method of narration itself. In *Men at Arms* the narrator used pri-

2. Richard J. Voorhees, "Evelyn Waugh's War Novels: A Toast to Lost Causes," *Queens Quarterly* 65 (Spring, 1958) : 57.

marily a detailed summary technique in presentation
of the action. As a result the novel was developed more
organically, from within; there did not appear to be
the random cinematic-like selection of events as in some
of the earlier novels. In *Officers and Gentlemen* there was
a marked tendency to dramatize the action, as indicated
by the increase in dialogue and the narrator's own more
direct reporting of events; as a result, there seemed to
be a greater potential of ironic detachment on the part
of the narrator and also the reader, particularly in regard to characters other than the hero. In *Unconditional
Surrender,* there is a balance of these two methods: there
is crisp, directly reported dialogue and dramatic scenes
(see p. 49); but there is also detailed narrator summary
(see pp. 77, 81, 96, 169, 245). The first moves the narrative in an entertaining, cinematic manner from without; the second, from within, allows and is demonstrated
in the telescoping of chronology, narrative transitions,
and interpretive elaborations on the events. While the
narrator is controlling externally the narrative, he is also
developing the narrative internally by close identification with a host of characters. Therefore, throughout the
novel there runs a counterbalanced attachment-detachment potential: the narrator is external "maker" but he
also functions as an internal controlling, shaping factor;
when the attachment-detachment potential is extended
to practically every character as it is in this novel, it
very likely means that the author has not only expanded
his narrative range but also his sympathy.

The narrator's external function is first apparent in
the structure of the novel. There is a prologue which
connects narratively and thematically this final installment
to the preceding novels; there is also an epilogue, con-
taining the account of events which are removed from
the main narrative in time by about six or seven years
and geographically by a continent, and this not only pro-

vides the narrative conclusion of the Crouchback crusade but also crystallizes the theme of the entire trilogy. But even more demonstrative of the narrator's external control is the "Synopsis of Preceding volumes," which positions the characters, primarily Guy, for the final act in the drama. Here the narrator quotes frequently from *Men at Arms* and *Officers and Gentlemen,* and even offers his own rather critical interpretation of the two preceding volumes. For instance, the narrator notes that the early Guy saw the war "as an opportunity to re-establish his interest in his fellow men and to serve them" (2). What seemed at the time in *Men at Arms* a rather cruel reproach by Virginia, becomes now at the narrator's suggestion merely "mild ridicule" (2). He also supplies information about the preceding volumes which was lacking in them; for example, he notes that "it is to be supposed that Ludovic perpetrated or connived his [Hound's] murder" (3). This is a necessary inference from *Officers and Gentlemen,* but another bit of information supplied here might not be so apparent from the text of the earlier novel:

> Ludovic believes that Guy knows the truth of the disappearance of 'Fido' Hound. He does know and has proof in the written orders to the rearguard, the full culpability of Claire's desertion (3).

In *Officers and Gentlemen,* it is implied that only Julia Stitch knows this, but that Ludovic more likely thinks that Guy knows the truth about the death of the sapper who vanished overboard during the escape from Crete. Thematically, there is the narrator's brief account of the alien's struggle with an ideal and a summary of the state of the alien after two volumes of little or no success:

> As Guy, in the late Autumn of 1941, rejoins his regiment he believes that the just cause of going to war has been forfeited in the Russian alliance. Personal honour alone remains.

> The hallucination was dissolved, like the whales and turtles on the voyage from Crete, and he was back after less than two years' pilgrimage in a Holy Land of Illusion in the old ambiguous world, where priests were spies and gallant friends proved traitors and his country was led blundering into dishonour (4).

This kind of obvious narrator manipulation and commentary is not confined to the synopsis or the epilogue, but shows up continually throughout the novel in ways by now familiar in Waugh's fiction. For example, there is first a great deal of dramatic shifting of scenes, although here not so abruptly as before:

> Then she informed him, without any extenuation or plea for compassion, curtly almost, that she was with child by Trimmer.
> Ian and Kerstie Kilbannock returned to London from Scotland on the night of Childermas (189; see also 23–34, 144, 160).

Such shifts are effective not only as a subtle ironic counterpointing technique, but they also provide a realistic panorama of simultaneity; some, in fact, seem designed not so much for dramatic effect as for a continuing unification of the various subplots:

> 'Do you think things will ever be normal again?'
> 'Oh, no,' said Peregrine Crouchback. 'Never again.'
> Meanwhile Guy and Virginia were together in London (185).

> After the Absolution he said: 'You are a foreigner?'
> 'Yes.'
> 'Can you spare a few cigarettes?'
> In Westminster Cathedral at almost the same time Virginia made her first confession (220; see also 185, 205, 238, 259).

That the narrator has complete external control of the material is noted also in at least one subtle narrator flashback, which, by the way, springs from Guy, regarding the Loot's background (22–23). But this same kind of omniscience, if not the same degree of narrator control, is demonstrated in less dramatically informative passages:

Captain Fremantle was a simple man. Before the war he had served in a lowly capacity in an insurance company. His post for the last three years had given him an occasional glimpse into arcane matters. Too many strange persons had briefly passed through his narrow field of vision for him to be totally unaware of the existence of an intricate world of deception and peril that lay beyond his experience. Roughly speaking he was ready to believe anything he was told. De Souza confused him only by suggesting so much (141).

Again, the narrator functions omnisciently as a historian who not only has at hand detailed information regarding the histories of the characters but also can provide genuine historical information about countries and events of World War II. As as example of the first, the narrator is still particularly concerned with Guy's heritage:

The Catholic parish church is visible from the little station yard; a Puginesque structure erected by Guy's great-grandfather in the early 1860's at the nearer extremity of the village street. At the further end stands the mediaeval church of which the nave and chancel are in Anglican use while the north aisle and adjoining burying ground are the property of the lord of the manor. It was in this plot that Mr. Crouchback's grave had been dug and in this aisle that his memorial would later stand among the clustered effigies and brasses of his forebears (72–73).

Regarding events of actual history the narrator admits to being something of an external summarizer:

At the end of the first week of that December, History records, Mr. Winston Churchill introduced Mr. Roosevelt to the Sphinx. Fortified by the assurances of their military advisers that the Germans would surrender that winter, the two puissant old gentlemen circumambulated the colossus and silently watched the shadows of evening obliterate its famous features (63).

But there is a new refinement in the blending of the historical with the fictional which makes *Unconditional Surrender* outdistance even *Men at Arms* in seriousness of narrative material. The lengthy passage introducing Bari is an excellent example of the narrator's fusing fictional and historical material. In the narration, he begins his description of that city with a reference to its antiquity:

> Few foreigners visited Bari from the time of the Crusades until the fall of Mussolini. Few tourists, even the most assiduous, explored the Apulian coast. Bari contains much that should have attracted them; the old town full of Norman building, the bones of St. Nicholas enshrined in silver; the new town spacious and commodious. But for centuries it lay neglected by all save native businessmen (215–16).

Here are genuine historical events, people, and places; he concludes the first paragraph with "Guy had never set foot there" (216). The next paragraph relates a relatively recent and historically significant occurrence in Bari ("the only place in the Second World War to suffer from gas" because a ship full of "mustard" blew up in the harbour); then, the city is described in its present confused condition:

> Now, early in 1944, the city had recovered the cosmopolitan, martial stir it enjoyed in the Middle Ages. Allied soldiers on short leave, some wearing, ironically enough, the woven badge of the crusader's sword, teemed in its streets; wounded filled its hospitals; the staffs of numberless services took over the new, battered office-buildings which had risen as monuments to the Corporative State. Small naval craft adorned the shabby harbour (316).

As easily, the fictitious characters become caught up in the horror and reality of the war:

> Belgrade fell to the Russians, Bulgarians and partisans. A day of rejoicing was declared in Begoy by the Praesidium. The concert and the *Vin d'Honneur*, postponed in mourning, were held in triumph. On order from high authority a *Te Deum* was sung in the church, re-opened for that day and served by a new priest whom the partisans had collected during their expansion into

Dalmatia. At nightfall the anti-fascist choir sang. The anti-fascist theatre group staged a kind of pageant of liberation. Wine and slivovic were copiously drunk and Guy through the interpreter made a formal little acknowledgment of the toast to Winston Churchill (296).

The narrator also provides throughout the novel omniscient descriptions as before (see pp. 93, 198, 212, 213, 223). But as it might be expected in this novel in which the narrator tends to identify closely with the several characters, most of the description is handled through the points of view of the characters:

> He had chosen these rooms because they were secluded from the scaffolds and platforms where the training exercises took place at the front of the house. He faced, across half an acre of lawn, what the previous owners had called their 'arboretum.' Ludovic thought of it merely as 'the trees.' Some were deciduous and had now been stripped bare by the east wind that blew from the sea, leaving the holm oaks, yews and conifers in carefully contrived patterns, glaucous, golden and of a green so deep as to be almost black at that sunless noon; they afforded no pleasure to Ludovic (114).

All of this brings up an interesting point regarding the narrator's role. In *Unconditional Surrender* the narrator, operating more freely than in any novel since *Black Mischief,* relies heavily upon "minor" characters for progression of the narrative. This method demonstrates the narrator's externality, particularly in the cases where the ironic potential is partially or fully realized as with Trimmer and Hound in *Officers and Gentlemen.* But on the other hand it has the effect of bringing the narrator into the narrative, especially when the narrator's identification with the characters is either straightforward or less ironical than before. The narrator's exact attitude toward the various characters will be discussed later in regard to tone, but the fact that the narrator is free to enter the minds of any of the several characters in a progressive, unified drama and thus become an internal narrative factor, yet all the while maintain his own identity and objective perspective, is an indication of the technical achievement of this novel.

The narrator uses Ludovic more than any other minor character; to do this he often identifies with this character and his narrative stance is not generally withdrawn. A second narrative figure is Virginia; the narrator seems even closer to her than to Ludovic. A third is Ian. There are several others, but the narrator's relationship to these is indicative of the manner in which both the necessary externality and desired identification are simultaneously achieved; in no case is the narrator completely withdrawn, but he usually closely identifies with the character under consideration. On the one hand externality is demonstrated by the very fact that the narrator can move from one character's mind to another's; on the other, by reporting even their mental activity in what appears to be internal detailed summary, he is drawn into the narrative itself. As might be expected, it is the narrator's identification with the hero that is the central factor both in narrative progression and narrative unity. But this identification is not an unbroken narrative thread as it is in *Men at Arms;* it is an intermittent relationship which, even in its absence, serves as the narrative reference point.

It is not until rather late in the novel that the real narrator identification with Guy begins. Before this the same relationship between narrator and character found in *Men at Arms* and *Officers and Gentlemen* has been more or less implied, but little other than the "synopsis" and prologue has necessitated the hero's presence or the narrator's identification with him in the narrative. The narrator, quite apart from the character, in the first three chapters of "State Sword" introduces the conditions on the home front, Lieutenant Padfield, Major Ludovic, the Kilbannocks, Virginia, and several other less important characters, new and old. But at the beginning of chapter 3, there is reestablished the narrator identification with the hero that is to be sustained through the entire narrative:

> Guy felt that he had been given a birthday present; the first for how many years? The card that had come popping out of the Electronic Personnel Selector bearing his name, like a 'fortune' from a seaside slot-machine, like a fortune indeed in a more real sense—the luck of the draw in a lottery or sweepstake— brought an unfamiliar stir of exhilaration, such as he had felt in his first days in the Halberdiers, in his first minutes on enemy soil at Dakar; a sense of liberation such as he had felt when he had handed over Apthorpe's legacy to Chatty Corner and when he broke his long silence in the hospital in Alexandria (53).

From this point on, this identification with the hero carries the burden of the narration and also controls the tone (see pp. 146, 197, 230–31, 268). As the narrator continues to identify with the hero, the narrative points of view become indistinguishable, much as in *Men at Arms*.

So interfused are the identities of the narrator and the character that they become one not only in narrative but also, as will be noted later in detail, in sentiment. Therefore, there is not here the narrative, nor the tonal, tension between the narrator and character that is found in the earlier works, because narrator and hero are essentially the same in sensibility and world view; there is not the absolute identification found in *Brideshead Revisited* if for no other reason than the third-person point of view and the dramatic distance of person; there is restraint if not dramatic tension.

As a result of this close narrative identification, Guy serves as more than a mechanical device for entering various social areas; Guy is indeed a "spectator" (290) or a "tourist" (218) who circumambulates among the strata of the civilized world, but here he does so obviously with and through the sensibilities of the narrator:

Guy went out and found the farmyard and the lane beyond
thronged. There were some children in the crowd, but most
seemed old, too old to be the parents, for they were unnaturally
aged by their condition. Everyone in Begoy, except the peasant
women, was in rags, but the partisans kept regimental barbers and
there was a kind of dignity about their tattered uniforms. The
Jews were grotesque in their remnants of bourgeois civility. They
showed little trace of racial kinship (226).

It is in this way that Guy provides opportunity for narrator commentary and reaction to the several areas of
society. Generally, the responses are not the bitter satirical
jabs characteristic of the previous novels; nor can they
be, for the narrator is too close to the material; there is
a "new spirit abroad" in the part of the narrator, a
spirit of compassion, perhaps wisdom, which is reflected
in the closer narrative identification of the narrator with
the several characters, but which finds its full expression
in the subdued tone of the novel.

As suggested in the discussion of narrative formulation,
there is in the posture of the narrator a great deal of
ironic potential, yet, as also indicated, this irony is generally suppressed by the narrator's closer identification
with the various characters and by his obvious special
identification with the hero. As one reviewer of *Unconditional Surrender* notes, Waugh "has grown and expanded the range not only of his expression but also of
his sympathies."[3] Thus, the dominant tone of the novel
becomes one that reflects not only an uncolored objective
vision of the decadent modern society, but one also that
implies a kind of wise, benevolent acceptance of the decadence, yet, at the same time, sympathy with the alien.
It is in this novel that Waugh's ironic realism emerges
as a philosophy of life. Here as in *Men at Arms* and *Officers and Gentlemen*, there is an ironic dual vision which

3. "The New Waugh," *Times Literary Supplement* (October 27, 1961),
p. 770.

makes for satiric possibilities; as Carens suggests, this novel "reveals an intense satiric vision of the social and moral consequences of the Second World War."[4] Yet the irony of *Officers and Gentlemen* is tempered by sympathetic identification even with the representatives of moral and social decadence.

The comparative gentle irony that pervades this novel and the potentiality for more bitter ridicule is evidenced in several of the narrator's methods. First, he reveals his ironic detachment, and hence the ironic capability, in many cases by parenthetically supplying knowledge which is designed to call attention to ironies in the situation at hand which might go unnoticed otherwise. For example, of General Whale, he says:

> Sometime back General Whale had forfeited the kindly sobriquet of 'Sprat' and was now known in the lower and more active regions of his command as 'Brides-in-the-Bath'; for the reason that all the operations he sponsored seemed to require the extermination of all involved (26).

Nor are the observations always touched with humor; later of Major Marchpole, the narrator notes in passing:

> This man was in fact at that moment busy despatching royalist officers—though he did not know it—to certain execution (304).

At other times, the narrator himself ventures his own observations and commentary on the events, this also from a relatively detached position; there are subtle variations in the tones of these comments. First, he objectively suggests the dramatic nature of the situation or the character under consideration. Of Sir Ralph Brompton he says:

> He seemed a figure of obsolescent light comedy rather than of total war (27).

---

4. Carens, p. 173.

He describes the conversation between Virginia and Guy as "light as the heaviest drawing-room comedy" because as he points out "each had a dread at heart" (186). Or he may ironically reveal personal secrets of the characters:

> There was a mood of exuberance, almost of exultation, in the ante-room that evening. The eleven surviving members of the squad had made their second jump in weather of undisturbed tranquillity. They had overcome all their terrors of the air and were confident of finishing the course with honour. Some sprawled at their ease in the armchairs and sofas; some stood close together laughing loud and long. Even Gilpin was not entirely aloof from the general conviviality. He said: 'I don't mind admitting now I didn't quite like the look of it the first time,' and accepted a glass of bottled beer from the despatching officer who had that morning ignominiously bundled him into space and stepped on his fingers as he clutched the edge of the man-hole in vain resistance to the force of the slip-stream (131).

Second, the narrator may offer rather sly but apparently harmless notes on the characters and the events, yet in some of these there is still a tinge of bitterness and almost always serious overtones. For example of Virginia and Kerstie, he says:

> So the two of them, who had 'come out' the same year and led such different lives, the one so prodigal, the other so circumspect and sparing, spread out Virginia's possessions over the grubby sofa and spent all that evening like gypsy hucksters examining and pricing those few surviving trophies of a decade of desirable womanhood, and in the end went off to bed comforted, each in her way, and contented with their traffic (52).

Rising to a kind of compassionate ridicule, the narrator describes Peregrine's reaction to Virginia's visiting Guy:

> What did he suspect? Assassination? Seduction? He stood studying the pair of them as the statesmen had studied the Sphinx,

not really expecting an utterance, but dimly conscious of the existence of problems beyond his scope (166).

Somewhat in the old wildly satiric vein, he comments on HOO HQ:

> In HOO HQ there was stagnation in the depleted offices. The more bizarre figures remained—the witch-doctor and the man who ate grass—but the planners and the combatants had melted away. In the perspective of 'Overlord,' that one huge hazardous offensive operation on which, it seemed, the fate of the world depended, smaller adventures receded to infinitesimal importance (239).

But, even the most caustic satire and the most rollicking humor is always tempered by the narrator's awareness of the dead seriousness of the activities in the real world; these he continually blends into the narrative: "There was a congress at Teheran at the time entirely occupied with quantitative judgments" (162).

There is yet a third manner in which the narrator demonstrates his ironic detachment from the characters; that is, by his style. In this method especially one cannot fail to catch a glimpse of the mischievous narrator of the early satiric novels. Some of the stylistic devices are merely stock comic tricks of language. Of Spruce's secretaries, he says: "They gave him their full devotion; also their rations of butter, meat and sugar" (43). Of the Loot's providing escort for Guy and Ian: "The Lieutenant had fulfilled his manifest destiny in bringing them here" (57). Other similar turns in language reflect a greater distance from the characters, although not so great as in earlier novels; there is a kind of gentle mockery predicated on dignified Keatsian or Biblical phrases. Possibly reflecting Keats are comments such as, "It was the *season of mists* and Guy felt the chill of anticipated failure" (294); or "Leisure, *bonhomie* and futility *had him in thrall*" (218, italics mine). The style in such instances calls attention to the narrator's detached and mildly ironic view; but the Biblical or religious phrases are more apparent and more easily adaptable to high ridicule:

> Into this jolly company Ludovic entered like the angel of death (131).

> There was no longer peace in the valley (285).

> The grocer and lawyer had gone ahead into the promised land (296).

> It was indeed as though the Red Sea had miraculously drawn asunder and left a dry passage between walls of water (302).

Such stylistic irony seems at its sharpest when aimed at Ludovic or Virginia; in descriptions of both, the style at times reaches burlesque proportions:

> And Ludovic was writing. Since the middle of December he had without remission written 3,000 words a day; more than a hundred thousand words. His manner of composition was quite changed. Fowler and Roget lay unopened. He felt no need now to find the right word. All words were right. They poured from his pen in disordered confusion. He never paused; he never revised. He barely applied his mind to his task. He was possessed, the mere amanuensis of some power, not himself, making for— what? He did not question. He just wrote. His book grew as little Trimmer grew in Virginia's womb without her conscious collaboration.

This passage contains the harshest satire in the novel. But even here the satirical potential obviously is not exploited; the gentleness with which these passages are handled is reminiscent of the mock heroic passages describing William Boot's reports from Ishmaelia. So even though there is satiric potential, the narrator's closer identification with the several characters precludes its being fully realized. This is the same attachment that is reflected in the narrative formulation: as the narrator moves freely into the minds of the characters, the ironic distance is decreased; but even more than this there seems to be a change in the personality of the narrator from a critical to a compassionate disposition. There is none of the external "mock-identification" with the characters here as in the case of Hound or Trimmer in *Officers and Gentlemen;* the repulsive has become tolerable, if not pitiable.

The character who should be, by all indications of the earlier novels, the principal object of a satirical attack is Ludovic, the articulate, scheming pansy who as a corporal did away with Major Hound and who is now, ironically enough, himself major and in charge of a parachute training school. Yet, even in the narrator's admittedly ironic portrait of Ludovic, there is more than a suggestion of pathos; there is at least implied a capacity for compassion:

> Ludovic walked alone among the trees. What had been paths were ankle deep in dead leaves and cones and pine needles. His glossy boots grew dull. Presently he turned back and, avoiding the French windows, entered by a side door and the back stairs. On his table lay a great plate of roast meat—a week's ration for a civilian—a heap of potatoes and cold thick gravy, and beside it a pudding of sorts. He gazed at these things, wondering what to do. The bell did not work nor, had it done so, were the mess orderlies trained to answer it. He could not bear to sit beside this distasteful plethora waiting to see what would become of it. He took to the woods once more. Now and then an aeroplane came in to land or climbed roaring above him. Dusk began to fall. He was conscious of damp. When at last he returned to his room, the food was gone. He sat in his deep chair while the gathering dusk turned to darkness (116–17).

If such passages do imply a degree of narrator sympathy, it may be significant that the epilogue finds Ludovic, unlike Hound, Ambrose, or even Tony Last, who are destroyed, happily situated and busily engaged in what has turned out to be a quite successful career (310). This kind of narrator identification with character is extended also

to more odious, more tedious characters: Peregrine, Sir
Ralph Brompton, Gilpin, and others; although they do
not fare so well as Ludovic in the novel, they are never
subjected to the harsh satire found even as late as the
previous novel. Virginia, particularly, offers an excellent
example of the narrator's sympathetic identification with
the characters and this is seen nowhere better than in her
interview with Peregrine:

> 'Peregrine, have you never been to bed with a woman?'
> 'Yes,' said Uncle Peregrine smugly, 'twice. It is not a thing I
> normally talk about.'
> 'Do tell.'
> 'Once when I was twenty and once when I was forty-five. I
> didn't particularly enjoy it.'
> 'Tell me about them.'
> 'It was the same woman.'
> Virginia's spontaneous laughter had seldom been heard in re-
> cent years; it had once been one of her chief charms. She sat
> back in her chair and gave full, free tongue; clear, unrestrained,
> entirely joyous, without a shadow of ridicule. . . .
> 'Oh, Peregrine,' said Virginia at last with radiant sincerity,
> 'I love you' (173–74).

Carens thinks that Virginia in this novel, and particularly
in this novel, "has a genuineness and warmth never
glimpsed in her predecessors."[5] In this way the narrator's
(and the author's) sympathies are extended inside the
ironic framework; thus, the author approaches again
within the exigencies of the ironic mode a tone of ironic
realism, a tone at once too light for tragedy and too
serious for comedy, yet a fusion of both.

While it is true that the tone is influenced greatly by
the mellowed responses of the narrator to less heroic characters, it is the narrator's identification with Guy that
provides the primary tonal factor in the book. And his
view of Guy is not blurred by the rose-tints of romanti-

---

5. *Ibid.*, p. 170.

cism as in *Brideshead Revisited;* he has a well-defined, objective view of the hero, yet there is no doubt that it is Guy who commands his deepest sympathies, so deep in fact that there is little if any humor in the activities of Guy in this novel. In *Unconditional Surrender* this relationship does not have to be established for it continues from *Men at Arms* and *Officers and Gentlemen* which ended on a note of tragedy—complete disillusionment; it is on the same low note that *Unconditional Surrender* begins. In this final novel of the trilogy, as narrative points of view merge, so does the sentiment of the narrator with his character. There is very little irony and no satire involved in his portrayal of Guy in this novel. In fact, one or two examples of ironic detachment almost exhaust the supply:

> At length the Lieutenant departed on his work of mercy, leaving Guy to *Survival.*
> This was the issue on which little Fido had gorged. It had gone to press long before Everard Spruce received Ludovic's manuscript. Guy turned the pages without interest. It compared unfavourably in his opinion with the Squadron Leader's 'comic' particularly in the matter of draughtsmanship. Everard Spruce, in the days when he courted the marxists, dissembled a discreditable, personal preference for Fragonard above Leger by denying all interest in graphic art, affirming stoutly and correctly that the Workers were solidly behind him in his indifference. 'Look at Russia,' he would say. But the Ministry of Information in the early days of *Survival,* before the Russian alliance, had pointed out that since Hitler had proclaimed a taste for 'figurative' painting, defence of the cosmopolitan *avant garde* had become a patriotic duty in England. Spruce submitted without demur and *Survival* accordingly displayed frequent 'art supplements,' chosen by Coney and Frankie. There was one such in the current issue, ten shiny pages of squiggles. Guy turned from them to an essay by the pacific expatriate Parsnip, tracing the affinity of Kafka to Klee. Guy had not heard of either of these famous names (156).

There is little satire of Guy in this or any other passage;

however, in other ways, the narrator allows Guy to come under cross-fire examination which may produce ironic overtones. After agreeing to remarry his wife, now pregnant by Trimmer, Guy is challenged by Kerstie:

> 'You poor bloody fool,' said Kerstie, anger and pity and something near love in her voice, 'you're being *chivalrous*—about *Virginia*. Can't you understand men aren't chivalrous any more and I don't believe they ever were? Do you really see Virginia as a damsel in distress?' (192).

However, even this episode is colored by the narrator's obvious sympathy for Guy and his ideal.

Amis therefore notes with disapproval that most of the comic or serio-comic narrator response is to the antic Ludovic (as previously it had been to Hound and Trimmer), and that Guy escapes scot free any indignities:

> Ludovic draws the laughs Crouchback cannot be allowed to draw, Hound and Trimmer meet the serio-comic humiliations reserved for persons who have no dignity to start with.[6]

As a result, Amis says Guy is crimped into something less than real by his not being able to share in the activities around him and by the narrator's refusal to view him also ironically. There is possibly one exception in which Guy is allowed to cut somewhat of a comic figure; that is the hospital incident, but even this episode has serious overtones in regard to Guy's situation. Only the attendant, who reads comic books, is in the least satirized; Guy's problem is a serious one:

> With pain and enormous effort he hobbled across the ward supporting himself by the ends of the empty beds. In a corner stood the almost hairless broom with which the attendant was supposed to dust the floor. Using this as a crutch, Guy stumbled into the open. He recognized the buildings; the distance across

6. Kingsley Amis, "Crouchback's Regress" *The Spectator* (October 27, 1961), p. 581.

the asphalt yard to the officers' mess would have been negligible to a whole man. For the first time since his unhappy landing Guy felt the full pain of his injury (146–47).

But there is ample reason for this benevolent view of the hero. The narrator is seriously emotionally involved in the struggles of Guy and is obviously sympathetic with him in his frustration:

> Guy's prayers were directed to, rather than for, his father. For many years now the direction in the *Garden of the Soul*, 'Put yourself in the presence of God,' had for Guy come to mean a mere act of respect, like the signing of the Visitors' Book at an Embassy or Government House. He reported for duty saying to God: 'I don't ask anything from you. I am here if you want me. I don't suppose I can be of any use, but if there is anything I can do, let me know,' and left it at that.
>
> 'I don't ask anything from you'; that was the deadly core of his apathy; his father had tried to tell him, was now telling him. That emptiness had been with him for years now even in his days of enthusiasm and activity in the Halberdiers. Enthusiasm were not enough. God required more than that. He had commanded all men to *ask* (80).

Yet despite the emotional attachment, there are maintained throughout the novel separate dramatic roles and some degree of ironic perspective. The narrator's "hardness of mind" thus allows him to accept realistically the incompatibility of Guy's original, heroic ideal with the valueless contemporary society, and yet quietly exult in Guy's personal paradoxical triumph; a comparison of his (and Guy's) view of the quest at the beginning of the novel with the attitude toward the same quest at the end of the novel is revealing:

> But it was not for this that he had dedicated himself on the sword of Roger of Waybroke that hopeful morning four years back (13).
>
> Guy had come to the end of the crusade to which he had devoted himself on the tomb of Sir Roger. His life as a Halber-

dier was over. All the stamping of the barrack square and the
biffing of imaginary strongholds were finding their consummation
in one frustrated act of mercy (301).

Irony is not compromised; but the narrator's (or author's) sympathy with Guy and his crusade is not disguised.
It is, rather, turned into a tolerant, resigned wisdom. By
lessening the intensity of the satire aimed at representatives of a decadent society and by adopting a more realistic, even resigned, view of the incompatibility of the
hero's ideals with that of his society, but while never
losing sight of the nobility of the hero's quest, Waugh
through tone alone formulates an ironic realism that
provides the philosophic substructure of the novel, a philosophy conducive to and active in the final crystallization
of theme. The tone at last can sustain the theme and
convey an attitude which finds traditional human values
and contemporary human needs not only compatible but
also complementary, and this not in a fantastically contrived world, not in a many-splendored Arcadia, not even
in the manner in which the author at first supposed and
lately hoped, but in the real world, in the physical suffering and confusion of war, within the individual human
spirit.

Unconditional Surrender blends previous thematic
components into a lucid final pronouncement regarding
the decline and fall of civilization and the foredoomed
quest of the alien to fulfill the demands of his own personal values, which somehow no longer have any meaning
among other men. The emphasis in *Unconditional Surrender* is on both the decadence of British society and the
plight of the alien. The conditions of the nation during
the war period are more than a backdrop to add a touch
of reality or seriousness to a tale of romantic, if noble,
notions turned into a quest; and the central character is
more than a mechanical device for exploring these areas.

The theme thus becomes at once a commentary on the otiosity of the real contemporary society and a realistic appraisal of the alien's plight in view of the surrounding adversity.

These two thematic factors have appeared before, in fact, even from *Decline and Fall*; consistently each has been defined chiefly by the contrary features of the other. In *Unconditional Surrender* there is not only mutual delineation, but, of paramount thematic significance, there is what must be considered a reconciliation of the two. *Unconditional Surrender* begins with the lines drawn, a carry-over from *Officers and Gentlemen*; but the entire novel, rather than merely circumscribing the hero with hostility and then lamenting his destruction as the earlier novels tend to do, actively pursues and, to the degree possible, achieves integration of the hero and his society. Yet the peculiar identity of each of the thematic antitheses is scarcely lessened in intensity.

Regarding the first element of theme, the decline of civilization, there are at least three social areas that are depicted as being in a terminal stage of decline and these areas, at the heart of civilization, are broad enough to cover all things that pertain to culture, authority, tradition, morals. First is the concern with nationalism, patriotism, and public honor; second, the declining aristocracy which is supposed to supply the leadership in times of crises; third, religion or, specifically, the Catholic church, which is still the only source of either public or private morality. All these are inextricably and shamefully caught up in a web of dishonor and disgrace; all three are interrelated, yet each receives its own emphasis in the novel.

The national, perhaps universal, decline of honor is vividly portrayed at the beginning of the novel with the brilliant dramatization of the public reaction to the "state sword," a sword which for the English populace has come to represent something far less than the sword of Captain Montagu (who "firmly grips his hilt" and prepares for the day of "victory and death") or the sword of Roger of Waybroke (on which Guy had dedicated himself "four years back"); this is not because the people have "sheathed their swords and composed their hands in prayer" or because they "have donned the toga" symbolic of the age of reason (19); rather, the new age has forsaken religion, reason, and valor and as a result has forfeited the "sword of honor." In the midst of chaos, the sword the people follow is not that of gallant Montagu; it is "another." This sword, forged and displayed as a token of the British–Russian alliance, seems itself to provide an ironic commentary on the moral compromise inherent in the alliance. Although some of the observers find comfort in the fact that it is "evidence that ancient skills have survived behind the shoddy improvisations of the present" (18), there is really little of the past order demonstrated by the sword, for as the American lieutenant points out, the escutcheon on the scabbard is wrongly put, upside down in fact. This is a less than subtle analogy of the topsy-turviness of the moral code and concept of honor held by the English people at the moment. As Carens notes, this section, indeed all of Book One, "intensifies Waugh's depiction of the betrayal of national honor." As the narrator says in the synopsis, the "country was led blundering into dishonour" (4).

Thus the "state sword" of chapter 1 represents the compromise of honor and principle with economic and military expedience, possibly, survival; this is completely a reversal of British military and moral tradition. Hollis notes the decline of public morality, national pride, and human dignity portrayed in the first few pages of *Unconditional Surrender*. This book, he says, "depicts the total decline of English standards which resulted from the nation's abandonment of principle in the closing years of the War." For the British there is no longer any question of justice, at least to Guy's mind, for "he believes that the just cause of going to war has been forfeited in the Russian alliance" (4). Motives for war and for coalition or alliance are now certainly other than honorable; obviously there is little concern with defending good from evil, because there is now only little if any distinction between them.

But there is second and possibly even a deeper implication of the "state sword"; this centers not so much on the sword itself as upon the reverential languor with which the people respond to the sword; somehow, it seems, the moral fibre and the consequent mettle of the Englishmen of modern day are pathetically diminished from that of their predecessors of a more glorious day:

> It was not his sword but another which on Friday, 29th October 1943, drew the column of fours which slowly shuffled forward from Millbank, up Great College Street, under a scarred brick wall, on which during the hours of darkness in the preceding spring a zealous, arthritic communist had emblazoned the words, SECOND FRONT NOW, until they reached the door under the blasted and bombed west window. The people of England were long habituated to queues; some had joined the procession ignorant of its end—hoping perhaps for cigarettes or shoes—but most were in a mood of devotion. In the street few words were exchanged; no laughter (17).

This offers quite a contrast to the formerly implied medieval "quest" of Waybroke and of heroic independence; here the flocks follow meekly blind leaders to destruction moral if not physical. For, as Carens suggests, the sword, which is "exposed for adoration" to the drab queues shuffling through Westminster Abbey, is a symbol, not of the nation's heroic past or present valor, but of the public's sentimental regard for its Russian ally.

It is, therefore, appropriate that the crowds enter the Abbey "as though they were approaching a *corpse lying in state"* (18, italics mine). Indeed this seems to be the fact, at least as Waugh sees it. The entire novel is demonstrative of the moral decadence of the nation. The brand of maudlin, whimpering patriotism portrayed in the first few pages pervades the entire book; besides this, the whole war effort is depicted here, much more seriously than in any preceding novel, as characterized by foolish futility and general carelessness. This point is also established rather early in the novel and continues throughout. One or two examples say more of the nature of the British military effort than could pages of explication:

> The intention of 'Hoopla' was to attack some prodigious bomb-proof submarine-pens in Brittany. A peremptory demand for Immediate Action against these strongholds had been received from the War Cabinet. 'If the Air Force can't destroy the ships, we can kill the crews,' General Whale had suggested. Twelve men were to perform this massacre after landing in a Breton fishing boat.
>
> The latest minute read:
>
> *In view of Intelligence Report C/806/RT/12 that occupied France is being supplied with ersatz motor fuel which gives an easily recognizable character to exhaust fumes, it is recommended that samples of this fuel should be procured through appropriate agency, analysed, reproduced and issued to Hoopla Force for use in auxiliary engine of fishing boat.*
>
> Someone before Guy had added the minute: *Could not a substance be introduced into standard fuel which would provide a characteristic odour of ersatz?*
>
> Someone else, an admiral, had added: *It was decided (see attached minute) that auxiliary engine should be used only under a strong offshore wind. I consider risk of detection of odour negligible in such circumstances.*
>
> Guy more modestly wrote: *Noted and approved. Guy Crouchback, Capt. for Brig. Commanding S. S. Forces,* and squeezed past the megalosaurus to carry the file on its way (25–26).

Moreover, there are a host of characters involved in the military who reflect the general preposterousness of the whole organization; there is not one heroic figure in the British military machine. Perhaps Mr. Oates, evidently a civilian employee, comes closest:

> No one could be reasonably described as 'out of place' in HOO HQ, but Mr. Oates, despite his unobtrusive appearance (or by reason of it), seemed bizarre to Guy. He was a plump, taciturn little man and he alone among all his heterogeneous colleagues proclaimed confidence. Of the others some toiled mindlessly, passing files from tray to tray, some took their ease, some were plotting, some hiding, some grousing; all quite baffled. But Mr. Oates believed he was in his own way helping to win the war. He was a profoundly peaceful man and his way seemed clear before him (29).

In view of these insights into the national and military circumstances, one can appreciate the irony in the origin of the sword:

> 'By the way, do you realize it was Trimmer who gave the monarch the idea for this Sword of Stalingrad? Indirectly of course. In the big scene of Trimmer's landing I gave him a 'commando dagger' to brandish, I don't suppose you've even seen the things. They were an idea of Brides-in-the-Bath's early on. A few hundred were issued. To my certain knowledge none was ever used in action. A Glasgow policeman got a nasty poke with one. They were mostly given away to tarts' (48).

These ironic, gravely satiric commentaries on the nature of English society might reach toward humor were they not undermined by the consistent tone of despair which arises out of the ignominy and the real human suffering resulting from loss of moral perspective universally; although this tone is present from the beginning, it reaches its highest intensity near the end of the novel:

> 'Is there any place that is free from evil? It is too simple to say that only the Nazis wanted war. These communists wanted it too. It was the only way in which they could come to power. Many of my people wanted it, to be revenged on the Germans,

to hasten the creation of the national state. It seems to me there was a will to war, a death wish, everywhere' (300).

Thus, translated into the hero's own experience, the sword symbolizes a thorough national decay which makes public morality something quite impossible, something even quite undesired, because it is no longer valued: "It was not for this that he had dedicated himself on the sword of Roger of Waybroke" (13).

But there is another social area other than those directly concerned with politics and war that reflects the decay of the nation not only morally but culturally as well; no doubt the author thinks these two factors, as they may well be, inseparably combined and mutually influential. This decline also is depicted very early in the action and its presence suffuses the entire novel. This decline, with all the social implications, is signaled by the death of Mr. Crouchback. Of course, the passing of the aristocracy is inherently connected with the deterioration of society in general, morally and culturally, for it is the aristocratic class who are supposed to embody the virtuous principles of personal morality and public responsibility. Hollis notes:

> In the older generation alone is there to be found virtue and any full conception of what life is about. In the early chapters the death of Guy Crouchback's father is described. . . . With his death a last relic of decency has gone from the world.[7]

Perhaps it is with this in mind that the author allows the narrator to describe the final rites with a sorrowful, resolute dignity; the ceremony itself reflects an antiquated grandeur:

> The pall was removed, the coffin borne down the aisle. Angela,

7. Christopher Hollis, *Evelyn Waugh* (London: Published for The British Council and the National Book League by Longmans, Green & Co., 1966), pp. 33–34.

uncle Peregrine and Guy fell in behind it and led the mourners out. Box-Bender modestly took a place behind the Lord Lieutenant. The nuns sang the Antiphon and then filed away from their gallery to their convent. The procession moved down the village street from the new church to the old, in silence broken only by the tread of the horse, the creaking of harness and the turning of the wheels of the farm cart which bore the coffin; the factor walked at the old mare's head leading her (81).

The last sentence is significant for other than its narrative function: "Then it was ended" (82). Likewise, there is more being catalogued in the description of Guy's clearance of Broome than worthless accumulation of the past:

And then in the six days' sale silver and porcelain and tapestries, canopied beds, sets of chairs of all periods, cabinets, consoles; illuminated manuscripts, suits of armour, stuffed animals; no illustrious treasures, not the collection of an astute connoisseur; merely the accumulations and chance survivals of centuries of prosperous, unadventurous taste; all had come down into the front court where Guy now stood, and had been borne away and dispersed, leaving the whole house quite bare (87).

This is a not-too-subtle reminder of a more glorious age of the nation, and of a finer hour for both the aristocracy and religion. In one paragraph there is summarized the passing of an order:

All Guy's early memories of his father were in these spacious halls, as the central and controlling force of an elaborate regime which, for him, was typified by the sound of hooves on the cobbled forecourt and of the rake in the gravelled quadrangle; but in Guy's mind the house was primarily his mother's milieu. . . . He had lost the solid image of his father as a man of possessions and authority (for even in his declining fortunes, up to the day of leaving Broome, Mr. Crouchback had faithfully borne all his responsibilities, sitting on the bench and the county council, visiting prisons and hospitals and lunatic asylums, acting as president to numerous societies, as a governor of schools and charitable trusts, opening shows and bazaars and returning home after a full day to a home that usually abounded with guests) and

saw him now only as the recluse of his later years in the smell
of dog and tobacco in the small seaside hotel. It was to that image
he had prayed that morning (87–88).

Mr. Crouchback thus epitomizes Waugh's later statement: "To have been born into a world of beauty, to die
amid ugliness, is the common fate of all us exiles."[8] It
is therefore significant that throughout passages dealing
with the passing of Mr. Crouchback, there is a sharp contrast drawn between the old order and the new. For
instance, immediately after the funeral, "Guy encountered Lieutenant Padfield in the street" (82); later de
Souza observes rather dolefully that "the new young gentlemen were a dreary lot; until one suddenly realized
that the whole thing had changed" (119).

Finally, it seems that the author admits to the inade-
quacy of the Church to offer any solace or solution either
because of her own moral infirmity or because of the
calloused irresponsiveness of those her charge. Hollis
supposes, quite wrongly, that this novel "leaves us with
a picture of the world in which one institution alone—
the Catholic Church—remains in protest against the nihilistic pointlessness of the modern age."[9] There is very
little, if any, of this kind of assurance in the novel. In
fact, the Church is introduced in *Unconditional Surrender* exactly as she was depicted in *Officers and Gentlemen*
—caught up in a political and apparently valueless "ambiguous world, where priests are spies" (4), where "un-
frocked priests" live by the charity of destitute old men
(9), and where those who still retain their ecclesiastical
function are more interested in cigarettes than absolu-
tion (220). It is little wonder that any kind of religious
profession becomes disrespectable, even odd:

Elderberry remembered that Box-Bender had had trouble with

8. Quoted by Carens, p. x.
9. Hollis, p. 35.

his son. What had it been? Divorce? Debt? No, something odder than that. He'd gone into a monastery (311).

It is significant then, in a world in which the church has fallen prey to political power-plays and intrigues and has lost sight of her real purpose, and, consequently, her effectiveness, that the Abbey church becomes not a sanctuary for worship but a place in which to display the sword of *dishonor*; to this ignominious symbol the people are drawn, people who have never felt the slightest tug of the church, primarily because the church is inactive:

As they reached the abbey church, which many were entering for the first time in their lives, all fell quite silent (18).

Perhaps the most damning testimony to the ineffectuality of the church is the complete absence of any evidence of her power to cope with contemporary problems or to redirect men toward the good life; she is no longer a positive force for good, an authoritative voice demanding order and discipline, and providing a guiding light in a world of darkness. And it is not just a case of the "light shining in darkness and the darkness comprehending it not"; the light of the world has been extinguished. No doubt this is why Waugh himself later admitted that:

On reading the book I realized that I had done something outside my original intention. I had written an obituary of the Roman Catholic Church in England as it had existed for many centuries. . . . It never occurred to me, writing *Sword of Honour* that the Church was susceptible to change. I was wrong and I have seen a superficial revolution in what then seemed permanent.[10]

In these ways—that is, through investigation of the nation at large, the aristocracy, and the church—the author is able to present a realistically conceived portrait

---

10. "Preface," *Sword of Honour,* p. 9.

of contemporary society, and to imply his attitude toward it; the fact that the portrait is more realistic makes the author's attitude seem even more pessimistic than in the earlier novels. A nondramatic, two-dimensional or, perhaps, fantastic presentation of such moral anarchy and social listlessness would be indictment enough, but the aura of reality deepens the tone into nearly absolute pessimism.

The author has indeed created on the pages of *Unconditional Surrender* a cycloramic "vision of the last war as an epochal defeat of Christian civilization, as a tragedy on a more than human scale."[11] But the decadence of contemporary society is delineated and emphasized by the noble quest of the alien to achieve through service to God and country some kind of heroic stature while maintaining strict moral integrity. It is under these adverse societal conditions that the hero continues his idealistic pursuit of outworn values and forgotten morals. But he himself by now has had his vision blurred or, perhaps, sharpened, for at the beginning of *Unconditional Surrender,* the hero has already suffered what he must think the most bitter disillusionment possible in the cowardly action of Ivor Claire, the "flower of the nation." Therefore, Guy is far from the idealist he was at the outset of *Men at Arms.* Perhaps, it is to give this novel self-contained unity, but certainly to trace the hero's quest up until the experiences of *Unconditional Surrender,* that there is an attempt in context of the quest to identify his present state of progress. The narrator reviews Guy's early activities and his original, romantically heroic ideals. At first, Guy was sure of the war and his place in it: "Whatever the outcome there was a place for him in that battle" (1). Guy enters the battle with highest motives: "He sees the war as an opportunity to re-

---

11. Patrick O'Donnovan, "Evelyn Waugh's Opus of Disgust," *The New Republic* (February 12, 1962), p. 22.

establish his interest in his fellow men and to serve them" (2). As noted in *Men at Arms* and *Officers and Gentlemen,* the hero is aware of his duty as an aristocratic Catholic Englishman to serve both his country and God.

Thus, the war becomes clearly a matter of right opposed to wrong; it is for him another "holy crusade," for him a war in which he is defending both church and nation against the advancing pagan hoards—just as Sir Roger might have done. But when at last Guy comes "to the end of the crusade to which he had devoted himself on the tomb of Sir Roger" (301), it is not what he had expected even in the depths of his initial disillusionment. After the episode in Crete, Guy can never retain his original vision, for he realizes all too well that his ideals have been shattered by a sharp, vicious reality. Obviously, the war no longer is a matter of justice to either side; the Russian alliance and the declaration of war on Finland forever establish, at least for Guy, this fact. His realization of his country's real motives, or lack of them, destroys any hope of heroically serving in an honorable war. Guy confesses his disappointment: "I don't think I'm interested in victory now" (8); "It doesn't seem to matter now who wins" (8).

But there is yet for Guy hope of satisfying his own private honor; although justice is not in question, national honor, already forfeited, no longer at stake, one glimmer of nobility spurs him on: "Personal honor alone remains" (4). Ironically, however, he continues to try to satisfy this noble aspiration through the machinery and opportunities of war and as one who is himself a participant in the chaos that produces terror and human suffering. Returning to duty after an extended absence he feels "an unfamiliar stir of exhilaration" (53). He feels that "now there is hope" (53), if not for regaining national honor, then at least for fulfilling his own heroic "destiny." Even so, his original lofty expectation of his purpose in life seems tempered; first because in his past experiences Guy has to a degree realized that "no good comes from public causes"; second because his father's philosophy that "quantitative judgements don't apply" is beginning to redirect his thinking along more realistic lines. The latter truth haunts Guy during the funeral of his father; his private meditation with God is in many ways premonitory if not the actual turning point in the hero's quest: he begins here to picture himself not as Roger of Waybroke, gallant Christian knight, but as a commoner "earthen vessel," even as a servant.

> In the recesses of Guy's conscience there lay the belief that somewhere, somehow, something would be required of him; that he must be attentive to the summons when it came. They also served who only stood and waited. He saw himself as one of the labourers in the parable who sat in the market-place waiting to be hired and were not called into the vineyard until late in the day. They had their reward on an equality with the men who had toiled since dawn. One day he would get the chance to do some small service which only he could perform, for which he had been created. Even he must have his function in the divine plan. He did not expect a heroic destiny. Quantitative judgments did not apply. All that mattered was to recognize the chance when it offered. Perhaps his father was at that moment clearing the way for him. 'Show me what to do and help me to do it,' he prayed (80–81).

Although this prayer shows his capacity for more realistic acceptance of a common lot, it still, nevertheless, has heavy overtones of romantic notions of duty and purpose; his quest retains something of the aura of the heroic, if not the egotistical, and it will until the end of the book. Two major incidents help demonstrate to Guy the incompatibility of the chivalric or heroic notions with necessary anthropocentric dictums. First, there is the episode involving Virginia and Guy's willingness to accept her again as his wife; but there is no love on either side: Virginia needs a father for Trimmer's child and Guy's own ego demands that he perform this "service" as a knightly duty to a damsel in distress. The remarriage for Guy becomes an act not of love and compassion, but of chivalric duty. There is a great deal revealed by Kerstie's taunt; and his own reply indicates even more his preoccupation with the knightly code of duty; the remarriage not only serves Virginia's purposes, but it also is a means of aiding both the church and the nation: a soul will be saved and the Crouchback line will be preserved.

> Guy regarded Kerstie from his bed. The question she asked was not new to him. He had posed it and answered it some days ago. 'Knights errant,' he said, 'used to go out looking for noble deeds. I don't think I've ever in my life done a single, positively unselfish action. I certainly haven't gone out of my way to find opportunities. Here was something most unwelcome, put into my hands; something which I believe the Americans describe as "beyond the call of duty"; not the normal behaviour of an officer and a gentleman, something they'll laugh about in Bellamy's.
> 'Of course Virginia is tough. She would have survived somehow. I shan't be changing her by what I'm doing. I know all that. But you see there's another—' he was going to say 'soul'; then realized that this word would mean little to Kerstie for all her granite propriety—'there's another life to consider. What sort of life do you think her child would have, born unwanted in 1944?'
> 'It's no business of yours.'
> 'It was made my business by being offered' (193).

He justifies his action with the thought that his "insane" action is in accordance with his father's belief that "quantitative judgments don't apply" (194).

But there is another episode in which again Guy is given the opportunity to respond to human needs. This is the activity involving the Jewish refugees whom Guy attempts to aid, but obviously, he does so with the same motivation as in the case of Virginia. Even in the attempt to serve, in what can only be taken as a most pathetic situation, his view of reality is still obscured by the glimmer of heroic destiny; this time, appropriately enough, it is not medieval but Biblical heroes that he would emulate, especially Moses:

> It seemed to Guy in the fanciful mood that his lonely state engendered, that he was playing an ancient, historic role as he went with Bakic to inform the Jews of their approaching exodus. He was Moses leading a people out of captivity (293).

It is not, however, until what the narrator calls "the end of the crusade" that Guy comes to a personal awareness that honor is not the most important thing in the world; in fact, he finds that it is in the name of honor, and particularly private honor, that the atrocities he is witness of and participant in are being committed:

> 'It seems to me there was a will to war, a death wish, everywhere. Even good men thought their private honour would be satisfied by war. They could assert their manhood by killing and being killed. They would accept hardships in recompense for having been selfish and lazy. Danger justified privilege. I knew Italians—not very many perhaps—who felt this. Were there none in England?'
> 'God forgive me,' said Guy. 'I was one of them' (300).

Here, as Carens notes, "Guy comes to understand not only that he was wrong in imagining that he might restore his own personal honor through acts of warfare, but that he, in common with all of Europe, has given himself not to life but to death."[12] The very next paragraph in the text suggests Guy's resulting transformation from one concerned only with satisfying private honor to one who is motivated by "mercy" and compassion: "All the stamping of the barrack square and the biffing of imaginary strongholds were finding their consummation in one frustrated act of mercy" (301). "Guy finally learns

---

12. Carens, p. 167.

that character is far more important than honor."[13] Bergonzi notes that "at this point, Guy's self-knowledge is complete. . . . Reality is too terrible and too various to be accounted for by any simple myth, any easy pattern of heroics, no matter how splendid."[14] Moreover, it is as though Guy has learned to appreciate more "those who stand and wait" (80). He has been made aware of the fact that "God does not need either man's work or his own gifts; who best bear his mild yoke, they serve him best." It is compassion that is required, not heroism and honor, for it is through divine providence, the "operation of divine grace" (176), that He overrules in the affairs of men—not through their own heroic efforts: "It was indeed as though the Red Sea had miraculously drawn asunder and left a dry passage between walls of water" (302).

Carens suggests, and quite correctly, that *Unconditional Surrender* is an account of Guy's spiritual "return to life after disillusionment, descent into hell, and discovery of self."[15] Yet there is discovery of much more fundamental truth; Guy's journey to reality is predicated on his recognition of an eternal purpose and an eternal power in the history of man. This is made clear in the epilogue. Here Guy is found about six years after the incident involving the Jewish refugees, married and living not in the ancestral house but on a farm. His wife is Domenica, who also had once had visions of grandeur in the service of humanity but who is now less fanciful than even a "damsel in distress":

> Domenica, now aged 25, who . . . tried her vocation in a convent, failed, and now drove a tractor on the home farm, an occupation which had changed her appearance and manner. From

13. *Ibid.*
14. Bernard Bergonzi, "Evelyn Waugh's Gentlemen," *Critical Quarterly* 5 (Spring, 1963): 35.
15. Carens, p. 169.

having been shy and almost excessively feminine, she was now rather boisterous, trousered and muddied and full of the rough jargon of the stock-yard (260).

The "destiny" of Guy, as it was spoken of at the beginning of the quest, appears to have no glamorous or heroic overtones; in fact, "destiny" is not too prestigious a word. One should say, as Box-Bender, that "things have turned out very conveniently for Guy" (311).

Ironically, and of thematic significance, there is in the epilogue an emphatic dramatic contrast between Guy's first noble vision and his present acceptance of reality, the overriding providence of God, and the manner in which best to serve Him. Ludovic, the romantic pansy, becomes somewhat of a parody of the early Guy; he now owns the Castello, is isolated from society, and is writing esoteric novels. Guy on the other hand, tends a farm, has been fully integrated into his society, and is involved in the common affairs of men; significantly, he is rearing Virginia's child by Trimmer. His private cause has not separated him from the rest of the world as it has Ludovic; Guy's has brought him to the world. In fact, Bergonzi may be very near the truth when he suggests that "Guy's heir represents a union, no matter how oddly contrived, between the Upper Classes and the People."[16] Thus, there is in Guy's experience a recognition of self, almost, perhaps, a "tragic awareness,"[17] but there is no recovery in the strict sense of the word; there is, however, an acceptance which is reflected in a "resigned cosmic melancholy" (205). This is not to say, however, for all the pessimism of the conclusion that Guy represents "Waugh's final, infinitely reluctant surrender to the modern world."[18] Neither Guy nor Waugh has surrendered unconditionally to modernity; both are determined that

16. Bergonzi, p. 36.
17. Carens, p. 169.
18. Bergonzi, p. 36.

at least the morality and code of human values inherently a part of the original ideal, though now transformed into principles compatible with the needs of real human beings, will continue to exert a positive force in the world.

Early in the novel Ludovic describes a good officer as one who on rainy days commands, "with drawn swords, dismount," not "return swords" (38), for in this way the sword does not get rusty. Waugh, the good officer, has not returned swords, but has dismounted with sword in hand—not to surrender, but to continue the good fight, on foot.

CONCLUSION

Waugh's fiction, diverse to the point of incongruity and even contradiction, covers the spectrum between farce and melodrama and finally arrives at a kind of realism within the discipline of the conventional novel. He may, therefore, be judged as a writer of various subgenres— satires, comedies, near tragedies, melodramas, or realistic novels. In all these, because of an exceptional command of the English language and a remarkable felicity in the craft of fiction, Waugh achieves a level of excellence equal or superior to that of the contemporary masters of these various modes. Yet, this cannot be the final evaluation of Waugh as an artist.

This study has shown that when Waugh's fiction is viewed collectively as a progressive artistic critique of contemporary civilization the discrepancies among novels or groups of novels are resolved. A close examination of his basic technique as it discovers and develops theme in novel after novel reveals that the later realistic works are in direct line of succession of the early satires; his fiction is progressively united in theme and artistry chiefly through the uniquely contrived personae technique which is based on the variable relationship of the narrator-persona with a special character-persona. This technique, formulated early within the technical exigencies of the satiric-ironic mode, is continuously modified and refined to conform ever more closely to the discipline of the conventional novel and to delineate an increasingly serious theme and sustain a maturing world vision. The technique provides in all the novels narrative structure, the basis of thematic development, and tonal control; studied variation of the relationship of narrator and character in all three areas gives the novels their singular characteristics yet binds them together in a progressive study of twentieth-century civilization, a critique, literally, which begins in satirical denunciation and ends in realistic, perhaps compassionate, acceptance.

In the first novel, *Decline and Fall,* Waugh introduces the personae technique as a means of gaining authorial detachment artistically and emotionally from the character-persona; in this way he is able to satisfy the "exit author" requirement of satire, effect a scathing ironic attack of contemporary society, yet at the same time have the narrator-persona begin to imply a genuine interest in the alien. Thus, not only is the basic technique established, but the essential theme and thematic device of all the following novels are inaugurated. Central to both narrative and theme is the character-persona, an *ingénu,* who is relentlessly persecuted by a hostile modern world; thematic emphasis therefore is on the plight of the alien rather than on the panorama of decadence and chaos. Although the narrator does imply interest in the hero, Paul Pennyfeather, there is not enough sympathetic identification of the narrator with the hero to raise the general tone of the novel above comic satire. Nevertheless, this first novel contains the germinal narrative, thematic, and tonal factors of all the various subsequent novels.

Vile Bodies, the second novel, while essentially the same in narrative material and theme, is remarkably different from the previous novel. The author, by placing the burden of narration solely on a narrator who is absolutely detached from the events and the characters, gains the detachment necessary for a caustic attack of the foibles and corruption of contemporary civilization. There is no identification with the hero, Adam Fenwick-Symes, a two-dimensional observed participant, who exists, it seems, merely as an internal unifying device. The thematic emphasis is on the decadence and confusion of modern civilization, not on the plight of the alien. Without the implied sympathy for or even interest of the narrator in the hero, the novel, although potentially serious to the point of tragedy, becomes a satirical farce.

Black Mischief brings not only changes in locale, societies, and characters, but also an extension of the personae technique. Perhaps the most significant feature is the narrator's new freedom in narrative process; he is no longer restricted by the hero's immediate adventures and is not reliant upon him for narrative continuity or progression of plot. However, the character-persona still is the primary internal unifying device in the otherwise far-flung activities. The character-persona has changed also; the innocent or *ingénu* is translated into Basil Seal, an adolescent cad, semi-aware and energetic, but bearing obvious likenesses to his predecessors. Isolated, alienated from his society, the hero through his search provides a critical review of European and African societies; the narrator's harmoniously controlled identification with the hero, described best as attachment-detachment, allows both cruel and comic satire to exist simultaneously, but the final note of the novel is toward serious realism.

In *A Handful of Dust* the increasingly balanced function of the narrator-persona and character-persona reaches its first culmination, producing, in what may well be Waugh's best work, a tone near tragedy. The narrator's control of the narrative is more subtle though no less positive than before; the hero's story provides the narrative progression as well as plot and thematic unity. In fact, at times the narrator completely absents himself from the narrative, not merely to achieve a dramatic effect as in *Black Mischief,* but to intensify the sympathetic identification of the reader with the hero. Tony Last is the culmination of the *ingénu* tradition; tedious, ineffectual, yet a visionary, he is destroyed spiritually by the cruelties of modern society, annihilated physically by the jungle. Here emerges the thematic motif common to later novels of the predoomed, romantic quest. It is in this novel that Waugh approaches tragic irony for the first time. The tension created by the conflict of the narrator's artistic detachment with his implied emotional sympathy in the hero, coupled with the stark realism of even the most fantastic events, bring this novel amazingly near the tragic end of the spectrum and to a consummate intensity in pessimism. This novel alone is convincing testimony to the greatness of Waugh's art; master craftsmanship, a serious concern for a universal moral dilemma, and human compassion are blended into one of the century's most significant novels.

If the novels are considered in chronological order, the next, *Scoop,* becomes something of a comic relief from the pessimism and tragedy of *A Handful of Dust.* Here the personae technique, quite similar to that in *Black Mischief,* is adjusted to allow a tandem-like relationship between the narrator-persona and the character-persona which results in an extended comic routine complete with straight man and fall guy. The theme remains essentially the same—the plight of the alien in a hostile world, but there is one significant development. For the first time, the hero, William Boot, triumphs over the confusion and decadence of his society. The nature of the events and the personalities of both the comically naïve hero and the congenial mischievous narrator combine to make this Waugh's one truly funny novel.

Put Out More Flags is in many ways a *pivotal* novel, for it provides the culmination of all the preceding works and at the same time forecasts all the succeeding fiction right down to the last installment of the war trilogy. The fantastic world of the Bright Young Things, the unlikely characters who frequented the early novels, the comic cruelty, even Basil Seal are neatly set aside with the conclusion of this novel, because of the gradual intrusion of the real world and the very serious implications of war. Consequently, the narrator, who while the dominant factor in narrative progression, relinquishes much of his previous ironic detachment. Even though there is a great deal of irony, the narrator is generally closer to the events and is sympathetic even toward minor characters, who in this novel play an important thematic role. The theme is essentially the same as in the earlier novels, but here there are three aliens—Basil Seal, Ambrose Silk, and Cedric Lyne. Through these characters the theme is extended into a study of the individual's moral responsibility in his society—the "cenobitic" versus the "conventual"—a conflict which is resolved only in the hero-cad's reformation and his acceptance of personal responsibility which integrates him into the society. This extension of theme into realistic human terms and the narrator's implicit discerning judgment of the heroes' values forecast the serious realism of the later novels; there is a new spirit abroad.

Brideshead Revisited, while unique in Waugh's canon, is a logical development of the early fiction in every way. The previous novels are characterized by an increasing closeness of the narrator-persona to the character-persona; in this first-person narrative, the identification is made complete. Previously, the dominant theme has gradually taken on more and more realistic proportions; here a combination of war, romance, and religion blends strangely the early fantasy and the realism of *A Handful of Dust* and *Put Out More Flags*. The tone of the preceding novels is increasingly modulated, less bitter and more compassionate, less negative and more optimistic; in *Brideshead Revisited* the tone is characterized by a kind of reluctant optimism, suspended somewhere between romance and realism. But this novel is not an unqualified success; in it Waugh pushes too far the variation in the technical exigencies of the ironic—technique clashes with sentiment and the latter proves stronger than the restraint of the former. First, although Waugh attempts to gain within the first-person point of view an ironic perspective similar to the earlier novels by the use of three levels of "I" personae—a narrator, a narrator-character, and a character, the too-close identification of the narrator or "now I" with the character or "then I" both in narrative and tone invalidates the intrinsic ironic potential of the "intermediate I." As a result the ostensible memories of Captain Ryder are illogically omniscient; the tone, although sometimes ironic, is generally romantic because the events are filtered through the consciousness of the romantic narrator. The theme while essentially that of the earlier novels, is thus translated into the hero's romantic quest for identity, which leads him through Arcadian innocence, adolescent cynicism, and finally religious certainty; pervading all is the illicit but beautiful love affair of the hero and Julia. The narrator's nostalgic, somewhat sentimentalized response to the events colors all and moves the tone of the novel inevitably toward the melodramatic; the ironic spectrum is broken through; technique conflicts with the material. Yet, if *Brideshead Revisited* is a failure, it is an impressive failure if for no other reason than the greatness of the attempt.

Waugh apparently realized the shortcomings of *Brides-*

head Revisited for in several "interludes," pieces immediately following this novel, he returns to the techniques
and themes of the early novels. It is not until *Men at
Arms* that he confidently resumes the development of
the expanding thematic concerns and the maturing artistry of the novels preceding *Brideshead Revisited*. In this
first of the war trilogy, and in *Officers and Gentlemen*
and *Unconditional Surrender*, Waugh demonstrates an
assured handling of the exigencies of the ironic mode,
particularly the personae technique, toward the formulation of a serious and plausible moral statement; the
result is a trilogy which in sheer artistry surpasses all of
the previous fiction and which in thematic impact identifies Waugh as an outstanding moralist of the age. In
narration, Waugh has learned to manipulate the relationship of the narrator-persona and the character-persona to
achieve a variable dual-vision; the narrator is the external
"maker" of the novel and has ironic perspective on the
character, yet he is able, especially near the end of the
last installment to gain an almost "absolute" identification with the hero, Guy Crouchback; distinction between
them is impossible. As a result the narrator maintains
an ironic overview of society and constantly projects an
awareness of the inevitable failure of the hero to realize
his ideals, yet all the while he can explicitly sympathize
with the hero to the point of asserting the superiority of
his ideals over the decadence of modern civilization.
Irony is not compromised; it is rather disciplined into a
"hardness of mind" which can realistically accept the fact
that the hero's quest is predoomed and at the same time
ungrudgingly extend sympathy to less chivalric but no
less noble segments of the society. This is but a culmination of the growing realism of the previous novels. Although the quest is characterized by a note of high
romance (Captain Truslove style) at the outset of *Men
at Arms,* and although the original vision of knightly

duty to church and state is never destroyed, it eventually finds its fulfillment not in the Arcadian splendor of Brideshead nor in the chivalric world of Roger of Waybroke, nor even in the Royal Corps of Halberdiers, but in the physical suffering and spiritual chaos of war, within the individual human spirit. In fact this pervasive "ironic realism" ultimately comes to sustain a whole philosophy of life—not the harsh repudiation of *Decline and Fall* or *Vile Bodies,* not the mere seriousness of *Put Out More Flags,* nor the optimism of *Brideshead Revisited,* but a resigned and compassionate wisdom.

It is Waugh's uniquely contrived personae technique—working through all the various novels, simultaneously and purposefully developing narrative, controlling tone, and discovering and extending theme—which proves that the author is both a master craftsman and a sincere moralist whose works, viewed collectively and in context, are a single earnest attempt to identify and to reconcile within the artistic medium of the novel a moral dilemma of universal proportions. The attempt is a tribute to the man; the astounding degree of success is testimony to the greatness of his art and to his status as a major novelist of the twentieth century.

Bibliography

I. PRIMARY SOURCES

Waugh, Evelyn. *A Handful of Dust*. Boston: Little, Brown and Company, 1934.

———. *A Little Learning*. Boston: Little, Brown and Company, 1964.

———. *Black Mischief*. Boston: Little, Brown and Company, 1946.

———. *Brideshead Revisited*. Boston: Little, Brown and Company, 1945.

———. *Decline and Fall*. London: Chapman & Hall, 1928.

———. *Edmund Campion*. Garden City: Doubleday & Company, Inc., 1956.

———. *Helena*. Boston: Little, Brown and Company, 1950.

———. *Love Among the Ruins*. London: Chapman & Hall, 1953.

———. *The Loved One*. Boston: Little, Brown and Company, 1948.

———. *Men at Arms*. London: Chapman & Hall, 1962.

———. *The Ordeal of Gilbert Pinfold*. Boston: Little, Brown and Company, 1957.

———. *Officers and Gentlemen*. London: Chapman & Hall, 1955.

———. *Put Out More Flags*. London: Chapman & Hall, 1942.

———. *Scoop*. Boston: Little, Brown and Company, 1949.

———. *Scott-King's Modern Europe*. London: Chapman & Hall, 1947.

———. *Sword of Honour*. Boston: Little, Brown and Company, 1961.

———. *Tactical Exercise*. Boston: Little, Brown and Company, 1954.

———. *Unconditional Surrender*. London: Chapman & Hall, 1961.

———. *Vile Bodies*. London: Chapman & Hall, 1930.

———. *Work Suspended*. London: Chapman & Hall, 1949.

II. SECONDARY SOURCES

Amis, Kingsley, "Crouchback's Regress," *The Spectator* (October 27, 1961) , pp. 581–82.

Benedict, Stewart H. "The Candide Figure in Waugh's Novels," *Papers of the Michigan Academy of Science, Arts, and Letters,* 48 (1963) : 686–89.

Bergonzi, Bernard. "Evelyn Waugh's Gentlemen," *Critical Quarterly* 5 (Spring, 1963) : 23–36.

Booth, Wayne C. *The Rhetoric of Fiction*. Chicago: The University of Chicago Press, 1961.

Braybrooke, Patrick. *Some Catholic Novelists: Their Art and Outlook*. Freeport, New York: Books for Libraries Press, 1966.

Bredvold, Louis I. "A Note in Defense of Satire," *A Journal of English Literary History* 7 (December, 1940) : 252–64.

Carens, James F. *The Satiric Art of Evelyn Waugh*. Seattle: University of Washington Press, 1966.

Churchill, Thomas. "The Trouble with *Brideshead Revisited,*" *Modern Language Quarterly* 28 (June, 1967) : 213–28.

"A Concert of the Persona in Satire: A Symposium," *Satire Newsletter* 3 (Spring, 1966).

Davis, Robert Murray, "Evelyn Waugh's Early Work: The Formation of a Method," *Texas Studies in Literature and Language* 7 (Spring, 1965) : 97–108.

———. "Evelyn Waugh on the Art of Fiction," *Papers on Language and Literature* 2 (Summer, 1966) : 243–52.

Delasanta, Rodney and Mario L. D'Avanzo, "Truth and Beauty in *Brideshead Revisited,*" *Modern Fiction Studies* 11 (Summer, 1965) : 140–52.

DeVitis, A. A. *Roman Holiday: The Catholic Novels of Evelyn Waugh*. New York: Bookman Associates, 1956.

Didion, Joan. "Gentlemen in Battle," *National Review* 12 (March 27, 1962) : 215–17.

Dyson, A. E., "Evelyn Waugh: And the Mysteriously Disappearing Hero," *The Crazy Fabric: Essays in Irony*. New York: St. Martin's Press, 1965. Pp. 187–96. Also in *Critical Quarterly* 2 (Spring, 1960) : 72–79.

Ehrenpreis, Irvin, "Personae," *Restoration and Eighteenth-Century Literature*, C. Carrol Camden, ed. Chicago: The University of Chicago Press, 1963. Pp. 25–37.

Feinburg, Leonard. *The Satirist: His Temperament, Motivation, and Influence*. Ames, Iowa: Iowa State University Press, 1963.

Fielding, Gabriel, "Evelyn Waugh: The Price of Satire," *The Listener* 72 (October 8, 1964) : 541–42.

Forster, E. M. *Aspects of the Novel*. New York: Harcourt, Brace & World, Inc., 1927.

Frye, Northorp. *Anatomy of Criticism*. Princeton: Princeton University Press, 1957.

———. "The Mythos of Winter: Irony and Satire," published (also) in *Modern Satire*, Alvin B. Kernan, ed. New York: Harcourt, Brace & World, Inc., 1962. Pp. 155–64.

Greenblatt, Stephen J. *Three Modern Satirists: Waugh, Orwell, and Huxley*. New Haven: Yale University Press, 1965.

Greene, George. "Scapegoat with Style," *Queens Quarterly* 71 (Winter, 1964–1965) : 485–93.

Greenfield, Meg. "Half-People in a Double World," *Reporter* 18 (June 26, 1958) : 38–39.

Hall, James. "Stylized Rebellion," *The Tragic Comedians*. Bloomington: Indiana University Press, 1963. Pp. 45–65.

Hardy, John Edward. "*Brideshead Revisited:* God, Man, and Others," *Man in the Modern Novel*. Seattle: University of Washington Press, 1964. Pp. 159–74.

Highet, Gilbert. *The Anatomy of Satire*. Princeton: Princeton University Press, 1962.

Hollis, Christopher. *Evelyn Waugh*. London: Published for the British Council and the National Book League by Longmans, Green & Co., 1966.

Johnson, Edgar. *A Treasury of Satire*. New York: Simon and Schuster, 1945.

Karl, Frederick R. "The World of Evelyn Waugh: The Normally Insane," *The Contemporary English Novel*. New York: Farrar, Straus and Cudahy, 1962. Pp. 167–82.

Kernan, Alvin B. *The Plot of Satire*. New Haven: Yale University Press, 1965.

———. "A Theory of Satire," *Modern Satire*, Alvin B. Kernan, ed. New York: Harcourt, Brace & World, Inc., 1962. Pp. 164–79.

———. "The Wall and the Jungle: The Early Novels of Evelyn Waugh," *Yale Review* 53 (Winter, 1963) : 199–220.

Kierkegaard, Søren. *The Concept of Irony*, Lee M. Capel, trans. London: William Collins Sons & Co., Ltd. 1966.

Kleine, Don. W. "The Cosmic Comedies of Evelyn Waugh," *South Atlantic Quarterly* 61 (April, 1962) : 533–39.

Knox, Norman. *The Word Irony and its Context, 1500-1755*. Durham: Duke University Press, 1961.

LaFrance, Marston. "Context and Structure of Evelyn Waugh's *Brideshead Revisited*," *Twentieth Century Literature* 10 (April, 1964) : 12–18.

Long, Richard A. and Iva G. Jones, "Toward a Definition of 'the Decadent Novel,'" *College English* 22 (January, 1961) : 245–49.

Mack, Maynard. "The Muse of Satire," from *Studies in the Literature of the Augustan Age*, Richard C. Boys, ed. Pp. 219–31. Also in *The Yale Review* 41 (1951) : 80–92.

Martin, Graham. "Novelists of Three Decades: Evelyn Waugh, Graham Greene, C. P. Snow," *The Pelican Guide to English Literature* 7. Baltimore: Penguin Books, 1963.

"The New Waugh," *Times Literary Supplement* (October 27, 1961) , p. 770.

Nichols, James W. "Romantic and Realistic: The Tone of Evelyn Waugh's Early Novels," *College English* 24 (October, 1962) : 46–56.

O'Donnovan, Patrick, "Evelyn Waugh's Opus of Disgust," *The New Republic* (February 12, 1962) , pp. 21–22.

O'Faolain, Sean. *The Vanishing Hero: Studies in Novelists of the Twenties*. London: Eyre & Spottiswoode, 1956.

Rogers, Franklin R. *Mark Twain's Burlesque Patterns*. Dallas: Southern Methodist University Press, 1960.

Rolo, Charles J. *The World of Evelyn Waugh.* Boston: Little, Brown and Company, 1958.

Ruff, Lawrence A. "Comments on the 'Decadent Novel,' " *College English* 23 (October, 1961) : 63–64.

Schorer, Mark "Technique as Discovery," from *Approaches to the Novel,* Robert Scholes, ed. San Francisco: Chandler Publishing Company, 1961. Pp. 249–68. Originally published in *Hudson Review,* Spring, 1948.

Sedgewick, Garnett G. *Of Irony, Especially in Drama.* Toronto: University of Toronto Press, 1948.

Spender, Stephen. *The Creative Element.* New York: British Book Center, 1954.

Stopp, Frederick J. *Evelyn Waugh: Portrait of an Artist.* Boston: Little, Brown and Company, 1958.

Voorhees, Richard J. "Evelyn Waugh's War Novels: A Toast to Lost Causes," *Queens Quarterly* 65 (Spring, 1958) : 53–63.

Waugh, Evelyn. "Fan-Fare," *Life* (April 8, 1946), pp. 53–60.

———. "Felix Culpa?" *Commonweal* 48 (July 16, 1948), 322–25.

Wasson, Richard. "A Handful of Dust: Critique of Victorianism," *Modern Fiction Studies* 7 (Winter, 1961-1962): 327–37.

Worcester, David *The Art of Satire.* New York: Russell & Russell, 1960.

Index

Amis, Kingsley, 264, 272
Aristophanes, 26
"Attachment-detachment," 48, 50–53, 72–74, 88, 90–92, 105–7, 109, 115, 124–25, 140–41, 146–47, 173, 189–90, 207, 256–58, 274, 275, 282, 283–84, 285, 286, 302, 311, 313, 314, 315, 319, 339

Benedict, Stewart H., 54, 112
Bergonzi, Bernard, 37, 91, 136, 139–40, 239, 256, 268, 335, 336
Booth, Wayne C., 74
Bredvold, Louis I., 29, 32

Cad, 120–21, 167, 178, 179, 183, 231, 267
Carens, James F., 23, 25–26, 29, 34, 39, 40–41, 55–56,, 72, 76–79, 91–92, 95–97, 111, 115–16, 119, 123, 132, 139, 143, 148, 149, 161, 165–66, 209, 214–15, 220–28, 238, 246, 256, 257, 262, 267, 272, 275, 295, 311, 316, 322, 323, 334, 335
Candide, 54, 208
Catholicism, 37, 38, 194, 195, 215, 217, 221, 233, 253, 263, 265, 266, 268, 269, 289, 297, 321, 328, 331
Comedy, 29, 46, 49–53, 72–73, 82, 85, 112, 145–46, 163–65, 167, 257, 282, 283

Davis, Robert M., 41, 51, 63, 67, 72, 90, 91, 95, 140
Decadent novel, 27–28
DeVitis, A. A., 62, 74, 95, 109, 115, 120, 133, 135, 148, 150, 159, 166, 209–10, 217–19, 226–27, 240–44, 256, 264–68, 271, 281

Didion, Joan, 263, 268, 283
Dramatic narratives, 52
Dyson, A. E., 55, 71, 75, 78, 131, 136

Farce, 25, 49, 99, 139–40
Feinberg, Leonard, 32, 35, 50, 51
Fielding, Gabriel, 34
Forster, E. M., 68, 148; *Passage to India*, 148
Fraser, G. S., 34
Frye, Northrop, 27, 29, 45–48, 52–53, 134, 142–43

Greenblatt, Stephen J., 54, 76, 95, 112, 116, 117, 120, 123, 133, 136
Greenfield, Meg, 98

Hegelian triad, 242
Hemingway, Ernest: *Farewell to Arms*, 208
Highet, Gilbert, 27
Hollis, Christopher, 74, 92, 115, 123, 149, 187, 218, 219, 234, 322, 326, 328

Ingénu, 50, 53, 54, 55, 78, 120, 132, 156, 158, 161, 180, 183, 190, 226, 237, 242
Interior monologue (stream of consciousness), 98, 140, 173, 186
Ironic authorial stance, 31, 32, 35, 41. *See* attachment-detachment
Ironic mode, 10, 42–53, 91, 124, 143, 147, 197, 237, 243, 245, 262, 274, 316
Ironic realism, 283, 284, 310, 320
Ironic spectrum, 98, 143–44, 207, 208, 243, 257, 342

Irony, 42–49, 50, 106, 138, 142, 208, 213

James, Henry, 225
Johnson, Edgar, 43–44

Karl, Frederick R., 195, 197, 266
Keats, John, 313
Kernan, Alvin B., 19, 27, 28, 49, 53–56, 63, 69, 84, 92, 116, 131
Kierkegaard, Søren, 43

LaFrance, Marston, 146, 193, 195–96, 209
Lewis, Wyndham, 26

Mack, Maynard, 50
Martin, Graham, 136, 148
Melodrama, 49, 145, 207
Melville, Herman: *Moby Dick*, 208
"Mock oral tradition," 87
Modes, 20, 21, 23, 27, 42, 43, 45–53

"Narrative plank technique," 145
Nichols, James W., 24, 40, 41, 57, 64, 70, 91, 113, 141

O'Donnovan, Patrick, 267
O'Faolain, Sean, 34, 36, 54, 73, 220, 221
O'Neill, Eugene, 33
Orwell, George, *Burmese Days*, 148

Persona, 50–59, 66, 67, 82, 151, 167, 198–201, 204–5, 207, 237, 244, 251, 255, 257, 266, 272, 275, 284, 300
Personal narrative, 51
Poetics, 52

Quest motif, 121, 124, 135, 165, 180, 267, 268, 271, 273, 290, 291, 294, 319, 320, 323, 330, 333, 336

Rolo, Charles J., 27, 31, 32, 34, 56, 219
Ruff, Lawrence, 34

Satire, 19, 23, 24, 26, 27, 42–49, 52, 53, 85, 207

Satirical novel, 17, 18, 19, 20
Savage, D. S., 136, 141
Schorer, Mark, 38, 39, 49
Sedgewick, Garnett G., 44
Shaw, Bernard, 31
Spender, Stephen, 74, 98, 102, 116, 121, 218, 219, 227
Stopp, Frederick J., 25, 28, 35, 37, 54, 62, 84, 85, 98, 116, 134, 135, 156, 216, 227, 239, 260, 271
Swift, Jonathan, 33; *Gulliver's Travels*, 208; *A Modest Proposal*, 208
Symposium, 47

Technique, artistic, 38–42, 49, 60, 61, 71, 72, 82, 93, 100–101, 145–46, 155–56, 166–67, 174, 185, 197, 207–9, 210–11, 225, 237, 246, 247, 254, 272, 274, 299, 300, 302, 304
Tone, elements of, 56–59
Tragedy, 46–49, 137, 146, 167, 207, 257, 268, 273, 282, 283
Twain, Mark: "A Dog's Tale," 208; *Huckleberry Finn*, 208

Voorhees, Richard J., 260

Wasson, Richard, 37, 134
Waugh, Evelyn: *The Balance*, 41; *Black Mischief*, 100, 101–22, 123–24, 126, 128, 144, 148, 149, 170, 174, 177, 180, 183, 210, 242, 244, 251, 307, 339, 340; *Brideshead Revisited*, 22–24, 30, 35–40, 145–47, 166, 193–235, 237, 239, 243–45, 256, 258, 262–63, 265, 275, 299, 309, 317, 341–44; *Crouchback Novels*, 30, 37, 40, 123, 166, 226, 235, 239, 242, 246, 256, 297, 303; *Decline and Fall*, 21, 22, 38, 41, 60, 61–82, 84, 87, 90–92, 95, 97, 100–101, 104–5, 117, 123, 147, 154, 159, 170–71, 187, 236, 237, 243, 244, 256, 262, 266, 274, 283, 321, 338, 344; *Edmund Campion*, 236; *A Handful of Dust*, 22, 37, 100, 121, 122–44, 145–47, 150, 159, 165, 207, 210, 244–45, 283, 294, 300,

339, 340, 342; *Helena,* 28, 236, 237, 239; *Love Among the Ruins,* 236, 237; *The Loved One,* 32, 37, 236, 237, 239; *Men at Arms,* 238–71, 272–75, 279, 281, 284, 286, 289, 295, 298–99, 301, 303, 305, 308–10, 317, 330–31, 343; *Officers and Gentlemen,* 238, 239, 246, 271–97, 298, 300–3, 307–8, 310, 311, 315, 317, 321, 328, 331, 343; *The Ordeal of Gilbert Pinfold,* 236, 237; *Put Out More Flags,* 145–47, 165–92, 210, 225–26, 238–42, 266, 298, 341–42, 344; *Scoop,* 145, 147, 148–65, 210, 226, 251, 298, 340; *Scott-King's Modern Europe,* 236, 237, 239; *Sword of Honour,* 263, 266, 272; *Unconditional Surrender,* 22, 238, 241–42, 246, 253, 264, 295, 296, 297–337, 343; *Vile Bodies,* 21, 60, 82–99, 100–101, 104, 105, 109, 117, 123, 126, 128, 144, 145, 210, 266, 273, 275, 338, 344; *Work Suspended,* 210, 239

Wilson, Edmund, 31, 219

Worcester, David, 43–44, 46, 49

World War II, 177, 179–80, 183, 263, 305–6, 311, 331